The
White House
Speaks

The
White House
Speaks

Presidential Leadership
as Persuasion

Craig Allen Smith and Kathy B. Smith

Praeger Series in Political Communication

Westport, Connecticut
London

Library of Congress Cataloging-in-Publication Data

Smith, Craig Allen.
    The White House speaks : presidential leadership as persuasion /
Craig Allen Smith and Kathy B. Smith.
        p.   cm. — (Praeger series in political communication, ISSN
    1062–5623)
    Includes bibliographical references and index.
    ISBN 0–275–94394–1 (alk. paper)
    1. Presidents—United States. 2. Presidents—United States—
Messages. 3. Political leadership—United States. 4. Political
oratory—United States. I. Smith, Kathy B. II. Title.
III. Series.
JK518.S583 1994
353.03'23—dc20   93–23468

British Library Cataloguing in Publication Data is available.

Library of Congress Catalog Card Number: 93–23468
ISBN: 0–275–94394–1
ISSN: 1062–5623

First published in 1994

Praeger Publishers, 88 Post Road West, Westport, CT 06881
An imprint of Greenwood Publishing Group, Inc.

Printed in the United States of America

∞

The paper used in this book complies with the Permanent
Paper Standard issued by the National Information Standards
Organization (Z39.48–1984).

10 9 8 7 6 5 4 3 2 1

To our daughter Debbie, a very able persuader.

Contents

Series Foreword

Those of us from the discipline of communication studies have long believed that communication is prior to all other fields of inquiry. In several other forums I have argued that the essence of politics is "talk" or human interaction.[1] Such interaction may be formal or informal, verbal or nonverbal, public or private, but it is always persuasive, forcing us consciously or subconsciously to interpret, to evaluate, and to act. Communication is the vehicle for human action.

From this perspective, it is not surprising that Aristotle recognized the natural kinship of politics and communication in his writings *Politics* and *Rhetoric*. In the former, he established that humans are "political beings [who] alone of the animals [are] furnished with the faculty of language."[2] In the latter, he began his systematic analysis of discourse by proclaiming that "rhetorical study, in its strict sense, is concerned with the modes of persuasion."[3] Thus, it was recognized over twenty-three hundred years ago that politics and communication go hand in hand because they are essential parts of human nature.

In 1981, Dan Nimmo and Keith Sanders proclaimed that political communication was an emerging field.[4] Although its origin, as noted, dates back centuries, a "self-consciously cross-disciplinary" focus began in the late 1950s. Thousands of books and articles later, colleges and universities offer a variety of graduate and undergraduate coursework in the area in such diverse departments as communication, mass communication, journalism, political science, and sociology.[5] In Nimmo and Sanders's early assessment, the "key areas of inquiry" included rhetorical analysis, propaganda analysis, attitude change studies, voting studies, government and the news media, functional and systems analyses, technological changes, media technologies, campaign techniques, and research techniques.[6] In a survey of the state of the field in 1983, the same authors and Lynda Kaid found additional, more specific areas of concerns such as the presidency, political polls, public opinion, debates, and advertising.[7] Since the first study, they have also noted a shift away from the rather strict behavioral approach.

A decade later, Dan Nimmo and David Swanson argued that "political communication has developed some identity as a more or less distinct domain of scholarly work."[8] The scope and concerns of the area have further expanded to include critical theories and cultural studies. Although there is no precise definition, method, or disciplinary home of the area of inquiry, its primary domain comprises the role, processes, and effects of communication within the context of politics broadly defined.

In 1985, the editors of *Political Communication Yearbook: 1984* noted that "more things are happening in the study, teaching, and practice of political communication than can be captured within the space limitations of the relatively few publications available."[9] In addition, they argued that the backgrounds of "those involved in the field [are] so varied and pluralist in outlook and approach, . . . it [is] a mistake to adhere slavishly to any set format in shaping the content."[10] More recently, Swanson and Nimmo have called for "ways of overcoming the unhappy consequences of fragmentation within a framework that respects, encourages, and benefits from diverse scholarly commitments, agendas, and approaches."[11]

In agreement with these assessments of the area and with gentle encouragement, in 1988 Praeger established the series entitled "Praeger Studies in Political Communication." The series is open to all qualitative and quantitative methodologies as well as contemporary and historical studies. The key to characterizing the studies in the series is the focus on communication variables or activities within a political context or dimension. As of this writing, nearly forty volumes have been published and numerous impressive works are forthcoming. Scholars from the disciplines of communication, history, journalism, political science, and sociology have participated in the series.

I am, without shame or modesty, a fan of the series. The joy of serving as its editor is in participating in the dialogue of the field of political communication and in reading the contributors' works. I invite you to join me.

Robert E. Denton, Jr.

NOTES

1. See Robert E. Denton, Jr., *The Symbolic Dimensions of the American Presidency* (Prospect Heights, IL: Waveland Press, 1982); Robert E. Denton, Jr., and Gary Woodward, *Political Communication in America* (New York: Praeger, 1985; 2d ed., 1990); Robert E. Denton, Jr., and Dan Hahn, *Presidential Communication* (New York: Praeger, 1986); and Robert E. Denton, Jr., *The Primetime Presidency of Ronald Reagan* (New York: Praeger, 1988).

2. Aristotle, *The Politics of Aristotle,* trans. Ernest Barker (New York: Oxford University Press, 1970), p. 5.

3. Aristotle, *Rhetoric,* trans. Rhys Roberts (New York: The Modern Library, 1954), p. 22.

4. Dan Nimmo and Keith Sanders, "Introduction: The Emergence of Political Communication as a Field," in *Handbook of Political Communication,* eds. Dan Nimmo and Keith Sanders (Beverly Hills, CA: Sage, 1981), pp. 11–36.

5. Ibid., p. 15.

6. Ibid., pp. 17–27.

7. Keith Sanders, Lynda Kaid, and Dan Nimmo, eds. *Political Communication Yearbook: 1984* (Carbondale, IL: Southern Illinois University: 1985), pp. 283–308.

8. Dan Nimmo and David Swanson, "The Field of Political Communication: Beyond the Voter Persuasion Paradigm," in *New Directions in Political Communication,* eds. David Swanson and Dan Nimmo (Beverly Hills, CA: Sage, 1990), p. 8.

9. Sanders, Kaid, and Nimmo, *Political Communication Yearbook: 1984,* p. xiv.

10. Ibid.

11. Nimmo and Swanson, "The Field of Political Communication," p. 11.

Preface

This book takes Richard Neustadt's dictum that presidential power is the power to persuade and Jeffrey Tulis's description of *The Rhetorical Presidency* seriously enough to argue that we can profitably study presidential leadership rhetorically. Such a study requires exploration of the permeable boundaries between political science and communication studies. We argue that recent theories of presidential leadership have emphasized persuasion without studying it rhetorically, and that many studies of presidential rhetoric have failed to fully appreciate the political dynamics of the American presidency. We present our interpretive systems approach to persuasion and use it to analyze several important cases of presidential leadership. Our case studies have been selected for their theoretical significance, and our presentation of them purports to be neither chronological nor comprehensive. Many other cases might have been included, but they must wait for a different volume.

Two housekeeping matters deserve mention at the outset. First, our references to *The Public Papers of the Presidents* bracket the year of the speech instead of providing the copyright year in parentheses to minimize confusion. Second, we use masculine pronouns when referring to past presidents because all of them have been male, and we use gender-free references to those who might someday occupy the American presidency.

We wish to acknowledge Wake Forest University's generous support of this project with an R. J. Reynolds leave and grants from the Archie Fund, the Research and Publications Fund, and the Research and Creative Activities Fund. The archivists at the Harry S Truman, John F. Kennedy, Gerald R. Ford, Jimmy Carter, and Ronald Reagan Presidential Libraries provided invaluable assistance over several years. So did Jo Lee Credle and Elide Vargas, who assisted greatly with the preparation of the manuscript and index.

The
White House
Speaks

1

Presidential Leadership as Persuasion

When Richard Neustadt wrote in 1960 that "Presidential *power* is the power to persuade" (1980, p. 10), he forced us to reconceptualize the presidency. Unfortunately, portions of that reconceptualization have confounded scholarly efforts to understand presidential leadership. The purpose of this book is to refine the study of presidential leadership as persuasion by treating it as a rhetorical process. Our thesis is that political circumstances invite presidents to make rhetorical choices, each of which has political consequences.

This chapter begins our examination of presidential leadership with a critical synthesis of several of the major theories of presidential leadership advanced by political scientists since the publication of Neustadt's *Presidential Power*. That synthesis will lead to the presentation of a theoretical framework for studying presidential leadership as persuasion. Subsequent chapters will use that approach to illuminate a variety of case studies.

POLITICAL SCIENTISTS ON PRESIDENTIAL LEADERSHIP

Prior to the publication of Neustadt's *Presidential Power* in 1960, the presidency was studied from the perspective of roles and powers. The foremost proponents of the roles and powers approach were Clinton Rossiter (1956) and Edward S. Corwin (1957). Corwin examined the office by studying its constitutional and statutory powers, and

Rossiter examined the various hats worn by every president, including those of commander in chief, head of party, and so forth. Implicit in both books was the principle that presidential leadership could best be understood through the powers of the office rather than the uses made of those powers by individual presidents. It was with this view of the presidency that Neustadt took issue.

Neustadt and Presidential Power

Neustadt hypothesized that if presidential leadership could be understood solely, or even primarily, through its roles and powers then that approach would surely have to account for presidents' "self-executing" orders. He regarded as "self-executing" any presidential command that met five criteria: the command was a widely *publicized* and *unambiguous* statement of the president's *personal* and *legitimate* directive, for which the "order-taker" *possessed the resources* needed to implement it. Three cases met those criteria: President Truman's seizure of the steel mills, his firing of General Douglas MacArthur, and President Eisenhower's use of federal troops to quell opposition to the integration of Little Rock's Central High School. He concluded that instances of self-executing orders were rare, that they constituted these presidents' strategy of last resort, and that the results proved to be less than these presidents had sought. Concluding that even these three cases of presidential command failed to fulfill the predictions of the rules and powers approach, Neustadt offered an alternative formulation.

Neustadt's new formulation derived from his interpretation of the constitutional doctrine of "separation of powers" as separate institutions sharing powers. Viewed from that perspective the Constitution had created multiple institutions each with partial resources, such that government action required the cooperation of multiple agencies. Thus he observed that "The essence of a President's persuasive task is to convince such men that what the White House wants of them is what they ought to do for their sake and on their own authority" (p. 27). In an environment of separated institutions sharing power, then, the president must bargain with his counterparts.

The roles and powers therefore function less as "powers" than as sources of influence or bargaining chips in a process of give and take. Neustadt argued that individual presidents maximize or squander their sources of influence through actions that affect their professional reputation, their public prestige, and their range of choices. Presidential actions that enhance their professional reputation, public prestige, and options are like deposits in a political bank account, whereas actions that expend their political capital complicate the process of leadership.

Neustadt's approach gained favor because it made presidential leadership personal and dynamic rather than structural and rigid. It also seemed to explain presidential leadership during the early 1960s, at least partly because President Kennedy relied on Neustadt's book as a user's guide to the presidency. But because of its shortcomings, the book misdirected our attention. Those shortcomings merit discussion.

The first problem with Neustadt's original analysis derives from the fact that it was written at the dawn of the television age. True, television was born in 1939, and it had reached adolescence in the 1950s. But by the late 1950s, when Neustadt wrote his book, the west coast had just begun to receive live telecasts, there had been no televised political debates, and network newscasts were only fifteen minutes long. It is, therefore, not surprising that Presidents Truman and Eisenhower had rarely used television directly to mobilize public opinion. Also, Neustadt did not foresee the extent to which television coverage of presidents would undermine the vitality of political parties.

The second, and related, problem with Neustadt's analysis is that it was written at a time when most presidential bargaining could be conducted among the elite behind closed doors. During the last three decades, omnipresent public scrutiny and the declining influence of party loyalty and congressional seniority have made private bargaining less effective and more suspect than in Neustadt's day.

The third problem with Neustadt's analysis is that he mistakenly equated persuasion with bargaining. When Neustadt writes of inducing others to do what the White House wants them to do in their own interest and on their own authority, he is describing persuasion. The problem arises because he assumes that the only way for a president to induce compliance is through the trading of bargaining chips and that public persuasion is but one of those chips.

Persuasion and bargaining are discrete communication processes. In bargaining one wins by relinquishing something; in persuading one wins by justifying one's policy with the audience's needs, reasons, and priorities. Bargaining involves persuasion to the extent that the president's bargaining partners must believe that he has the chips, the cards, and the ability and willingness to play them. But persuading does not require the president to relinquish anything for the sake of compliance.

For these and other reasons, many political scientists have sought to repair, revise, and redirect Neustadt's work. Let us consider seven of these alternative conceptualizations.

Barber and Presidential Character

James David Barber expanded Neustadt's emphasis on the president's personal choices. If presidential success and failure are to be understood in relation to the individual president's personal choices, he reasoned, then it should be profitable to understand our presidents' idiosyncratic tendencies. Barber explored presidential biographies for pre-presidential hints of presidential performance.

Barber argued that presidential performance was influenced by the president's character, world view, and style. He further argued that character was determined in childhood, world view in adolescence, and style in early adulthood. Barber suggested that the most important of these three dimensions, but not the only important predictor, was the president's character. To facilitate the prediction of presidential performance, Barber proposed a four-part typology of character types based on two dimensions of character: activity/passivity and orientation toward life.

"Active-positive" presidents are flexible and adaptive people who value success. They enjoy the process of leading and consequently invest much of their energies in it. Active-positive presidents are like football quarterbacks: they call plays, run them, and then regroup to call new plays. Exemplified by Franklin Roosevelt and John F. Kennedy, active-positives are the people best suited by character to the demands of the presidency.

"Passive-positive" presidents such as William Howard Taft and Warren G. Harding need to be liked. They tend to act in ways that are consistent with their advisors' recommendations and public opinion, content to revel in their popularity. "Passive-negatives," on the other hand, treat leadership as a duty. Because they do not enjoy themselves, these presidents (such as Calvin Coolidge and Dwight Eisenhower) invest little of their energy in leading. Instead, they withdraw.

The most intriguing of Barber's character types is the "active-negative," who pours all of his energies into tasks that he hates. It is this very psychological contradiction that worries Barber about active-negatives. Their obsessive-compulsive nature inclines them toward rigidification and endangers their presidencies. Woodrow Wilson's refusal to negotiate with Senate moderates over the Treaty of Versailles, Herbert Hoover's intransigence on the issue of Depression era relief measures, Lyndon Johnson's escalation of the Vietnam War, and Richard Nixon's Watergate conduct all suggest to Barber the dangers of putting an active-negative in the Oval Office.

Barber's approach provides a helpful guide to presidential choice-making. To the extent that presidential leadership is contingent upon the character of individual presidents, his concern for presidents' personal needs and orientations must be addressed in any model of presidential leadership. But Barber's work is not without its difficulties.

The first shortcoming is that Barber underestimated the roles and powers of the office that impinge on the president. Barber has repeatedly bristled at the suggestion that he ever suggested that character *alone* determines presidential performance, and indeed that was never his position. Nevertheless, he has said (as a visitor to our own classrooms, as a matter of fact) that there is no such thing as the presidency, there is only one president after another. Just as the roles and powers view underestimated the part played by personal idiosyncrasies, so Barber overestimates personality relative to the external factors and expectations that make the presidency an office. In so doing, Barber overestimates the president's ability to do as he pleases and underestimates his interdependence with others.

The second problem with Barber's model is that his method is tautological. Barber's central thesis is that we can predict much of a president's performance if we can understand the development of his character in childhood and adolescence. How, then, do we learn about our presidents' childhoods? Barber's answer is to scour presidential biographies for evidence of character formation. Unfortunately, all such biographies are written *after*, not before, the public character of the adult is sufficiently well known to warrant biographies. Where Barber argues that presidential biographies offer clues to presidential performance, it might also be argued that presidential performance offers clues to the biographies' depictions of each president's early life. Barber looked where he could for evidence, and his research is exhaustive. But we must be cautious: his accurate predictions may indicate a good model, a biography inspired by adult success, or some of each.

Buchanan and the Presidential Experience

Bruce Buchanan advanced a model of the relationship between the presidential office and the person that offers a more balanced position than Barber's. In Buchanan's view the presidential office forces each president to tackle a set of roles, and each role provides its own set of psychological pressures (1978). The modern presidency requires each of its occupants to function as a policy advocate, as a national symbol, as a mediator, and as a crisis manager. Policy advocacy exposes the president to the psychological pressures of frustration and dissonance. His symbolic status exposes the president to expectations of deference and, when others do not defer, to dissonance. The functions of mediator and crisis manager similarly expose the president to stress. Consequently, every president faces a transcendent psychological environment of stress, frustration, dissonance, and anticipated deference that constitutes a uniquely presidential experience. It is the president's own personality, particularly his self-esteem, that determines how he will cope with both policy matters and the psychological environment of stress, frustration, dissonance, and deference. Buchanan's notion of presidential experience provided a reasonable way to frame the role-character controversy, but it left unanswered the question of how presidents lead. Buchanan attacked that topic in a subsequent book, *The Citizen's Presidency* (1987).

The key to reducing the psychological pressures on a president is public support. The presidential job description and the president's personality may be important, but it is "public support" that "empowers the contemporary presidency" (1987, p. 7). Public support, Buchanan observes, empowers presidents through increased congressional support for their legislative agenda, an enhanced ability to conduct foreign policy, favorable news coverage, enhanced credibility among government and policy professionals, and increased self-confidence. "A president is elevated, empowered, and enlarged or diluted, drained, and reduced," writes Buchanan, "according to the magnitude of public support mustered." In fact, he goes so far as to say that "public support is justly considered the enabling energy of the presidency, the only consistently reliable force available to the president for transcending constitutional weakness and even personal limitation" (1987, p. 16).

Because it is difficult for the president to function, either administratively or psychologically, when public support wanes, political professionals try to influence public opinion or to insulate the president from it. Fortunately for presidents already stressed and frustrated by the psychological demands of their office, Buchanan attributes the cause of declining support less to presidential behavior than to citizens' means of evaluating presidents. A series of controlled surveys revealed to Buchanan three distinguishable sets of priorities being used to evaluate presidents. Moreover, each of these groups was found to be associated more closely with political ideology than any of the other variables.

For his population, Buchanan identified policy liberals (accounting for about 18% of the electorate at the time) who wanted a "Humane Presidency" devoted to the reduction of international tensions and light on the exercise of military or economic toughness. Policy conservatives (36% of the electorate) wanted a "Potent Presidency" in which a competent individual with a clear sense of purpose used the office as an instrument of power. They regarded idealism and generosity as signs of weakness. Finally, policy moderates (about 40% of the electorate) wanted a "Pragmatic Presidency" characterized by neither empathy nor potency, but by an emotionally detached pursuit of results, including crisis management and peace.

If Buchanan's analysis and preliminary data are correct, indeed if they are even partly correct, then we have a presidency that requires public support but encounters at least three divergent public views of the ideal president, none of which is a majority view. With their views properly understood, presidents might expect the support of anywhere from 18 to 40 percent of the electorate—hardly enough to accrue the benefits of strong public support. The continuing absence of that strong support is likely to frustrate and stress presidents who are otherwise accustomed to deference, and thus tempt them to stretch, or even to break, the constitutional leash.

Buchanan's two books are valuable because they draw our attention to the interdependence of the president's and the citizens' cognitive and affective processes. More clearly than Barber, Buchanan has recognized that each of us has psychological needs and pressures, some of which find gratification or release in presidential politics. Thus, quite apart from substantive policies, a president can affect his public support by acting out the humane, potent, or pragmatic view of the office. But Buchanan's interest in psychological dimensions of the president-citizen relationship hampers his investigation of presidential coalitions.

Seligman and Covington's Coalitional Presidency

Lester Seligman and Cary Covington have made coalitions the heart and soul of their approach to presidential leadership (1989). To win election a candidate must assemble an electoral coalition from diverse financial backers, professional strategists, party factions, interest groups, and demographic voting blocs. But to govern after the election the president must assemble a governing coalition from members of Congress, interest groups, the bureaucracy, the media, the public, and personal appointees. To win re-election the president must reconstruct an electoral coalition; to govern during the second term he must retain or rebuild his governing coalition. Rarely are all of these coalitions congruent.

Seligman and Covington regard the translation of coalitions as the key to the process of presidential governance. A president has a "consensus coalition" when an "alliance of groups share similar views on a range of issues, or even a common ideology" (p. 9). Consensus coalitions are as rare as they are stable. Short of consensus, presidents can forge a "conglomerate coalition" from groups that share little beyond their support of the candidate/president. The translation of an electoral conglomerate into a governing conglomerate, and back again, is a delicate process that risks alienating important groups. Finally, there are "exclusive coalitions" based on groups supporting a single issue or concern. Because exclusive coalitions are the most prevalent in contemporary American politics, the translation of coalitions is now a permanent concern for presidents and their advisors.

The coalitional model advanced by Seligman and Covington echoes Neustadt's view of the president as a broker of interests who is sometimes able to reformulate interests and resources. Because it emphasizes translation and mobilization, their model captures far more of the dynamism of presidential leadership than could the roles and powers theory.

Given the centrality of mobilization and translation to their model, one might expect Seligman and Covington to echo Neustadt's view of presidential power as the power to persuade. But Covington has been reluctant to recognize the role of persuasion in the translation process (Smith, Tulis, & Covington, 1990). Interests are somehow known to citizens, and presidential actions somehow inspire these citizens to modify their issue positions, their group affiliations, and their allegiance to presidents. But those cognitive and affective changes occur, Covington maintains, apart from presidential rhetoric, news coverage, campaign commercials, debates, or interpersonal conversation.

How, then, do mobilization and translation occur, if not through communication? How do individuals acquire information without communication? How do leaders mobilize without persuasion? A model that defines presidential leadership in terms of its need to build, to maintain, to modify, and to rebuild coalitions and then ignores the processes through which building, maintaining, modifying, and rebuilding occur is a model that is at best partial. Fortunately, several other political scientists have recognized, explicitly, the relevance of persuasion to presidential leadership.

Edwards and the Public Presidency

Whereas Neustadt meant to say that the power of the president was the power to bargain, and while others were emphasizing the role of mobilization, George Edwards (1983) advanced the strongest arguments for the central role of persuasion in the presidency. He launched into his study of *The Public Presidency* with the following words, which merit quoting at length:

"Public sentiment is everything. With public sentiment nothing can fail, without it nothing can succeed." These words, spoken by Abraham Lincoln, pose what is perhaps the greatest challenge to any president: to obtain and maintain the public's support. It is this ceaseless endeavor that is at the heart of the public presidency.

Why is the public presidency such a critical component of presidential politics? The answer is straightforward. As every student of the presidency quickly learns, the president is rarely in a position to command others to comply with his wishes. Instead, he must rely on persuasion. (1983, p. 1)

Edwards was particularly interested in the public relations techniques used by presidents to persuade the public to enhance presidential influence with the Congress.

Edwards examined presidents' uses of addresses to the nation, press conferences, symbolic acts, and the manipulation of economic and foreign policy problems. One chapter of his book is devoted to direct leadership of public opinion through presidential addresses. It recognized that:

Language is not only a vehicle for expressing ideas. Words can also shape people's ideas by affecting what is expressed and how it is remembered, by evoking emotions, and by classifying objects of attention into categories that influence how they will be evaluated and what information will be relevant to them. (p. 65)

Edwards went well beyond the positions taken by his predecessors by recognizing the centrality of words, arguments, and discourse to presidential leadership.

But Edwards's intellectual interest and methodological expertise concern the analysis of public opinion. Consequently, his argument that language and reasons are central to presidential leadership did not lead him to examine the inner workings of presidential persuasion, for that is the province of rhetorical criticism.

Moreover, Edwards was more concerned with aggregate public opinion than with the opinions of diverse publics or constituencies. But to emphasize aggregate opinion is to risk underestimating crosscurrents of opinion in relation to public preferences and political coalitions. For example, presidential confrontations with Congress can enhance the president's aggregate public opinion even as they alienate the congressional moderates needed to achieve his goal. Because it underplays the role of evolutionary political coalitions, Edwards's perspective is more helpful for understanding presidential influence in times of unity than in times of division.

Kernell's Strategy of "Going Public"

Persuasion, specifically presidents' use of public persuasion to form coalitions, is also the subject of Samuel Kernell's book *Going Public* (1993). He distinguishes between the politics of bargaining and the politics of persuasion. Bargaining, he observes, is appropriate in a system of "institutional pluralism" wherein members of the elites can persuade one another in private, secure that they are insulated from direct public scrutiny. A variety of lower level "protocoalitions" form among legislators, bureaucrats, courts, interest groups, state governments, and political factions around policy directions, political cleavages, and friendships. As Kernell explains, protocoalitions arise as participants in the policy process seek out mutual needs and complementary resources at all stages of the policy process, from enactment to implementation. Many protocoalitions are transient, but the important ones endure:

Those that matter most tend to be constructed more coherently and durably. They arise not from some fleeting issue but from kindred interest or the continuing need of proximate participants to work together. . . . Rarely are these entities self-sufficient . . . a protocoalition typically must join with others if its bill is to be passed or its policy implemented effectively. (p. 14)

Some protocoalitions may be able to block others' efforts to set the policy agenda, but protocoalitions are, by definition, too narrow to set the policy agenda.

In institutional pluralism, presidents sometimes have used persuasion to nudge protocoalitions toward compromise or to increase their status among Washingtonians. This was the nature of American politics in Neustadt's day, and this was the bargaining president he described. Kernell argued that presidents in those days rarely sought to focus aggregate public opinion against their adversaries.

But even as Neustadt drafted his first edition during the late 1950s, other writers were describing changes in the political order. The New Deal began, and subsequent policies fostered, the emergence, energizing, and empowerment of a plethora of new interest groups. As these new interest groups engaged more and more actively in national and subnational politics, the protocoalitions found themselves beset by more diverse and more powerful competing pressures. Additionally, historic developments in communication and transportation technologies began to break through some of the walls that had insulated the bargaining elites from public scrutiny. These changes served to accelerate both the fragmentation of political parties and the decline of party loyalties, and to diminish the power of congressional leaders. These centrifugal forces transformed the politics of institutional pluralism into a free-for-all, a system Kernell calls "Individualized Pluralism," in which simple bargaining has become increasingly difficult.

Today's context of individualized pluralism, says Kernell, has increased the president's prospects for influence. As protocoalitions weaken and diversify, it is the president who can best attract free agents. Presidents do this by "Going Public": campaigning around the country to "create uncertainty for [the protocoalitions] while offering refuge in their support for his policies" (1993, p. 25). The individuation of the political system has not eliminated bargaining; in fact, the centrifugal forces make negotiated compromises all the more necessary. Presidents such as Jimmy Carter and Bill Clinton who come to the presidency as outsiders, and those like Ronald Reagan who are master persuaders, are especially likely to go public to improve their bargaining positions—as are presidents like Richard Nixon who face opposition party control of the Congress.

But for all its apparent advantages, warns Kernell, the strategy of going public can easily backfire and damage the president's bargaining position. This is especially likely when the president proves to be ineffective at public persuasion; this happened to Jimmy Carter, to Richard

Nixon during Watergate, and even to Ronald Reagan as he campaigned for aid to the Nicaraguan Contras.

Going public also can backfire when the president's advocacy offends the very members of Congress whom the president needs to persuade. Kernell cites a telling exchange between House Speaker "Tip" O'Neill and President Carter:

> O'Neill: Mr. President, I want you to understand something. Some of the brightest men in America are in this Congress of the United States. Don't make the mistake of underestimating them. . . . We want to work together, but I have a feeling you are underestimating the feeling of Congress and you could have some trouble.
> Carter: I'll handle them just as I handled the Georgia legislature. Whenever I had problems with the Georgia legislature I took the problems to the people of Georgia. (1993, p. 39)

The ultimate objective is agreement, and agreement cannot always be achieved with coercive strategies.

Kernell's analysis addresses the relationship between presidential bargaining and persuasion, and it locates them in the context of an evolving political order. Yet, as helpful as his analysis proves to be, it concerns macroscopic aspects of presidential persuasion. Kernell stops short of analyzing the argumentative and language choices made by presidents who do go public. He concludes that a presidential strategy of going public encourages issue posturing and strategic planning, and it also encourages the president's adversaries to go public as well. These same practices concerned Theodore Lowi.

Lowi's Personal Plebiscitary President

In *The Personal President* Theodore Lowi warned of the dangers inherent in Neustadt's conception of presidential power. He traced his view of the evolving presidency from its early dependence on the House of Representatives, through the rise of patronage in the 1830s, and the demands of populists and progressives at the turn of this century. According to Lowi, modern presidents have presided over a series of revolutions in which the national government took on responsibilities previously left to others, invoked direct and coercive authority over citizens, and empowered interest groups and bureaucrats by leaving unresolved policy questions to be settled during implementation.

Additionally, said Lowi, President Franklin Roosevelt began to create and nurture personal popularity through direct personal contact with the public. The consequence was the rise of the "plebiscitary presidency" in which the president's personal popularity is central. Today, according to Lowi:

the ultimate nominee of the so-called party does not possess a coalition, does not represent a coalition, and does not contribute in the quest for a nomination to the formation of a coalition. . . . A coalition is a fusion of unlike parts, an association formed by compromising conflicts into an interdependent organization, with something of a common history, a common sense of purpose, and even a set of common goals. (p. 112)

Lowi's conception of a coalition was far more restrictive than that of either Seligman and Covington or Kernell. As a result, Lowi saw presidents elected on the basis of personal popularity and personal promises that they could neither sustain nor fulfill. This presidency worried Lowi because he saw it as the centerpiece of an American system of government so nontraditional that he referred to it as "the Second Republic."

The national government of the late twentieth century is now president-centered. Presidential centrality spurs presidents to encourage public hopes and expectations with initiatives that divide the very constituencies needed for success; short of success, presidents turn to public relations techniques to create the appearance of success. It was Lowi's conviction that the personal presidency is unworkable and inescapable, until we create a system in which multiple parties hold each other accountable for their initiatives and failures.

Lowi's analysis is provocative and well argued, even if occasionally hyperbolic. His diagnosis of the body politic and the extensive surgery he prescribes require systemic change because he analyzes political behavior macroscopically. The trends of which he writes are undoubtedly important, but it might be prudent for us to examine the patient microscopically just in case simpler methods of treatment can help. Let us turn to the issue of presidential popularity.

Lowi said that presidential performance ratings tend continually downward unless the trend is interrupted by an international event associated with the president, even if his response is considered unsuccessful. Only Reagan's popularity diverged from this pattern, and Lowi attributed that to a unique charisma that confounds an understanding of the office. But how does an event become either "known" or "associated with the president"? And who "defines" it, as a success or failure? Even if such international events are beyond a president's formal control, their public meaningfulness is never beyond his rhetorical reach. To a considerable degree a "crisis" exists when a president says it does, and it ends when he says it has passed.

Because of his concern for long-term systemic and structural changes, including changes in communication technology, Lowi never tackled some very basic questions related to presidents' "exalted rhetoric," "inflated expectations," and their "associations" with issues and events. Is it possible for any of us to perceive associations among persons and events without some kind of language? Is it possible for citizens to have political expectations, inflated or otherwise, without a logic of cause and effect? Do all Americans need and want the same things? If not, then how do presidential actions uniformly inflate the public's diverse expectations, and thus disappoint them uniformly? In short, are there no political consequences attendant to presidents' choices of reasons and language? Lowi's sweeping critique of the presidency prematurely discounted these questions.

Tulis and the Rhetorical Presidency

"The modern presidency is buffeted by two 'constitutions,'" observed Jeffrey Tulis (1987). The first is, of course, the original Constitution as amended. This was a Constitution drafted by men who grudgingly added a chief executive late in the process, fearful that the young country might fall prey to some unscrupulous, silver-tongued demagogue. They created the electoral college as a buffer between the public and the president, and for good measure they routed electoral college stalemates through the House of Representatives. Presidents of the first century largely avoided policy debates, said Tulis. They spoke on ceremonial occasions and were careful to explicitly ground any other remarks in their constitutional duties.

The second "constitution" began to dawn toward the end of the nineteenth century in response to government corruption and legislative gridlock. Theodore Roosevelt was the first president to try this approach, using it to facilitate passage of the 1906 Hepburn Act. By pretending to support a tariff bill, Roosevelt created a bargaining chip that he could trade for some Republican votes for the railroad regulation bill that was important to him. Additionally, he used the "bully pulpit" of the presidency to reassure those distressed by the bill that it was less radical than they supposed. In both ways Theodore Roosevelt took unusual rhetorical steps in the direction of policy making.

But even as he was adopting a new form of leadership, Roosevelt grounded his actions in traditional principles. In his view, presidents periodically needed to take the perspective of founders if they were to achieve the founders' original intentions. This was especially important because the Congress had come to be dominated by political factions built around the sort of demagoguery feared by the founders. The president could restore the government to its principles by speaking out on the issues to undermine the demagogues.

It fell to Woodrow Wilson to set forth the second "constitution." As a professor at Princeton University, Wilson had diagnosed the problems endemic in congressional government during the 1880s, and by 1908 he had begun to emphasize presidential leadership as a solution. Tulis argued that Wilson pioneered two forms of presidential leadership—the visionary speech and the policy-stand speech—that marked the rise of the rhetorical presidency.

Beginning with Wilson, and especially since the presidency of Franklin Roosevelt, American presidents have used public addresses to lead. Technological advances such as radio, newsreels, television, and satellites have enabled presidents to make more extensive use of speeches, but the Roosevelt and Wilson cases demonstrate that the doctrine of the rhetorical presidency predates those technologies. Indeed, Wilson began the rhetorical presidency prior to the development of microphones and loudspeakers.

The doctrine of the rhetorical presidency is the second "constitution" that buffets contemporary presidents, and it differs markedly from the original Constitution. It provides just the sort of president-public relationship that worried the founders. It undermines the delicate system of checks and balances and encourages presidents to set the legislative agenda and to work for its enactment. Thus the contemporary presidency is a hybrid of the old and the new. The rhetorical presidency is, therefore, both good and bad. According to Tulis, "The rhetorical presidency is more deleterious than beneficial to American politics because the rhetorical presidency is not just the use of popular leadership, but rather the routine appeal to public opinion. Intended to ameliorate crises, the rhetorical presidency is now the creator of crises, or pseudo-crises" (p. 181). But for better or worse, the American political system of the late twentieth century revolves around the rhetorical presidency, as Wilson imagined and the founders feared; and presidents who ignore the second "constitution" court government gridlock and political disfavor.

Tulis's lucid analysis demonstrated the increasing role of public persuasion in the presidency of the twentieth century. Nevertheless, he paid scant attention to what these presidents have said and how they have said it.

Summary: Political Science on Presidential Leadership

So far this chapter has summarized eight different approaches to presidential leadership advanced by political scientists. Although each of these approaches has unique contributions, they have important points of convergence. Let us attempt to summarize the points on which we see widespread, if not always unqualified, agreement.

1.   The presidency of the late twentieth century is fundamentally different from the presidency envisioned by the founders (Kernell, Lowi, Seligman and Covington, Tulis).

2.   The presidency of the late twentieth century is actively engaged in policy making and the legislative process (Edwards, Kernell, Lowi, Neustadt, Seligman and Covington, Tulis).

3.   Presidential leadership in the late twentieth century entails the creation, mobilization, transformation, and maintenance of coalitions (Buchanan, Edwards, Kernell, Lowi, Neustadt, Seligman and Covington, Tulis).

4.   The creation, mobilization, transformation, and maintenance of coalitions requires presidents of the late twentieth century to influence a variety of other citizens: the Congress and the courts, political parties and interest groups, reporters and pundits, the powerful and the powerless, foreign and domestic groups, public opinion and posterity (Buchanan, Edwards, Kernell, Lowi, Neustadt, Seligman and Covington, Tulis).

5.   Presidents of the late twentieth century attempt to influence those other citizens by informing them, by bargaining with them, by persuading them; in short, by communicating with them (Barber, Buchanan, Edwards, Kernell, Lowi, Neustadt, Tulis).

6.   The effectiveness of a president's leadership in the late twentieth century depends heavily on his persuasive abilities (Barber, Edwards, Lowi, Neustadt, Tulis).

These six features of presidential leadership point unmistakably to presidential persuasion as a crucial component of presidential leadership.

Even though many political scientists have been interested in analyses of presidential leadership as persuasion, few have attempted to analyze presidential persuasion as persuasion: to examine the language and logical choices made by presidents in relation to the array of exigencies and constraints buffeting them and their contemporaries. That has been the work of many others who have been toiling in the fields of political communication and rhetorical criticism. The contributions from those fields are the next concern of this chapter.

COMMUNICATION STUDIES AND PRESIDENTIAL LEADERSHIP

The cliché that "politics is all talk" can be a convenient fig leaf for those who evade their civic responsibilities. But in a very real sense politics *is* all talk. Communication is the fundamental social process through which individuals build personal relationships and social communities. Only through communication can persons conceive of interests, political issues, constitutional authorities, sanctions, allies, and adversaries. Only through our silent internal arguments can we think and rethink our political choices (Billig, 1991).

The problem is not that "politics is talk," for there is no other way for humans to establish or employ abstract standards for behavior. The problem is that most citizens are poorly equipped to understand, and therefore to participate in, politics as talk; perhaps this is so because they are unaware of the relationship between self-governance and communication.

The framers of the Constitution devised a tripartite system with both separate and shared powers that would unify America by blending diverse representative mechanisms: state governments, state-appointed senators, sub-state representatives, a president chosen by citizens whose preferences were weighted in accordance with their congressional representation, and a court reflecting judicial expertise. The Constitution explicitly legitimized both the institutions' responsibilities for devising, executing, and applying laws and the enduring sovereignty of the states and people apart from their national government. By dividing authority the Constitution denied any individual the right to orient society, and it based government on the dialectic of emerging interests and coalitions. Thus communication among interests was central to governance in America from the beginning.

Because communication is the fundamental process of human interaction, it is only through communication that individuals find community. More specifically, institutions, legitimacy, statutes, leaders,
sanctions, interests, ideologies, and coalitions are all socially constructed through language. Young children are politically acculturated
with stories such as the familiar legend that links George Washington,
the cherry tree, and honesty. In later years, language becomes the only
way to comprehend the uniquely American institution of the electoral
college. Clearly, neither politics nor government can exist without communication. In fact, communication serves at least five functions in the
American system of government.

The Governmental Functions of Communication

Communication serves to *unify* a society by fostering a sense of
inclusion and efficacy among its varied people, interests, values, and
traditions. The basic act of addressing another person establishes a
sense of relational inclusion. Beyond that, any speech necessarily
blends a variety of symbols, myths, values, and reasons to evoke a
sense of recognition and identification among those in the audience.
But because of the diversity of citizens and their preferences, identification and polarization are inextricably related. Therefore, communication that is essential for unification paradoxically produces division,
which in turn creates a need for unifying communication.

Communication serves to *legitimize* by justifying the distribution of
power in society. The doctrines of Divine Right, Social Darwinism, and
Consent of the Governed have all been used to justify political influence. Powerholders and aspirants to political power alike ground their
claims in a socially accepted doctrine of legitimation that is created,
learned, and applied through communication.

Communication serves to *orient* a society by defining objectives
and problems in coherent narratives that integrate people, interests, values, traditions, power distributions, and spheres of influence. One of
these narratives attains temporary ascendency and frames an agenda for
ordering society's priorities. This occurs only through communication,
and the characterization of the political landscape frames political reality for the community.

Communication serves to *resolve conflicts* by drawing new distinctions, by transcending differences, by verifying factual claims, by
weighing arguments, by adjudicating arguments, and by choosing
between prospective futures. Reflecting on Karl Deutsch's *Nerves of*

Government (1966), Doris Graber (1992) observes that "the essence of governmental organization is decision-making, and the essence of decision-making is communication" (p. xv).

Finally, communication serves to *implement policies* by mobilizing or by narcotizing others. Mobilizing consists of activating and organizing people; narcotizing is the process of pacifying and distracting them. Effective persuasion mobilizes supporters and narcotizes adversaries, but it is possible to mobilize opponents and to narcotize supporters.

The presidency of the late twentieth century must be understood as the interface between the person and the office, between the leader and followers, between the Constitution and precedents, between the past and the future. It requires its occupants to reconcile their goals with practical constraints, their personal identities with role expectations, their agenda with the public's agenda, and personal coherence with social coordination. Through communication each president attempts to orient the country with words and symbolic actions.

This book is about our individual and collective efforts to make sense of the world we inhabit by having others use our logic (by force, when necessary). It is less about institutions, laws, and procedures than it is about the negotiation of consensual agreements that all too quickly outlive their usefulness. Because societies exist in the process of communing, political communication is more verb than noun. We agree with many of the political scientists, previously discussed, who say that presidents are now the central figures in the ongoing effort to make sense of the world and its oddities. If the contemporary presidency is as rhetorically driven as Tulis and Edwards contend, and as Seligman and Covington imply, then it is worth our while to study the rhetoric that it generates.

This is certainly not to say that presidential politics should *only* be studied rhetorically. Rather, it is to insist that studies of presidential politics should be mindful of fundamental rhetorical processes, even as our studies of presidential rhetoric must be mindful of relevant political variables and processes. Like Neustadt, we are interested in presidential power as the power to persuade; but unlike him, we are neither interested in the president's *personal* power nor do we equate persuasion with bargaining. Like Seligman and Covington, we regard coalitions and their transformation as crucial to presidential leadership; but unlike them, we regard persuasive communication as the crucial process through which those dynamic coalitions come and go. Like Lowi and Tulis, we regard the contemporary presidency as highly rhetorical; but more than they, we want to examine the rhetoric that it has generated.

And like Edwards and Kernell, we regard public persuasion as a crucial dimension of presidential leadership; but more than they, we want to explore the significance of what presidents say and how they say it.

The title *The White House Speaks* is, therefore, a reference to the nature of presidential leadership, to the collaborative nature of presidential speechwriting, and to the institutionalized genres of presidential discourse. Fortunately the field of presidential rhetoric has not gone unplowed. Let us therefore preface our studies of presidential rhetoric with a selective review of the pertinent literature.

Students of public discourse have traditionally been drawn to the study of individual orators. It is therefore hardly surprising that most presidents have been studied as individual orators, often with great value. But because the American presidency is a governmental role now heavily dependent on public persuasion, we cannot assume that the rhetoric of the rhetorical presidency is neither more nor less than the aggregation of personal rhetorical styles. We must look, at least initially, for the peculiarities of rhetoric that is *presidential*—for the impact of the office upon the discourse. Three dimensions of presidential rhetoric are its frequency, its genres, and its language.

Hart's Patterns of Presidential Speechmaking

Once we have entertained the hypothesis that presidents use public persuasion, it behooves us to test it. Roderick P. Hart, the most innovative student of presidential persuasion, tackled this task and more in *The Sound of Leadership* (1987). Hart explored empirical patterns in the relative frequency of various kinds of presidential speeches. He ignored what presidents said and how they said it; instead he focused on presidential speech acts. As he explained it:

The essential logic of this book is as follows: by choosing to utter words to another, a speaker makes at least these decisions—to speak to A and not B; to speak now and not then or never; to speak here and not there; to speak about this matter and not about all other matters; to speak for this period of time, not longer or shorter. These rhetorical decisions by a speaker contain "information" for us as observers if we are wise enough and patient enough to track these decisions. (p. xxi)

Hart and his associates coded every address from the Truman through Reagan administrations according to speaker as well as situational, temporal, social, political, and topical variables; and then they examined the data for statistical patterns. The data reveal some of the contours of the rhetorical presidency.

Presidents from 1945 to 1985 gave an average of twenty speeches per month, ranging from Eisenhower's ten to Ford's forty-three; but there was no statistical relationship between the frequency of speechmaking and public approval. Each new president's first year was busier rhetorically than that of his predecessor, and each president's second year was even busier than his first. Presidents Ford, Carter, and Reagan were far more likely to engage in ceremonial rhetoric than were their predecessors, and the recent presidents also had more multi-speech days. Hart's data suggest that President Kennedy reshaped the presidency for his successors by speaking more frequently in a wider variety of forums about a broader range of topics.

The presidents in Hart's sample engaged heavily and increasingly in ceremonial rhetoric (37.5%), as opposed to briefings (26.5%), political rallies (15%), organizational meetings (10.3%), and miscellaneous speaking activities (p. 69). All this ceremonializing is rhetorically significant, said Hart, because ceremonies reinforce the president's elevated symbolic status, they invite citizen participants to be politely deferential, and they fill participant observers with a host of thoughts and feelings that function both to reinforce communal solidarity and to distract them from their policy differences with the president (pp. 67–76).

Obviously, most presidential speeches have been delivered in Washington, DC. But 40 percent of those Washington speeches were given to interest groups and invited guests presumably in hope of, or in recognition of, their support. When Congress is controlled by the opposition party the president travels the country, resulting in a decrease in Washington speeches from 69.8 percent of the total to 54 percent (p. 83).

Presidential talk is also the subject of other people's talk, especially that of reporters. Being mindful of this, presidential aides plan their addresses to maximize favorable news coverage. Nevertheless, Hart's analysis suggested that although presidential activities provided the "news peg" for many stories, the presidential voice accounted for only 7.9 percent of the speaking time in network newscasts. Silent pictures of presidents provided the visual interest while reporters used their 46.8 percent of the speaking time to frame the conflicts that swirled around presidents and their political contemporaries, who got a combined 45.3 percent of the speaking time. In short, presidential speechmaking attracts news coverage, but it can hardly be said that the resulting coverage guarantees that the president's message, or even the president himself, will reach the public directly.

The research reported in *The Sound of Leadership* lends support to Tulis's argument that twentieth-century presidents rely heavily on public persuasion. It also suggests some of the resources, public expectations, and limitations faced by these eight presidents, as well as those that Presidents Bush and Clinton would later inherit. But because it is macroscopic in nature, it ignores most other aspects of presidential rhetoric.

Campbell and Jamieson's Genres of Presidential Governance

Karlyn Kohrs Campbell and Kathleen Hall Jamieson (1990) have made a substantial contribution to our understanding of the rhetorical dimensions of presidential leadership by describing the features of eight specific genres of presidential speechmaking, all derived from the presidency's tasks of governance. Each of these genres provides each new president with a set of public expectations, resources, and constraints to be addressed in the exercise of constitutional duties.

Inaugural Addresses. These addresses need to facilitate the rite of presidential investiture and smooth the potentially traumatic transition. Toward this end inaugural addresses invoke communal values, establish the political principles that will guide the new administration, and allow the new president to demonstrate that he can credibly enact the presidential role. As a type of epideictic (or ceremonial) discourse, any inaugural address must attempt to fuse past and future in the present and employ eloquent phraseology worthy of historic preservation.

State of the Union Addresses. These speeches facilitate institutional maintenance in two ways: by recognizing the president as both the symbolic and the real head of state, and by providing him with his most significant moment of legislative leadership. It is significant that Woodrow Wilson was the first president personally to speak to the Congress about the state of the Union as well as the first president to take an aggressive legislative role. State of the Union addresses simultaneously establish the separate identities of the White House and the Congress and invite legislative dialogue. Presidents intent on exercising legislative leadership use these addresses to extend the political principles articulated in their inaugural address and to use those principles to frame their legislative agenda.

Veto Messages. The requirement that presidents explain to the Congress the reasons for their vetoes institutionalizes these messages. Veto messages typically emphasize the president's role as that of a "legislator-judge" acting on behalf of the interests of "the people." Although vetoes occur only when the president and Congress are sharply divided, veto messages typically employ calm, objective, and impartial language and profess to be nonpartisan. The president can use the veto message to set forth his legislative requirements, thereby expanding his legislative leadership role.

War Addresses. These speeches derive from the constitutional separation of powers: the president is the commander in chief, but war is declared by the Senate. This sharing of the war powers by two institutions requires coordination and, ideally, cooperation. War messages reflect the president's need for Congress to legitimate his use of his war powers in pursuit of a goal that has been justified. When they work, war addresses unify the nation behind the president and the war and thus facilitate victory. War messages are typically thoughtful rather than angry narratives that explain the origins of the immediate crisis and the necessity for war. Presidents normally argue that military force is being used as a last resort and ask for congressional legitimation. Over time presidents have expanded the range of arguments used to justify independent presidential initiatives and have tended to announce actions already taken. The case of the 1991 Gulf War indicates that a successful war address is now more important than a formal declaration of war.

Rhetoric to Forestall Impeachment. According to Campbell and Jamieson, this type of speech is more common than we might imagine, largely because it has often worked. In addition to the impeachment of Andrew Johnson and the near impeachment of Richard Nixon, there were the responses of Presidents Jackson, Tyler, and Buchanan to formal congressional reports, President Lincoln's response to New York Democrats, and Ronald Reagan's response to the Iran-Contra charges. Without this rhetorical genre it would be much easier for Congress to back a president into a corner. One strategy of presidential defense is a personal "apologia" that supports the president's character. These speeches are personal in tone and strive to make the accusations seem impossible, implausible, or at least unworthy of impeachment. Presidents frequently admit mistakes by attributing their misjudgments to admirable traits of character. The alternative strategy is "forensic" as the president demonstrates that the constitutional duties and the oath of office were upheld. These speeches typically advance three arguments: the president kept his oath, his accusers undermine the Constitution, and the president is accountable not to his congressional accusers but to the Constitution and the people.

Formal Impeachment. Impeachment charges limit the president's freedom to use personal apologia, compel him to respond to specific charges, and require him to persuade a particular set of individuals who will vote formally to reach a verdict on his fitness for office. His case is made by legal experts rather than by the president himself, and the arguments helpful for mobilizing public opinion decline in utility.

Pardoning Rhetoric. A president's exercise of his constitutionally unlimited power to pardon is explained in these addresses. It is the pardon document that excuses the accused from punishment but the pardon rhetoric that protects the president from public disfavor. He must act as the symbolic head of state to justify the timing of the pardon and its contribution to the public good.

Farewell Addresses. These have become increasingly popular as the presidency has become increasingly rhetorical. Farewells combine the president's roles of leader and visionary so as to define his legacy to the country. For this to occur, say Campbell and Jamieson, the legacy must be consistent with the president's prior rhetoric, it must be offered for contemplation rather than action, and it should "encapsulate in a memorable phrase or sentence" an enduring truth about American society and government (p. 194).

Campbell and Jamieson's exhaustive analysis is important because it separates presidential actions from the presidential rhetoric explaining and justifying those actions. They enable us to better understand that President Ford's problem was not his pardon of Nixon but his inability to justify that pardon to the public. It helps us to see that Lyndon Johnson's problem was not the war in Vietnam but his failures to legitimate his exercise of his war powers and to mobilize the public behind his goal. Finally, their analysis shows how recurrent political exigencies, constitutional constraints, and rhetorical precedents affect each president's rhetorical elbow room. Presidents Lincoln, Wilson, and Roosevelt enlarged the scope of presidential powers with convincing rhetorical justifications; on the other hand, the scope of presidential powers was undermined by President Truman's inadequate justification for the steel seizure, by President Nixon's inadequate justification of executive privilege, and by President Ford's inadequate justification of the Nixon pardon.

Hart on Presidential Language

The books by Hart and by Campbell and Jamieson suggested ways in which the presidency shapes speechmaking and the lines of argument appropriate to the various tasks of governance. On a microscopic level, the presidency also affects its occupants' language. Hart (1984) used a computer-based analysis of presidential language to explain the unique properties of presidential talk. He compared presidential language with pre-presidential language, campaign language, and post-presidential language; and he compared the language of presidents with the language of corporate executives, political candidates, religious leaders, and social activists. Much as Bruce Buchanan tried to identify the impact of the presidential experience on the president's psyche, Hart's data enabled him to analyze the presidency's impact on the president's language.

Hart's data suggested that presidents, upon inauguration, begin to employ language that is both more concrete and more cautious. Apparently sobered by the powers and responsibilities of the office, they largely abandon the histrionic bravado of bold abstractions appropriate for political candidates. They are less belligerent and dogmatic than social activists; more abstract than corporate executives, but less so than religious leaders.

Hart also demonstrated some of the ways that presidential language changes over time. The language of Presidents Johnson, Nixon, Ford, Carter, and Reagan was more cautiously optimistic, more person- and self-oriented, and less assertive than had been the language of Presidents Truman, Eisenhower, and Kennedy. During their administrations, each president from 1945 to 1981 used language that was increasingly more certain and less simple, and the "clear, eloquent retort" was replaced by "the strong statement, even the overly strong statement" (p. 50).

Regularities are also apparent in various presidents' responses to circumstances. National strife is met with strong and certain language replete with self-references that attest to the president's resolute leadership. Discussions of values invite language that is complex, embellished, moderately self-referencing, and lacking in certainty. Pragmatic topics invite language that is certain and embellished. Moreover, presidential language changes when presidents speak on television. The language of presidential television was found to have more self-references, familiarity, human interest, and optimism than the language of personal appearances.

Presidential language is important because figures of speech are also figures of thought. The kinds of words used by presidents both shape and reflect the ways in which they perceive themselves and the world around them, and they invite their fellow citizens to conceive of the world in those same terms. As presidents increasingly refer to themselves, for example, they increasingly invite their citizenry to credit and to blame them for the course of events. And when they speak differently as presidents than they spoke as candidates, they invite their fellow citizens to see them as unfaithful to the images they projected to win election.

The approaches taken by Jamieson, Campbell, and Hart to study presidential rhetoric are all intended to reveal regularities and patterns. They are not, nor were they intended to be, approaches to particular episodes of presidential persuasion, to the idiosyncratic aspects of the rhetoric of presidents, to the responses of particular audiences and constituencies, or to illuminate the process of rhetorical coalition-building.

CONCLUSIONS

This chapter began our exploration of presidential leadership as persuasion with a review of several of the major approaches to presidential leadership advanced over the years by political scientists. All of those models suggest, directly or indirectly, the centrality of persuasion to the current state of the presidency and its need to perform important governmental functions.

The chapter closed by considering the ways in which the nature of the presidency itself has affected presidential discourse: the patterns of speechmaking, the genres of governance, and the language of the rhetorical presidency. But these institutional regularities hardly account for the variabilities of presidential leadership. To understand presidential successes, frustrations, and failures we must examine what presidents say and how they say it. That requires us to turn from the normal to the exceptional.

Chapter 2 presents the interpretive systems model of political communication that will frame our analysis of presidential persuasion. It explains how each individual's personal interpretive processes find coordination in four social interpretive structures: laws, language, logic, and ideologies. These structures define a multitude of interpretive communities, many of which become politically active. Presidents lead by weaving discourse from the interpretive threads available to them.

Chapter 3 analyzes the relationship between rhetoric and coalitions by reconsidering Gerald Ford's handling of the Nixon and draft-evader pardons. It emphasizes the ways in which Ford's handling of those pardons was constrained by his lack of either an electoral or a governing coalition.

Chapter 4 examines the presidential use of rhetoric to unify and to divide. It considers George Bush's mixed success with the rhetoric of division: he used it to win election in 1988, he used it with mixed results as president, and he used it unsuccessfully in his bid for re-election.

Chapter 5 considers the political significance of narratives as evidenced by the 1976–1978 debate over the Panama Canal treaties. Gerald Ford, Jimmy Carter, and Ronald Reagan were all involved in this debate, but it was Reagan's compelling narrative built from public recollections and fantasies that enabled him to win control of the Republican Party and the presidency.

Chapter 6 considers the political significance of political jeremiads from the "bully pulpit" of the presidency. The jeremiad was the first truly American rhetorical form, and it has been used by many aspirants to office. This chapter examines four presidential jeremiads—by Franklin Roosevelt, John F. Kennedy, Jimmy Carter, and Ronald Reagan—to analyze the advantages and disadvantages of presidential sermonizing.

Chapter 7 analyzes two presidential efforts to mobilize support for policies requiring public sacrifice: Harry Truman's famine relief campaign and Jimmy Carter's energy program. It explores the strategies available to presidents who need to induce public sacrifice.

Chapter 8 draws upon the Watergate and Iran-Contra scandals to explore the kind of "rhetorical crisis" that occurs when presidents become entangled in their own rhetoric. In Watergate Richard Nixon said too much and was trapped by his own words. Ronald Reagan, on the other hand, found that the rhetoric that had served him so well was inappropriate for his Iran-Contra defense.

In Chapter 9 we summarize our conclusions and offer some observations about the demise of the Bush presidency and the first hundred days of the Clinton presidency. We suggest that George Bush abdicated the rhetorical presidency years before he lost the election, and that Bill Clinton won the presidency by emphasizing persuasive communication that contrasted starkly with that of George Bush. The chapter concludes with several suggestions that could increase the rhetorical effectiveness of Bill Clinton's presidential leadership.

REFERENCES

Barber, J. D. (1985). *The presidential character: Predicting performance in the White House* (3rd ed.). Englewood Cliffs, NJ: Prentice-Hall.

Billig, M. (1991). *Ideology and opinions.* Newbury Park, CA: Sage.

Buchanan, B. (1978). *The presidential experience.* Englewood Cliffs, NJ: Prentice-Hall.

Buchanan, B. (1987). *The citizen's presidency.* Washington, DC: Congressional Quarterly.

Campbell, K. K., & Jamieson, K. H. (1990). *Deeds done in words: Presidential rhetoric and the genres of governance.* Chicago: University of Chicago Press.

Corwin, E. S. (1957). *The president: Office and powers* (4th rev. ed.). New York: New York University Press.

Deutsch, K. (1966). *The nerves of government.* New York: Free Press.

Edwards, G. C., III. (1983). *The public presidency: The pursuit of popular support.* New York: St. Martin's.

Graber, D. A. (1992). *Public sector communication: How organizations manage information.* Washington, DC: Congressional Quarterly.

Hart, R. P. (1984). *Verbal style and the presidency: A computer-based analysis.* New York: Academic Press.

Hart, R. P. (1987). *The sound of leadership: Presidential communication in the modern age.* Chicago: University of Chicago Press.

Kernell, S. (1993). *Going public: New strategies of presidential leadership* (2d ed.). Washington, DC: Congressional Quarterly. Originally published in 1986.

Lowi, T. J. (1985). *The personal president: Power invested, promise unfulfilled.* Ithaca: Cornell University Press.

Neustadt, R. E. (1980, rev. ed.). *Presidential power: The politics of leadership from FDR to Carter.* New York: John Wiley. Originally published in 1960.

Rossiter, C. (1956). *The American presidency.* New York: Harcourt, Brace & World.

Seligman, L. R., & Covington, C. (1989). *The coalitional presidency.* Chicago: Dorsey Press.

Smith, C. A., Tulis, J., & Covington, C. (1990). The rhetorical and coalitional presidency: An interdisciplinary seminar. Chicago: Speech Communication Association annual convention.

Tulis, J. K. (1987). *The rhetorical presidency.* Princeton, NJ: Princeton University Press.

2

The Interpretive Systems Approach
to Presidential Leadership

One of the present authors (Smith 1990, 1992) has suggested a conceptual model that treats politics as communication. It does this by emphasizing the innate, involuntary human processes through which individuals make their worlds personally coherent, even as they create structures to facilitate their social coordination with others. But the crosspressures toward individual coherence and social coordination nurture an array of interpretive communities that inevitably come into conflict with one another, thereby inviting struggles for dominance. During these struggles some individuals change communities and, therefore, some communities gain and lose members. Over time we observe the survival of the fittest, at least until the less fit are able to regroup and challenge again.

This chapter provides a revision of the interpretive systems model. It illustrates the model's principles and dynamics with presidential examples and suggests some of the ways to study presidential leadership as persuasion.

THE FOUR INTERPRETIVE PROCESSES AND STRUCTURES

There are four innate personal interpretive processes that each person uses to arrive at a personally useful conception of the world. Through these four interdependent processes we need, we symbolize, we prefer, and we reason. To coordinate our activities with others we create or learn laws to guide our need fulfillment, languages to guide our symbolizing, logics to guide our reasoning, and ideologies to guide our preferencing. Let us explore each of the four.

Needing and Laws

Needing is the process through which individuals (re)formulate their personal motives, drives, needs, and goals. It refers to each human being's personal need to have personal needs, and it includes each human's need to periodically (re)formulate those needs, sometimes in a public way (Lasswell, 1962; Lipset, 1960; Greenstein, 1969). The needing process is internal, personal, and private. For purposes of illustration we shall use Abraham Maslow's (1943) familiar hierarchy of needs and James David Barber's (1985) typology of presidential character types.

Maslow suggested that human needs range from the physiological and survival needs through safety and security needs, to the needs for love and belonging, respect and esteem, to—in some cases—the need for self-actualization. His hierarchy helps to explain, for example, why many of the upper middle class people who voted for George Bush in the prosperity of 1988 turned against him in 1992. They did so, Maslow might say, because the economy turned sour and threatened their safety and security and, in some cases, their physiological and survival needs. Consequently, those voters literally could no longer afford to use their political behavior to fulfill their higher level needs; they had to use their political behavior to fulfill their fundamental survival and security needs by voting for economic change.

Maslow's hierarchy also suggests a fundamental difference between the politically active and the politically passive. Few people can afford to become politically active until their physiological and safety/security needs have been satisfied because they are too busy trying to keep the wolf away from their doors. On the other hand, people whose needs allow them to run for office experience basic need issues from a vantage point of safety. When politicians say "I feel your pain," it is not their own pain. The relationship between personal needs and political leadership is still more evident in Barber's work on presidential character.

Barber's (1985) studies were based on the connections between presidents' personal needs and their behavioral tendencies. It is not that some presidents "have" needs or characteristics that other presidents "lack." Rather, Barber said, "We all have all of them, but in different amounts and in different combinations" (p. 4). He defined "character" as "the way the President orients himself toward life—not for the moment, but enduringly" (p. 5). Barber's explanation of character deserves to be quoted at length because it has often been oversimplified:

Character is the person's stance as he confronts experience. And at the core of character, a man confronts himself. The President's fundamental self-esteem is his prime personal resource: to defend and advance that, he will sacrifice much else he values. . . . A President who rates himself by the standard of achievement, for instance, may be little affected by losses of affection. (p. 5)

In short, we all want affection, success, self-worth, and we all want to feel needed. But relative to others some of us *need* to be liked, others *need* to achieve results, others *need* to establish their self-worth, and others *need* to be needed.

Barber argued that these inner needs interact with political forces to create an inner struggle between the rational person who calculates and the emotional person who feels. Because active-positive presidents (such as Franklin Roosevelt and John Kennedy) find their satisfaction in results, they are better equipped than the others to withstand assaults on their self-worth and affection. Because active-negative presidents (such as Lyndon Johnson and Richard Nixon) need to buttress their feelings of self-worth, they are less well equipped than the others to handle those same assaults. Because passive-positive presidents (such as William Howard Taft and Warren G. Harding) need to be liked, they are less well equipped than the others to lead the country in necessary but unpopular directions. And because passive-negative presidents (such as Calvin Coolidge and Dwight Eisenhower) need to perform duties that they do not enjoy, they are less well equipped than the others to take any presidential initiative at all. Barber's analysis reminds us that individual human beings are not interchangeable because their internal needs, world views, and styles of action are uniquely personal. Presidents enact the presidential job description in partial fulfillment of their personal needs.

Because individuals try to satisfy their personal needs in a world inhabited by other persons pursuing their own needs, social interdependence is important. Need satisfaction normally requires some other(s) to cooperate and many others to acquiesce. Moreover, it is never essential for every citizen to acquiesce, as long as those opposed to the need fulfillment do not control sufficient resources to thwart it. For example, a president ready to commit the armed forces to combat needs military personnel to cooperate and the rest of society to acquiesce. The context of separated institutions sharing power, therefore, requires that presidents discover or develop means for encouraging cooperation and disempowering opposition. Those means range from coercion to persuasion, and they lead us to consider the ways in which individuals coordinate their pursuits of need satisfaction.

Laws are the social interpretive structures created by individuals to coordinate their various need satisfaction behaviors. These laws can be formal and codified or informal norms. Laws, in either sense, proscribe some ways of satisfying needs for members of the community.

Laws facilitate the coordination of individual need fulfillment by setting behavioral limits to which community members are bound to acquiesce, usually under threat of punishment. To enact or accept one pattern of need fulfillment as law is, of course, to advantage some persons and to disadvantage others.

By living in a society of laws humans put limits on opportunities for need satisfaction. Most people want to accumulate wealth, but virtually all of us acquiesce to a shared system of taxation to avoid needing to build our own roads, bridges, security forces, and schools. People hurry, but they create a system of traffic laws lest they kill each other in the process of hurrying. People seek control over their lives, but they create legal entities and delegate responsibilities so that they know whom to blame for the decisions that inconvenience them.

The American presidency was created by the Supreme Law, the Constitution. It vested legislative, executive, and judicial authority in three branches of government to create what Neustadt (1980) identified as separated institutions with shared powers. Tulis (1987) observed that presidents during America's first century were careful to justify their actions with specific references to their constitutional authority. But he also observed that presidents since Woodrow Wilson, and especially since Franklin Roosevelt, have exercised increasingly independent action without justifying such action with reference to the Constitution. Instead, they justify their independent actions with moral arguments and with references to the actions of other presidents.

The views of Kernell (1993), Lowi (1985), Tulis (1987), and others who have argued that recent presidents' enactment of the presidency has gone far beyond the law of the Constitution were summarized in Chapter 1. The difference between the original and contemporary presidencies can be seen in the emergence of "the law of executive supremacy"—a dramatic phrase perhaps, but less dramatic than either Lowi's (1985) "second republic" or Tulis's (1987) "second constitution." Although informal and uncodified, the law of executive supremacy has been obeyed consistently for decades by presidents of both political parties. Under the law of executive supremacy Franklin Roosevelt took control of the banking system; Harry Truman nationalized the steel mills; John Kennedy sent federal troops to help citizens defy state segregation laws; Richard Nixon authorized a program of efforts to disempower his opponents; Ronald Reagan's aides violated a congressional ban on the sale of arms to the Nicaraguan Contras; Lyndon Johnson and Richard Nixon conducted a war in Vietnam, Ronald Reagan sent troops to El Salvador, Lebanon, and Grenada, and George Bush conducted the Gulf War all without declarations of war; Franklin Roosevelt tried to pack the Supreme Court with "reasonable" justices, and Richard Nixon and Ronald Reagan nominated unconfirmable justices on the grounds that it was the president's job to select new justices.

It can be argued that many of the presidential actions undertaken in accordance with the law of executive supremacy were important measures that could not otherwise have been taken. We do not disagree. Indeed, that is precisely the reason that America acquiesced to the law of executive supremacy: it broke government gridlock and produced action in the face of inaction. But it produced that action without regard to the constitutional conception of the presidency. We disagree with Lowi (1985) and Tulis (1987) who say, respectively, that we have today a "second republic" or a "second constitution." The distinction is important because it is the very informality of this "law" of executive supremacy that has enabled presidents to exploit it to their advantage. If we truly had a second republic it would be because we had adopted a second constitution through which we and our courts could adjudicate claims of constitutional and unconstitutional behavior. But there is no second formal, legal, founding document to which presidents, their critics, or citizens can turn.

The first aspect of interpretation, then, is the needing process. It is the involuntary personal process of needing to have personal needs. Individuals normally find it useful to protect themselves by establishing laws as shared social structures that coordinate and regulate their pursuit of need satisfactions. The presidency has been defined in law by the Constitution and other statutory grants of authority, and by the informal law of executive supremacy that has evolved during this century. Each person who becomes president is equipped differently for the job by virtue of his enduring needs, and he will respond to external demands, in part, on the basis of his personal needs.

Symbolizing and Language

Symbolizing is the process of (re)formulating semantic relationships among meanings and images. Individuals discover or create words and meanings that become their cognitive building blocks. It is through symbols, and only through symbols, that humans perceive the world around them. Notice that we say "perceive" rather than "sense" the world. We grant that any creature can sense its environment. But it is only through symbolization that humans (1) sense the world, (2) ascertain the essence of that sensation, (3) label it, (4) relate it to one or more sets of remembrances, (5) imagine the implications of the present sensation for the future, and (6) respond to the present sensation on the basis of its abstract qualities. Any dog can recognize a new bag of dog food as the replacement for the last bag, but it takes a human to perceive the abstract connection between an ad for dog food and a bag of dog food. That abstract connection is a product of the symbolizing process.

The relationship between symbolizing and perception is apparent in many aspects of human behavior. The development of vocabulary is an obvious example, since each individual needs a unique set of lexical categories to comprehend her or his environment. Moreover, the variation in personal needs and experiences leads each individual to invest each word or symbol with personally relevant associations. Symbols evolve in response to personal needs, such that terms like "liberal Republican," "abortion," and "Soviet menace" evoke a variety of meanings in different persons at different times.

Jesse Delia (1982) and others in the constructivist school of communication research have demonstrated that individuals' personal symbolic inventories vary along the dimensions of differentiation, articulation, and integration. First, the sheer number of words or constructs available to individuals affects each individual's ability to "differentiate" among similar phenomena. Some Arctic peoples have as many as twenty-five words for snow—or, as one of them might say, we have only one word for twenty-five kinds of precipitation.

Therefore, to create a new word is to create new potential for cognitive differentiation. Each figure of speech is also a figure of thought. President Gerald Ford was opposed to "blanket amnesty" for those who had evaded service in Vietnam, but he favored an "earned pardon." President Bill Clinton proposed to cut both taxes and spending, but he proposed that Americans "contribute" to the nation by "investing" in economic growth. In each case a president tried to coin new terms to differentiate among policy alternatives.

Second, a construct that is refined and detailed is said to be an "articulated" construct. Terms like "peace," "progress," and "freedom" are used frequently in political discourse because they are abstract, rather than well-articulated, constructs. For example, a speaker could fill in the blanks in the following sentence with "peace," "progress," and "freedom" in any order: "I am committed to _____, but not at the expense of _____ or _____." All six of the possible constructions sound bold, positive, and compelling; but none clarifies the speaker's meaning for any of the three terms.

One might reasonably expect a speaker to articulate an abstraction before making it a policy goal. But it is frequently more advantageous to pursue the goal as an abstraction because people who disagree about specific policies can often agree on abstract principles. Richard Nixon's "secret plan" for ending the Vietnam War enabled him to win votes from some who construed him to mean a secret plan to escalate the war and from some who construed him to mean a secret plan to withdraw from Vietnam.

The ways in which individuals relate and connect their constructs "integrate" their constructs. Some presidents have sought to integrate the constructs of economic growth, tax reduction, and reduced government spending; others have tried to integrate economic growth with redistributive taxation and economic stimulus packages. The semantic reconfigurations of differentiation, articulation, and integration shape, and are shaped by, discourse.

Theoretically, each individual develops a personal mode of symbolizing and a set of personal constructs, the better to achieve personal coherence. But each of us is born into a social group—or, more accurately, into a myriad of social groups—within which the members are able to coordinate their individual symbolizing. They are able to do so because of language—the social interpretive structure created by individuals to coordinate their individual symbolizing behaviors. Members of a community see that the formal, codified rules governing semantic and grammatical practices—their *language*—are learned by aspiring members of their community, whereas a variety of informal languages can be found among various subcultures. Any language advantages some persons and disadvantages others at several levels.

First, those born into the community's mainstream learn the mainstream language from the beginning. They are advantaged by virtue of the fact that they need never sacrifice their original language to gain access to the mainstream, and by their consequent ability to keep in tact their sense of social origin and family support. This is the dilemma captured so well in George Bernard Shaw's "Pygmalion" when the poor flower girl learns the Queen's English well enough to pass for royalty, only to discover that her father and former friends can no longer accept her as one of them.

Second, language advantages some persons at the expense of others as a consequence of depiction. Haig Bosmajian (1983) was one of the first scholars to observe the oppressive aspects of language. His analyses of the languages of anti-Semitism, white racism, Indian derision, sexism, and the language of war suggest the potential of language to dehumanize those who are not valued members of the language's community.

The result is that a pluralistic society like that of the United States is comprised of a variety of linguistic communities. When a quarter of the population speaks Spanish, bilingualism becomes an important political issue—but an issue more important to some people than others. More subtly and pervasively, America consists of a variety of political languages: populist language and administrative language, diplomatic language and military language, liberal language and conservative language, legal language and academic language, the language of confrontation and the language of conciliation. Thus individuals differ in the meanings they attach to words like "Republicans" and "Democrats," "liberals" and "conservatives," "we" and "they," "freedom" and "liberty." So too are some individuals unable to distinguish between "parties" and "Political Action Committees," "primaries" and "caucuses," "continuing resolutions" and "special orders."

Because each figure of speech is a figure of thought, it matters a great deal which language is used to set forth government policies and directions. It is frequently necessary for presidents to speak in the language of their domestic adversaries to bridge the gulf between them. Let us examine President John F. Kennedy's June 10, 1963, commencement address at American University as an important example of such a semantic reconfiguration.

A decade after Joe McCarthy's allegations of communist influence in the American diplomatic and military community, "peace" was still construed by many Americans as a euphemism for softness toward communism. Kennedy sought to make "peace" a rational policy goal just eight months after he had taken the world to the brink of nuclear war over the Soviet missiles in Cuba. To do so, he needed (1) to articulate his conception of peace, (2) to differentiate his conception of peace from other possible meanings, and (3) to integrate his conception of peace with other policy objectives.

The third paragraph of Kennedy's speech (1963) addressed these rhetorical tasks with themes developed throughout the speech:

What kind of a peace do I mean? What kind of peace do we seek? Not a Pax Americana enforced on the world by American weapons of war. Not the peace of the grave or the security of the slave. I am talking about genuine peace, the kind of peace that makes life on earth worth living, the kind that enables men and nations to grow and to hope and to build a better life for their children— not merely peace for Americans, but peace for all men and women; not merely peace in our time, but peace for all time. (1963, pp. 53–54)

Here, as in many of the speeches he wrote for Kennedy, Theodore Sorensen differentiated by saying explicitly what he "sought not." Thus, he neatly differentiated Kennedy's conception of peace from the "Pax Americana enforced on the world by American weapons of war," from "the peace of the grave," from "the security of the slave," from "merely peace for Americans," and from "merely peace in our time" (pp. 53–54). Later in the speech Sorensen also differentiated Kennedy's brand of peace from "the absolute, infinite concept of universal goodwill" (p. 55). These differentiations were important because they constrained his audience's latitude for misunderstanding him, and they constrained those adversaries who were tempted to misrepresent his position.

The speech articulated Kennedy's conception of peace, loosely at first, as "genuine peace, the kind of peace that makes life on earth worth living" (p. 53). But it proceeded to articulate a vision of peace that was rational and practical. Kennedy's version of peace derived from the premise that "peace is a process, a way of solving problems" (p. 55). By treating peace as a process of conflict resolution, Sorensen was able to transcend Soviet-American differences with their "mutual abhorrence of war" (p. 56) because the nations of the world "have a mutually deep interest in a just and genuine peace and in halting the arms race" (p. 57). Kennedy's brand of peace emphasized measured, practical, self-interested choices: "a gradual evolution in human institutions" and "a series of concrete actions and effective agreements which are in the interest of all concerned" (p. 55).

Kennedy's speech also effectively integrated his conception of peace with themes, values, and policy goals supported by most Americans. Kennedy's vision of peace would enable "men and nations to grow and to hope and to build a better life for their children" (p. 53). It was less altruistic than self-interested because "our most basic common link is that we all inhabit this planet. We all breathe the same air. We all cherish our children's future. And we are all mortal" (p. 57). This kind of peace, said Kennedy, was "practical" and "attainable" (p. 55), "the rational end of rational men" (p. 54).

Kennedy's address facilitated a shift in American-Soviet relations because Sorensen's language facilitated a perceptual shift. Theodore Windt's (1990) analysis of this address emphasizes Kennedy's need to prepare Americans to accept forthcoming arms control treaties, and the importance of Kennedy's decision to justify the change in relations not in the language of idealism but in the language of the hard-line "realists." Had Kennedy justified negotiating with the Soviets in the language of idealism, it would have been far more difficult for him to sell the treaties to hard-line anticommunists in the Senate. But by speaking the practical, cautious, self-interested language of the hard-liners, Kennedy improved his prospects for success. And by differentiating, articulating, and integrating his conception of peace, he provided Americans with a new set of constructs for the discussion of world peace.

The second interpretive process, then, is symbolizing through which we conceptualize, label, perceive, and describe all aspects of our environment. To coordinate our idiosyncratic symbolizing behaviors, we develop languages. Our personal verbal construct systems are dynamic responses to our needs for more, or less, semantic differentiation, articulation, and integration. Presidential leadership often relies on semantic transformation to (re)orient the public.

Reasoning and Logic

Reasoning is the process of "making sense" by (re)formulating explanatory accounts to reconcile one's needs, cognitions, and affects. This conception of reasoning is a uniquely personal process that must not be confused with the studied reasoning of the educated elite, the adversarial reasoning of the courtroom, or the homespun reasoning of conventional wisdom because it undergirds them all. It is the innate reasoning process that enables infants to notice that the random phonemes "ma-ma" and "da-da" produce nonrandom environmental improvements, and to hypothesize that the sounds actually cause those changes to occur. We can teach and learn ways to improve one another's reasoning, but each of us first discovers how to reason on our own.

To reason about politics is not necessarily to engage in complex policy debates. Each of us reasons about politics, in one way or another, because we cannot help it. Like needing and symbolizing, reasoning is an involuntary process. To understand the process through which diverse individuals reason about life and politics is to explore the various ways in which they "make sense" of it all.

Individuals engage in political reasoning, but often as a secondary enterprise (Popkin, 1991). We allocate our time and energies to fulfilling our various personal needs, among which making sense of politics is normally a low priority. But in the process of satisfying our high priority needs we have experiences, encounters, and relationships that provide us with a stockpile of personally meaningful facts, stories, and associates. When political reasoning is called for, we combine the information we have thus acquired with new political information to reach conclusions.

Popkin (1991) argues that individuals triangulate (1) their experiences, (2) the opinions of personal associates they have learned to trust, and (3) the opinions of familiar political figures. This process enables every citizen to form a political judgment, even in the absence of real interest, because the triangulation process offers a variety of information shortcuts.

The most prominent information shortcuts are interpersonal influence, party identification, ideological orientation, policy orientation, political style, and framing (Popkin, 1991; Sanders, 1990). Interpersonal influence enables individuals to rely on the political opinions of persons important to them, independent of the accuracy or sophistication of the opinion leaders' views. Party identification and ideological orientation provide symbolic signposts that often help individuals to orient themselves to the reasoning of "people like us," but they appear rarely to determine individuals' opinions (Sanders, 1990).

Individuals often reason about government policies, but some persons are more likely to emphasize policy than others (Sanders, 1990). And when individuals do reason in terms of policies they are more likely to draw on their personal experiences—their children's school, their own taxes, their own economic well-being—than they are to rely on policy information from candidates, governments, or the mass media.

Many individuals reason on the basis of political style. Some, for example, care less about a politician's policy preferences than about her perceived sincerity, accessibility, or toughness. This was an important ingredient in President Reagan's success, as he was always more popular than the policies he advocated. Buchanan's (1987) three visions of the presidency and Barber's (1985) emphasis on presidential character, both discussed in Chapter 1, are examples of stylistic reasoning, as is Sanders's (1990) discussion of macho politics and the politics of compassion.

Each of these informational shortcuts works because it provides the individual with a method of framing the decision to be made. At some point, the individual must decide whether an election is about policy or style, ideology or competence, party loyalty or self-interest. To adopt one frame rather than another is, in many cases, to move swiftly toward an opinion. Although a politician, a friend, and a reporter can all suggest that individuals should frame a particular subject in a particular way, it is the individual's retinue of personal needs, symbolic perceptions, and experiences that make some frames seem more reasonable than others.

So far our discussion of political reasoning has sought to emphasize that ordinary people cannot help but reason about politics even though it is not, for most of them, a high priority activity. The fact that this reasoning process is highly individualized complicates presidents' efforts to communicate with the American people. But to say that people do reason about politics and that they rely on informational shortcuts is not to explain the mechanics of their reasoning, which is our next concern.

Each individual relies on a mix of categorical, propositional, and narrative modes of reasoning. When we reason categorically, we deduce conclusions from factual statements about categories. This form of reasoning relies upon the terms "all," "some," "are," and "not." Thus, if "all politicians are crooked" and if "Jones is a politician," we must inevitably conclude that "Jones is crooked." This is a convenient form of political reasoning—especially for the marginally informed, for the politically disinterested, for those who are intolerant of ambiguities, and for those who are unaccustomed to disagreement. This is the kind of reasoning that enables so many people to get by with political convictions such as "Republicans are the party of the rich" and "Liberals are not patriotic." When we reason categorically (and we all do it sometimes), we need only identify the appropriate categorical frame to predetermine our conclusion.

When a categorical statement is disputed it becomes a proposition (conversely, when a proposition is universally accepted it becomes a categorical statement). Propositional reasoning works through a series of arguable statements to reach a conclusion. Its key terms are "and," "not," "either/or," and "if/then," but we normally presume part of the proposition. For example, *if* handguns are tightly regulated *then* handgun-induced injuries will decrease. By providing a way of structuring a set of arguable contingencies, propositional reasoning enables us to integrate our experiences, the opinions of our friends, and political statements that reach us. But precisely because each proposition is both arguable and contingent, propositional reasoning requires an expenditure of rational effort that can seem too costly. It is therefore difficult for two persons—one reasoning propositionally and the other reasoning categorically—to coordinate their reasoning, because the former finds the latter simplistic, closed-minded, or stubborn and the latter regards the former as confused, indecisive, or uninformed. This is as true for presidents and their constituents as it is for coworkers, neighbors, and spouses.

Narrative reasoning, the third mode, relies on stories. Each individual experiences life and politics personally, and it is through stories that each of us imposes shape and form on the flux of history. Individuals live in personal presents shaped by their remembrances and imaginings, and we each cast ourselves in unfolding stories and act them out. Our stories help us to reason by protecting what we "know" from counterargument, by defining what constitutes relevant evidence, by explaining the otherwise unexplainable, and by contextualizing otherwise ambiguous episodes (Kamler, 1983).

Logic is the social structure that enables individuals to coordinate their diverse reasoning activities. There are formal, codified logics to which all members of a community are expected to adhere, even if they are too often taught only to the elite. There are also informal logics without number, such as jurisprudential logic, paranoid logic, scientific logic, dramatic logic, and the logic of divine revelation. Each of these logics provides guidelines for members of its logical community. By arguing in accordance with the logic's rules of reasoning, members of the community can hope to lead their listeners toward a shared conclusion.

Traditional Aristotelian logic is, of course, the industry standard by which political discourse is judged. Politicians hold one another accountable for errors of fact, induction, deduction, and the litany of fallacies. But industry standards rarely conform to consumer expectations, and the logic of the political elite is often lost on everyday citizens who have logics of their own. For example, politicians can explain that unemployment is a lagging indicator of economic health, but citizens haunted by the spectre of joblessness are inclined to reason from their immediate personal needs.

People organize their social relationships and communities through the telling and retelling of shared stories (Carr, 1986). Shared stories and myths link us to our contemporaries, our predecessors, and our successors. The process of storytelling itself engages persons in communication through the narrator-audience relationship. Communities coalesce around clusters of stories as each "We" has its own folklore and narrators.

It is the narrator's vantage point—in time, intellect, wisdom, values, and character—that positions the narrative for the audience. People identify with narrators who enable them to step into the story, enact it, and retain the experience; and when repelled by a narrator they may use the narrative for its opposite lesson. Thus the narrator's image and audience appeal are important to the narrative, and personal identification overpowers logical rigor (Fisher, 1987).

If history is the creation of explanatory stories, and if social relationships form around these explanatory stories, then some of these narrative communities must inevitably conflict. Most American political communities have their own narratives of "The American Dream." Each of these narratives enacts a set of values that reinforces its community's categorical and propositional premises.

Walter R. Fisher (1987) says that we judge our narratives by their narrative coherence (does the story work?) and by their narrative fidelity (does the story fit the audience's experiences?). He argues that we regard as "good reasons" those stories that are (1) "true to and consistent with what we think we know and what we value," (2) "appropriate to whatever decision is pending," (3) "promising in effects for ourselves and others," and (4) "consistent with what we believe is an ideal basis of conduct" (1983, p. 194). Fisher's view of persuasion depends less upon the changing of beliefs, attitudes, or values than upon the integration of the desired beliefs and behaviors into a narrative regarded by the intended audience as coherent, relevant, compatible, promising, and proper.

Presidents who can establish the logic of policy debates have a tremendous advantage over their adversaries, because they can decide which means are logical and which are not. President Reagan confounded his economic critics by transcending their logic. When they charged that it would be impossible to increase military spending, to cut taxes, and to eliminate the deficit, Reagan sadly admitted that he had thought that way too—before grasping the higher logic of supply-side economics.

Preferencing and Ideology

We have suggested that humans are characterized by three innate, involuntary processes, which they coordinate through an array of socially constructed laws, languages, and logics. We have yet to identify a process through which individual humans arrange their needs, symbols, and reasons into functionally efficient hierarchies. Personal needs compel us to establish priorities, the symbolizing process forces us to differentiate and integrate, and reasoning entails the ordering of variably cogent arguments. Because all three processes lead us toward priorities, the process of establishing priorities deserves to be considered in its own right.

Allow us to coin the term *preferencing* to refer to the process of (re)formulating the hierarchical arrangement of one's needs, symbols, and reasons. By virtue of heredity, environment, and fateful exposures, some needs, symbols, and reasons begin early in life to form the nucleus of the individual's interpretive framework. These are the normally enduring elements of personality, first-learned language, and values. Each of these core elements enhances the credibility of some available authority figures, some of whose statements of preference are adopted.

Preferencing is multidirectional. Crucial to it is each individual's reevaluation of authority figures as she or he gains experience with the consequences of preferences derived from those authorities. Moreover, the loss of confidence in an authority figure can undermine confidence in the core preferences that made the authority figure preferable in the first place. The wild cards in this process are the personal needs for cognitive and affective consistency and the need to simplify the interpretive process. Thus do citizens, even those who know better, prefer information shortcuts such as single issue litmus tests, name recognition, and party affiliation to the careful study of political campaigns and controversies.

Although we may try to move carefully from needs through words and reasoning to preferences, we often begin with gut-level preferences and then back into our semantic associations and reasons. Humans are highly creative and adaptive, and they make sense of their environments with whatever symbolic inventories, modes of reasoning, and means of preferencing they find psychologically functional.

Indeed, the British social psychologist Michael Billig (1991) has argued that the process of thinking is inherently rhetorical. He suggests that orthodox social psychology, with its emphasis on problem solving and information processing, is flawed:

What is missing is a feel for the contentious and dynamic nature of thinking. This missing element can . . . be gathered from the old-fashioned and neglected study of rhetoric, which trained people to think argumentatively. In so doing, rhetoric revealed that a dimension of thinking is the silent conversation, or rather the silent argument, of the soul with itself. (1991, p. 38)

The essence of this silent argument, we suggest, is the preferencing process. Individual citizens decide whether to believe the president or the opposition, the Bureau of Labor Statistics or one's banking statement, a political pundit or a trusted friend.

In many ways preferencing is the interpretive process that is related most directly to politics. Each citizen reaches a voting decision based on an array of preferences: to follow the campaign or to ignore it, to consider policies or campaign style, to emphasize the record or the promise, to believe what candidates say or to discount it, and ultimately independent of all the foregoing, to vote or to stay home. Once elected, of course, the president continues to deal in preferences. In the abstract, every president wants to slash the deficit and to make the country a better place. But in the crunch, the president must prefer either foreign or domestic concerns (and some foreign or domestic concerns rather than others), tax increases or tax cuts (but which taxes on which people?), spending increases or spending cuts (but which programs by how much?).

As individuals carry on their silent internal arguments, they find kindred spirits. They "think out loud" in conversations with other people who either share or dislike their method of preferencing. Through these conversations they either buttress or modify their preferences. Over time they learn to coordinate their preferencing. They do this through conversations and arguments that are not silent. As they do so they create an *ideology* as a socially shared structure for coordinating their preferencing activities.

An ideology suggests the interpretive community's core principles, its authority figures or ways of determining how authority should be vested, and a set of preferences derived from them that can be modified without undermining the essential form and content of the ideology. Easton (1965) suggested that ideologies have "articulated sets of ideals, ends and purposes, which help to interpret the past, explain the present, and offer a vision for the future" (p. 290). Political interest groups, factions, and parties all have ideologies, some of which they are able to formalize.

Some people arrive at these shared preferences after careful thought, others by not bothering to think. Consequently, individuals are able both to prefer as a consequence of their reasoning and to rationalize their preferences. It is this kind of ideology that provides refuge for authoritarian and closed-minded individuals who need desperately some method for preferencing that works to establish and protect universal authority patterns (Adorno, 1950; Stewart, Smith, & Denton, 1994) or clearly differentiated beliefs and disbeliefs (Leathers, 1973; Rokeach, 1960).

Some individuals can adopt, modify, and switch ideologies almost as easily as they adopt new fashions. Indeed, one historian has suggested that periods of social reform come and go precisely because the ideology of reform comes in and out of fashion (Broesamle, 1990), not unlike the wide necktie. The reason for this is to be found in the fit between personal preferencing and personal needs. Some people prefer to buy new ties or ideologies that are fashionable, and some shop diligently for the familiar but unfashionable. Either the familiar or the new can be used or not used; and either choice can be rational or rationalized, according to one's personal needs.

Finally, it must be noted that individuals establish preferences among ideologies. This is evident, for example, when overworked and underpaid workers rail against ideologies that emphasize unionization or redistributive policies that would appear to benefit them. It is also evident when voters support a president whose style they like, even as they voice doubts about his policies.

INTERPRETIVE CONVERGENCE AND DIVERGENCE

So far we have described the process through which individuals create or adopt shared interpretive structures to coordinate their personal interpretive processes. We still need to explain the process through which individuals "connect" with one another, the process through which communities and coalitions arise, and the importance of this process to an understanding of presidential leadership.

Communication occurs when two or more persons try to understand one another's behavior through their respective interpretive processes and structures. Each tries to achieve social coordination by using the interpretive paraphernalia each has brought to the encounter. Occasionally one of us hears one of our own needs voiced by another person, one of our own preferences or reasons articulated by another, or one of our meaningful stories told by another narrator. When this happens we experience a momentary sense of recognition, unity, or "usness"—a feeling that has been called "consubstantiality" by literary critic Kenneth Burke (1969), "symbolic convergence" by rhetorical critic Ernest Bormann (1985), and "communitas" by anthropologist Victor Turner (1982).

The initial feeling of usness, or communitas, is spontaneous. It occurs when persons, "obtain a flash of lucid mutual understanding . . . when they feel that all problems, not just their problems, could be resolved, whether emotional or cognitive, if only the group (which is felt in the first person) as 'essentially us' could sustain itself" (Turner, 1982, p. 48). This momentary flash of recognition is crucial to the understanding of human behavior because it is the flashpoint at which "you" and "I" become "us." Robert Freed Bales (1970), for example, found that members of small groups reacted both cognitively and emotionally when they perceived others to be enacting, or "dramatizing," portions of their own life stories.

This feeling of communitas or symbolic convergence can occur when we read a poem or hear a song that speaks to our interpretations of our life experiences, and it can happen when an orator depicts life as we have been personally interpreting it. Bormann (1972, 1985) says that this happens when a speaker articulates our personal fantasies such that our symbolic worlds converge. As this happens the fantasy theme "chains out" with each new person embracing the theme and adding to it. Those who share the fantasy become a rhetorical community, united not only by their shared "rhetorical vision" but by the process of having mutually created it.

Discussing this same fundamental process, Kenneth Burke (1969) observed that persons attain identification with one another when they perceive themselves as being "consubstantial" (of the same substance). Thus do individuals become increasingly consubstantial as their symbolic worlds converge through identification. But Burke (1969) recognized that identification is inextricably linked to polarization and division, because it is impossible to converge with another without simultaneously diverging from some others. Thus, moments of communitas, identification, and symbolic convergence are also moments of disunity, polarization, and symbolic divergence from other persons.

Our interpretive systems model of communication therefore seeks to extend the insights of Burke, Turner, and Bormann in three ways. First, we agree with Bormann that persons coalesce into communities on the basis of their symbolic convergence; but we wish to refine his position by suggesting that they also can coalesce around need convergence, reasoning convergence, and preferencing convergence. This distinction results in a wider variety of interpretive communities: those that coalesce around a shared need in different ways, those that coalesce around a shared preference for a variety of needs and reasons, and those that coalesce around a shared mode of reasoning with different results.

Second, we agree with Bormann that communities arise around shared beliefs and fantasies, and we agree with Burke that identification and polarization are inherently compensatory. We therefore posit that communities can coalesce around shared dislikes as well as likes. Because individuals need, symbolize, reason, and prefer, they are able to ascertain what they need and what they need not, what they prefer and what they prefer not. Similarly, interpretive communities can be identified by their beliefs or by their disbeliefs (Rokeach, 1960; Leathers, 1973). It follows that disparate individuals and interpretive communities can come together through communication addressed to their shared beliefs or to their shared disbeliefs.

Third, the increasingly pluralistic nature of modern societies virtually precludes the existence of homogeneous national interpretive communities. In politics the key to success is the ability to create interpretive coalitions out of the available array of interpretive communities. This is most evident in electoral politics, where the goal is to get a majority of voters to coalesce around a preference for one candidate, with different communities preferring that candidate for their own reasons. It is also evident in legislative politics, where sponsors of a bill seek the votes of legislators, the executive's signature, and public acquiescence with a variety of reasons. An interpretive coalition can be pieced together with communication that addresses the needs of community A, in the logic of community B, and the language of community C. But precisely because the legislation is based on an interpretive coalition, each of the constituent communities is bound to experience some measure of disappointment.

The struggle of politics therefore derives from two sets of tensions. The first tension is inherent in any *social* structure that must satisfy *personal* needs. Social interpretive structures proliferate as we attempt to resolve this tension. Over time some of these interpretive communities win new adherents and outlive their founders. The second tension occurs as incongruent interpretive communities come into conflict—in election campaigns, in legislatures, in the streets, and on battlefields— over the "right" or "best" or "true" way to interpret the world. Thus, the tension between incongruent interpretive structures drives the struggle between incongruent interpretive communities as they seek the legitimate right to define social and political realities for the benefit of all (although the "all" inevitably have their own opinion of what is good for them).

This means that each of us is born and socialized into a set of overlapping interpretive communities including, but not limited to, a socioeconomic perspective, a religious orientation, a party orientation, and an ideological perspective. Our interpretation of unfolding events, framed and influenced by our communication with others, renders our interpretive frameworks functional or dysfunctional and we modify our interpretive patterns accordingly. Sometimes this means that we adopt the interpretive structures of the people we like, and sometimes it means that we join with new people who seem to share our revised way of thinking and preferring.

The result is a pluralistic society comprised of a wide array of overlapping interpretive communities that inevitably conflict. The struggles of politics are to be found (1) in the interplay of these interpretive communities, (2) in the interpretive mobility of people among these communities, and (3) in the ability of political leaders to mobilize interpretive coalitions that can, for a time, produce a dominant and legitimate interpretation of reality for most, if not all, citizens.

Political party platforms provide one example of such an interpretive coalition. Each platform sets forth certain needs, laws, reasons, and preferences as more important than others. Moreover, the platform embodies the effort of partisans to advance an interpretive statement that uses some people's language and other people's reasons to justify some other people's preferences. When it is well drafted, the party platform provides a broader and firmer foundation for its candidates than could any of the party's narrower constituent interpretive structures.

It is this struggle between competing interpretive structures that guarantees political argument. No out-group can either gain or regain power unless it disagrees with those in power. It is, therefore, always incumbent upon the out-group to disagree with those in power. The Republican Party's shift from support for, to opposition to, the 1978 Panama Canal treaties is an example of this phenomenon, and it will be discussed in detail in Chapter 5.

Convergence/divergence is the dynamic that drives the interpretive process. Interpretive visions stimulate recognition and empathy because they (1) articulate some audience member's needs, symbols, reasons, and preferences, (2) enhance the relational identification between audience and speaker, (3) induce the audience to participate vicariously in the speaker's narrative, (4) invite the audience to share in the creative process, (5) foster identification with like-thinking audience members, and (6) motivate the audience members to remember and to advance the story.

To the extent that one interpretive vision is widely shared by a community or a coalition of communities, it frames their categorical and propositional arguments. Presidents and other politicians normally argue within the prevailing vision, but occasionally the president must choose between defending the prevailing vision and helping the country to see a new vision. Such moments are crucial because they entail more than argument over a policy: they are arguments about the society's sense of historical progression, about its identification with its leadership, and about its way of thinking about governance.

In the continuing struggle among incongruent interpretive communities, the debates between conflicting interpretive visions embody the different communities' discrepant laws, languages, logics, and ideologies. In such debates, one community's reality is another's myth, and the struggle over images, heroes, villains, values, and motives is central. This struggle is profound because it reconfigures the ways in which policymakers, media pundits, scholars, and ordinary citizens experience their politics.

SUMMARY AND CONCLUSIONS

In Chapter 1 we discussed several theories of presidential leadership that suggested, directly and indirectly, the central role played by communication. But it is one thing to say that communication is central to presidential leadership and quite another to study presidential leadership as communication. Therefore, in Chapter 2 we have presented an interpretive systems model of political communication as a theoretical framework to guide our discussion of presidential leadership.

The interpretive systems approach posits four innate, involuntary personal interpretive processes: needing, symbolizing, reasoning, and preferencing. Barring disability, each person begins to develop these interpretive processes at a very early age. Reinforced and taught by parents, teachers, and others, each of us acquires a personally efficient way of interpreting the world around us. But at home, in school, and through public discourse, each of us is exposed to multiple ways of interpreting life's ebb and flow. As we become members of our relevant social communities we learn to use their social interpretive structures: their laws, languages, logics, and ideologies, some of which we find more useful than others.

We window shop a good deal, trying on old and new needs, words, reasons, and preferences to see how they fit us. Many of these needs, symbols, reasons, and preferences converge and diverge such that we find ourselves, if even for a moment, members of a new community. Political advocates and media pundits are the sales clerks who offer advice, and our friends and peers shop with us, complimenting this and disapproving that. Over time some of these overlapping interpretive communities come into conflict, and it is the function of political parties, interest groups, the institutions of government, and the mass media to (re)formulate interpretive coalitions to provide common ground, if only for a time.

Language, logic, ideology, and laws are interdependent. As elections empower an interpretive community they also empower its language, logic, and ideology. The language of the interpretive community in power necessarily disadvantages members of its competing communities, as when they operationalize anew words like "patriotic," "right," and "America." The temporarily ascendant ideology frames the nation's problems and solutions, such that the outgoing community's solutions often become the incoming community's problems. And the logic of the temporarily ascendant interpretive community defines the rationality of the government's policies, as when it tackles deficits by cutting taxes and spending, by increasing taxes and spending, or by increasing one and cutting the other.

The interpretive systems model also enables us to see how political advocates attempt to win and retain power by forging interpretive coalitions around the priorities of one community's ideology, by depicting it in the language of another community, and by justifying it in the logic of yet a third community.

The interpretive systems model is an integrative framework that can help us to see that political controversies arise because different people have incongruent needs, preferences, and verbal constructions of reality, each of which makes perfect sense to its own adherents. Moreover, it helps us to see that these interpretive structures are created and learned through communication. Thus, the interpretive systems model helps us to understand politics as communication.

To study presidential leadership as communication is, therefore, to study the ways in which presidents use the resources of laws, language, logic, and ideology to lead. More specifically, to study presidential leadership as persuasion is to study the ways in which (1) presidents depict some people's needs as their own, (2) presidents speak some people's language rather than others' language, (3) presidents reason in some people's logic rather than others' logic, (4) presidents prefer in some people's ideology rather than others' ideology, and (5) presidents use persuasion to create, to mobilize, to transform, and to sustain their governing coalitions.

To say that presidents use language and logic to create and sustain interpretive coalitions is not to say that presidential leadership is unprincipled or amoral. Nor is it to say that all needs, reasons, preferences, and symbols are, or should be, valued equally. Quite the contrary, our position is that it is possible for an infinite number of arguments to be made without presuming that those arguments have equal validity (Billig, 1991). It is impossible to understand the validity or desirability of, say, capitalism without acknowledging and examining the arguments for its alternatives, in this case socialism and communism. To acknowledge that some people prefer socialism to capitalism is not to concede that they are equally desirable economic systems. It is, rather, to seek the interpretive dynamics that explain how and why such people prefer as they do, so that the quality of political dialogue can be improved.

To better understand how the White House speaks, and to better appreciate the political significance of presidents' rhetorical choices, we turn now to critical analyses of several presidents' uses of language and logic to lead America.

REFERENCES

Adorno, T. W., Frenkel-Brunswick, E., Levinson, D. J., & Sanford, R. N. (1950). *The authoritarian personality*. New York: Harper.

Bales, R. F. (1970). *Personality and interpersonal behavior*. New York: Holt Rinehart.

Barber, J. D. (1985). *The presidential character: Predicting performance in the White House* (3rd ed.). Englewood Cliffs, NJ: Prentice-Hall.

Billig, M. (1991). *Ideology and opinions.* Newbury Park, CA: Sage.

Bormann, E. G. (1972). Fantasy and rhetorical vision: The rhetorical criticism of social reality. *Quarterly Journal of Speech, 58,* 396–407.

Bormann, E. G. (1985). *The force of fantasy: Restoring the American dream.* Carbondale: Southern Illinois Press.

Bosmajian, H. A. (1983). *The language of oppression.* Lanham, MD: University Press of America. Originally published in 1974 by Public Affairs Press.

Broesamle, J. J. (1990). *Reform and reaction in twentieth century American politics.* Westport, CT: Greenwood.

Buchanan, B. (1987). *The citizen's presidency.* Washington, DC: Congressional Quarterly.

Burke, K. (1969). *A rhetoric of motives.* Berkeley: University of California Press.

Carr, D. (1986). *Time, narrative, and history.* Bloomington: Indiana University Press.

Delia, J. G., O'Keefe, B., & O'Keefe, D. J. (1982). The constructivist approach to communication. In F. E. X. Dance (Ed.), *Human communication theory: Comparative essays* (pp. 147–191). New York: Harper and Row.

Easton, D. (1965). *A systems analysis of political life.* New York: John Wiley.

Fisher, W. R. (1987). *Human communication as narration: Toward a philosophy of reason, value, and action.* Columbia: University of South Carolina Press.

Greenstein, F. I. (1969). *Personality and politics: Problems of evidence, inference, and conceptualization.* Chicago: Markham.

Kamler, H. (1983). *Communication: Sharing our stories of experience.* Seattle: Psychological Press.

Kennedy, J. F. [1963]. What kind of peace do we want? June 10. In A. Bevins (Ed.), *The burden and the glory* (pp. 53–58). New York: Harper and Row, 1964.

Kernell, S. (1993). *Going public: New strategies of presidential leadership* (2d ed.). Washington, DC: Congressional Quarterly. Originally published in 1986.

Lasswell, H. H. (1962). *Power and personality.* New York: Viking.

Leathers, D. G. (1973). Belief-disbelief systems: The communicative vacuum of the radical right. In G. P. Mohrmann, C. J. Stewart, & D. F. Ochs (Eds.), *Explorations in rhetorical criticism* (pp. 124–137). University Park: Pennsylvania State University Press.

Lipset, S. M. (1960). *Political man: The social bases of politics.* Garden City, NY: Doubleday.

Lowi, T. J. (1985). *The personal president: Power invested, promise unfulfilled.* Ithaca: Cornell University Press.

Maslow, A. (1943). A theory of human motivation. *Psychological Review, 50,* 370–396.

Neustadt, R. E. (1980). *Presidential power: The politics of leadership from FDR to Carter.* New York: Wiley. Originally published in 1960.

Popkin, S. L. (1991). *The reasoning voter: Communication and persuasion in presidential campaigns.* Chicago: University of Chicago Press.

Rokeach, M. R. (1960). *The open- and closed-mind.* New York: Basic Books.

Sanders, A. (1990). *Making sense of politics.* Ames: Iowa State University Press.

Smith, C. A. (1990). *Political communication.* San Diego: Harcourt Brace Jovanovich.

Smith, C. A. (1992). Interpretive communities in conflict: A master syllabus for political communication. *Communication Education, 41,* 415–428.

Stewart, C. J., Smith, C. A., & Denton, R. E. (1994). *Persuasion and social movements* (3rd ed.). Prospect Heights, IL: Waveland.

Tulis, J. K. (1987). *The rhetorical presidency.* Princeton, NJ: Princeton University Press.

Turner, V. (1982). *From ritual to theatre: The human seriousness of play.* New York: Performing Arts Journal Publications.

Windt, T. O. (1990). *Presidents and protesters: Political rhetoric in the 1960s.* Tuscaloosa: University of Alabama Press.

3

The Coalitionless President and the Pardons

In Chapters 1 and 2 we established the coalitional nature of the contemporary presidency and the rhetorical nature of presidential coalition building. In this chapter we use the coalitional perspective on presidential leadership to analyze the efforts of the coalitionless president, Gerald Ford, to build working coalitions by healing the nation's wounds. This allows us to explore the ways in which one president sought to resolve political crises with rhetorical choices. Specifically, we analyze Ford's discourse justifying his pardons of Richard Nixon and the Vietnam era draft evaders—the most nettlesome issues of his first thirty days—as coalitionally based rhetorical problems.

THE COALITIONLESS FORD PRESIDENCY

The Ford presidency constitutes a unique test of the coalitional model because Ford remains the only president ever to take office without having been part of any national electoral coalition. Ford needed urgently (1) to forge a governing coalition from the ashes of the Nixon presidency without benefit of a personal electoral coalition, and (2) to forge a 1976 election coalition compatible with whatever governing coalition he might construct.

The Nixon-Ford transition is therefore unique in the history of the American presidency. Questions of presidential legitimacy, the shortness of time, and public disaffection from the national government set the stage for Ford's presidency. The United States prides itself on the orderly manner of transferring power and legitimacy to each succeeding president—a legitimacy grounded in the electoral process. However, President Ford assumed office under far different circumstances.

Other vice presidents have assumed the presidency, but no one had ever become president without having first been elected vice president. In accordance with Section 2 of the Twenty-Fifth Amendment to the Constitution, the resignation of Vice President Spiro Agnew led to the appointment, by President Nixon, of Gerald R. Ford to the vacant vice presidency. Then the Watergate episode led to the resignation of President Nixon and the transfer of power, under Section 1 of the Twenty-Fifth Amendment, to Vice President Ford. Thus, Gerald Ford rose to the presidency without ever being elected by a national constituency. The legitimacy of this transfer of power rested on the proper use of a law—the Twenty-Fifth Amendment—but not on the normal ideological basis of electoral success. Louis Koenig (1986) described this sequence of events as "abhorrent to democratic standards" (p. 86). This historic chain of events led scholars and President Ford himself to challenge the wisdom of retaining the Twenty-Fifth Amendment ("Move," 1973).

Beyond the cloud left by the legitimacy questions, Ford assumed the presidency with a very brief period for preparation. Although his preparation time was longer than that given to presidents following presidential deaths, it was still very short by historic standards. The Presidential Transition Act of 1963 provides for government funds to be spent for office space, staff, and other expenses incurred in planning the new administration from the November election onward until six months after inauguration. Even as Ford saw the Watergate scandal unfold, he could not work publicly on his own assumption of power without appearing to be both disloyal to President Nixon and personally ambitious (Hunter, 1974). He pre-empted these charges by maintaining a distance from transition plans until just before his inauguration. Thus, Ford was left with the rare problem of no time for public transition efforts prior to his assumption of office.

Finally, Ford entered the presidency at a time when the public was generally disenchanted with the presidency. The presidency is a position of great importance in the socialization of Americans, and Nixon's fall from that high pedestal was a hard one with many attendant aftershocks. Wariness toward governmental honesty and a particular distrust for the presidency aggravated Ford's transition problems.

President Ford was forced to address the problems of legitimacy, lack of preparation, and public disenchantment as he began his presidency. The approach he took in dealing with these problems affected the success of his transition period.

Many of Ford's associates, including Philip Buchen, assumed that Ford would quickly replace all of the Nixon holdovers except for Henry Kissinger (Buchen, 1989). The Presidential Transition Act of 1963 stipulates that a transition must strive for an orderly transfer of power with no disruption of governmental operations, and in normal transitions newly recruited loyalists are ready to take over. President Reagan, for example, even began compiling dossiers on prospective agency heads during the general election campaign. But Ford had no such cast waiting in the wings because he had no such transition period during which to identify, recruit, screen, and orient new people. Clearly, vice presidential staff cannot engage in all-out administration building during impeachment hearings without seeming impatient and disloyal.

The major considerations for any new president are the use of existing personnel and the hiring of a new team. But for Ford, the recruitment process had to occur after his inauguration. The immediate need was to get Nixon's staff to cooperate in insuring the smooth continuation of government services. Toward this end, a "Memorandum for the White House Staff" was sent out on August 9 by the vice president prior to his swearing in. After acknowledging their shared feelings of sorrow and encouraging staff to be "proud of the president you served and of your efforts for him and country," Ford asked each of them "to stay long enough to assure a steady and uniform transition of the presidency." One reason given them to stay on the job was their loyalty to Nixon: "You can still serve him [Nixon] and the nation by helping me to carry on the essential function of the presidency" ("Memo," 1974). Acknowledging their shared feelings and using their continuing loyalty to Nixon helped President Ford to bridge the immediate gap from the Nixon to Ford presidencies.

The people acquainted with the routines, the routing of information, the personal networks, and the intimate details and operations of the executive office were people selected by H. R. Haldeman and loyal to Nixon and, therefore, the object of widespread public suspicion. On August 10, the day after taking office, Ford sent to the heads of agencies and departments a memorandum describing how "President Nixon fought long and with all his might to serve the American people well, ending his presidency with a selfless and courageous act" (Ford, 1974a). Ford went on to acknowledge his dependence on them, the Nixon appointees:

Some of you may now want to pass your responsibilities on to others. But I need your help. I ask each of you to continue to carry on the mission of your agency and to give me the advice I need as I take on my new responsibilities. (1974a, p. 485)

Ford initially needed to learn from the Nixon holdovers so that he could, in time, create his own administration.

Clearly, Ford wanted and needed the Nixon loyalists' support, even if he did not want to need it. Ford's need for the Nixon holdovers, and their disloyalty to him, would be a continuing problem for the Ford administration. As Ford's chief of staff and speechwriter, Robert Hartmann was particularly sensitive to this cleavage between the Ford people and Nixon's "praetorian guard." Hartmann's view was that the Nixon praetorians continued to regard Ford not as president but as someone in place of the president, and therefore someone to be changed into a mini-Nixon. Had Ford removed them, suggested Hartmann, things would have been different (Hartmann, 1980). But Ford needed their expertise, and he had sought it on the basis of their shared devotion to Nixon.

In short, the coalitional approach to presidential leadership posits that a successful presidency requires electoral and governing coalitions, and that it is difficult for a president to succeed with only one. Gerald Ford had neither, and just twenty-seven months to mobilize both. The crisis for Gerald Ford and America was that a national government centered upon a coalitional presidency was to be led for at least two years by a coalitionless president. Ford needed desperately to find the persuasive arguments that would (1) keep the needed Nixon loyalists on board, (2) establish a favorable working relationship with both houses of Congress, (3) establish positive relations with the working press, (4) restore morale in the Republican Party during the remaining ninety days of midterm campaigning, and (5) transform the public's general good will into solid support for his leadership and candidacy.

Ford's problem was rhetorical in two ways. First, he became vice president, and later president, as a direct result of the failed apologia of Spiro Agnew and Richard Nixon, respectively. Second, and more important, Nixon had attributed his resignation directly to the collapse of his governing coalition, rather than to his own personal guilt: "I have concluded that because of the Watergate matter, I might not have the support of the Congress that I would consider necessary to back the very difficult decisions and carry out the duties of this office in the way the interests of the Nation will require" (1975, p. 627). Nixon conceivably could have attributed his resignation to his own failure to abide by his oath of office. Had he done so, Ford would have inherited at least the right to claim a governing coalition. But Nixon's decision to save face undermined Ford's claim to any pre-existing governing coalition. It was therefore crucial for Ford to establish immediately both his stature as president and the viability of his governing coalition.

Ford tackled this problem rhetorically. He gave more speeches than his recent predecessors had and he engaged in a variety of symbolic acts. He realized that he faced an unusual rhetorical situation, observing later that "unless I did something to restore [the public's] trust, I couldn't win their consent to do anything else" (Ford, 1979, pp. 124–125).

Ford and his speechwriters needed a rhetorical strategy, but the peculiar nature of the coalitional crisis left them facing dilemmas at every turn. The fundamental dilemma was that Ford could not even acknowledge, much less exploit, his crisis without making it worse. Imagine the Soviet, Democratic, journalistic, and even Republican communities responding to a Ford announcement that "I have no solid coalition of support outside of southwestern Michigan and no working relationships outside of the House." Whereas presidents normally create and/or exploit crises to enhance their effectiveness, Ford needed to tackle his rhetorical crisis indirectly, by establishing himself as the personal core of both coalitions.

The constituent elements of personal credibility or *ethos* are trustworthiness, competence, and dynamism; Ford moved quickly to stake out all three. He did so by using the resources at his disposal, however meager, to tackle four sets of interconnected problems: White House staffing, social polarization, economic distress, and midterm elections. Because of the fundamental dilemma Ford ran headlong into new dilemmas at every turn. But because these secondary dilemmas were more familiar, they were potentially more manageable.

Americans were sharply divided over Vietnam and Watergate in August 1974. Official U.S. involvement in Vietnam had ended seventeen months before, and while the Vietnamese continued fighting, Americans argued about the fate of those who had dodged or evaded the draft. One interpretive community felt that they should be treated as traitors, another camp felt that the resolution of the war had vindicated their opposition to the war, and animosity between the communities ran high. Meanwhile, Americans were divided over the fate of former President Nixon as well. One interpretive community argued that he had suffered enough, another that no one should be above trial and punishment; again, emotions ran high.

Presidents have the constitutional authority to grant pardons, and it is the pardon proclamation that accomplishes ipso facto the pardon. But because a president who went about pardoning people at will would rapidly dissipate his credibility, it is prudent for presidents to explain and to justify their pardons (Campbell & Jamieson, 1990). Ford therefore faced both *policy choices* relative to the punishment or pardoning of Nixon and the draft evaders, and *rhetorical choices* relative to his justification of his policy decisions.

What were Ford's policy alternatives relative to Nixon and the draft evaders? First, he could have ignored both issues, but they would have festered and undermined his ability to unify the public and to solve the nation's pressing economic problems. Second, he could have pardoned the draft evaders and punished Nixon, thereby losing the conservative and Republican support necessary for governance and eventual nomination. Third, he could have punished the draft evaders and pardoned Nixon, thereby incurring the enmity of those who had opposed Johnson and Nixon and who saw in Ford a new hope. Fourth, he could have punished all concerned, thereby inviting supporters of each to challenge the legitimacy of his presidential authority. Fifth, he could have pardoned Nixon and the draft evaders, thereby demonstrating his courage and good will while incurring the wrath of those in all quarters with a penchant for revenge.

Whichever policy path he chose, Ford would face equally difficult rhetorical choices. Karlyn Kohrs Campbell and Kathleen Hall Jamieson (1990) discussed presidential pardoning as a rhetorical genre in which "The impersonal tone, the archaic language, reliance on legalistic terminology, and the formality of the *document* [italics added] overpower individual style and give these *documents* [italics added] a quaint sameness" (p. 170). They observed that the rhetoric of pardoning has three key generic elements: "(1) acting in the presidential role as symbolic head of state; (2) demonstrating that this is an opportune time for action; and (3) justifying the pardon as for the public good" (pp. 168–169). Any decision to pardon would be especially dicey for Ford, given the tenuousness of his claim to presidential legitimacy. Moreover, it would be easier for him to justify the timeliness of postwar pardons than to justify a pretrial pardon of Nixon.

Ford therefore needed to lubricate public acceptance of any pardons he might choose to grant. The pardoning elements among his five policy choices could have been justified in a variety of ways. The actions of Nixon and the draft evaders could potentially be justified, for example, with any of the following reasons: (1) they had done nothing wrong, (2) they had made honest mistakes, (3) they had transgressed for laudable reasons, (4) they had transgressed because of extenuating circumstances, (5) they had transgressed because of others, (6) they had transgressed but should be forgiven, (7) they had transgressed and deserved punishment, which was being withheld out of mercy, (8) they had transgressed and deserved punishment but they had already suffered enough, and/or (9) they had transgressed and deserved an opportunity to make amends. Public acceptance of any of these rhetorical rationales for pardoning would mitigate the unavoidable challenges to Ford's legitimacy.

Ford faced a Rubik's Cube of a problem. One side of the cube aligned liberals and conservatives with the draft evaders and Nixon; the second side aligned his policy choices of avoidance, pardons, and punishments; and the third side provided an array of rhetorical justifications with which to explain his policy choices to his citizens. At stake were nothing more than his governing and electoral coalitions, the future of the Republican Party, and after their disappointments with Johnson and Nixon, Americans' confidence in the integrity of the presidency. Ford's moral, political, and rhetorical choices were certain to have far-reaching consequences for America's future as well as his own.

FORD'S VFW SPEECH OF AUGUST 19, 1974

Several of President Ford's advisors had encouraged him to address the draft evasion question in order to unify the country. Ford (1979) later recalled that Secretary of Defense James Schlesinger had suggested that Ford could hasten the healing process and differentiate between the Nixon and Ford administrations by doing something about the fifty thousand draft evaders and deserters from the Vietnam War. Former Secretary of Defense Melvin Laird and Ford's three sons agreed with him, and Ford himself was similarly inclined. But in what forum should he announce it?

Ford had previously agreed to address the annual Veterans of Foreign Wars (VFW) convention in Chicago on August 19, 1974; Nixon's resignation rendered it his first presidential address outside of Washington. He was a longstanding member of the Old Kent Post in Grand Rapids, and he could count on an enthusiastic reception from the conventioneers. "The more conservative VFW would be very disturbed" by his position, Ford (1979) observed, "but announcing it to them would indicate strength on my part. The Chicago address was the right occasion" (p. 141). In selecting the VFW as his audience the coalitionless president selected an interpretive community of which he was a respected member. One of their own was now president, and he chose to visit them almost immediately.

Ford's address dramatized his representation of those in his personal coalition. He alluded to his membership in the American Legion and the American Veterans of World War II, Korea and Vietnam (Amvets) as well as the VFW, and he promised an open office door for veterans "just as it was all my 25 years" in Congress. He announced his appointment of former Congressman Dick "Roudy" Roudebush (R-IN) to head the Veterans Administration (VA). Ford voiced the frustrations of veterans and others who were dependent on federal programs, saying that "As President, I want no arrogance or indifference to any individual, veteran or not. Our Government's machinery exists to serve people, not to frustrate or humiliate them" (1974e, p. 23). The president urged the improvement of VA hospitals and vowed to "humanize the VA" (p. 24). Applause and cheers filled the Conrad Hilton Hotel meeting hall.

In the advance text of the address Ford moved directly to support the VFW's new commander in chief, educational programs, the employment of veterans, democracy, free enterprise, and faith in America; and he came out against discrimination and inflation. The prepared text was music to the veterans' ears, and their cheers were the first public affirmation of Ford's presidency.

Had Ford delivered the advance text verbatim he would have signaled a presidency that would tell his supporters what they wanted to hear. Although that might enable a popular politician to maintain support, it neither wins new friends nor signals real leadership. But Ford surprised them by inserting previously secret material justifying selective pardons for draft evaders between his praise for all veterans and for their new commander, thereby accomplishing several instrumental goals.

The last-minute insertion precluded counterargument by advisors such as General Alexander Haig who opposed the plan. Haig had been Nixon's chief of staff, and his influence among the holdovers was considerable (Hartmann, 1980). Second, the surprise enabled the president, rather than the press, to make the announcement. It was important for Ford to announce personally a decision of this importance, lest he be perceived as a figurehead whose every action could be predicted by the press. Third, the insertion enabled Ford to wrap the unpopular policy in the spirit of camaraderie and identification with veterans. This was facilitated by inserting the material into a completed epideictic address, like putting the jelly into a jelly doughnut. Finally, Ford's maneuver enabled him to demonstrate to all Americans that his supporters would not be getting everything they wanted from his presidency, which is to say that his presidency would be less polarized than that of either of his recent predecessors. Gerald Ford wanted to be president of "all the people," and the VFW address dramatized that point.

Ford's handling of the announcement itself reflected the coalitional dilemmas he faced. He had to enact the role of president as defined by his predecessors and to complete the presidency inaugurated in 1973, while nevertheless distinguishing his administration from that of Richard Nixon. He did this by grounding his announcement in the relevant statements of Richard Nixon, the Pentagon, and previous presidents.

The first step was to find all public statements about amnesty by Nixon administration officials, statements that would narrow Ford's rhetorical alternatives. This process began well before Nixon's resignation, and it culminated in a March 5, 1974, memorandum from the Department of Defense's Lieutenant Kenneth R. Bailey to the vice president's naval aide, Commander Howard Kerr. Bailey's (1974) memorandum provided six statements on amnesty from Nixon, Laird, and others, and it served as the Ford team's basis for conceptualizing the pardon issue.

Congressional testimony by Major General Leo Benade defined the crucial terminology, differentiating "amnesty" from "pardon." The key distinctions between amnesty and pardon are not clearly drawn in Benade's testimony, but they seem to be these:

1. Both presume punishable misconduct and guilt.
2. Both release the offender from punishment.
3. "Amnesty" forgives the offense and removes the penalty, whereas a *"pardon" affirms the guilt as it removes the punishment.*
4. Amnesty is often extended to a group of persons before trial and punishment, whereas a pardon is usually granted to an individual after punishment has begun.
5. Amnesty is often extended to a group of persons contingent on the performance of certain conditions.
6. Both have traditionally been extended by the president.

The nagging semantic distinctions between amnesty and pardon would later complicate Ford's handling of the VFW and Nixon addresses.

Bailey's memorandum, as donated to the archives of the Ford Library, presented the administration's statements out of chronological order. This invites the reader to infer that the relatively conciliatory statements by Secretary Laird and General Benade were more recent than either Nixon's press conference of January 31, 1973, or his January 23, 1974, letter to VFW Commander Ray Soden. This was not the case. The most recent statement on the subject was, in fact, Nixon's reassuring letter to VFW Commander Ray Soden, who would eventually introduce Ford to the convention:

The few who refused to serve, or deserted their country, must pay a penalty for their choice. . . . We cannot provide forgiveness for them. Those who served paid their price. Those who deserted must pay their price. And the price is a criminal penalty for disobeying the laws of the United States. (Nixon, 1974)

It is difficult to discern the order in which the statements were read by President Ford. They might have been out of sequence, they might have been misfiled by Hartmann, or they might have been rearranged by Ford as he agonized over his position. Nevertheless, the net effect was to widen the gulf between Soden's expectations and Ford's announcement, further complicating Ford's rhetorical task.

The surprise insert employed a variety of techniques to advantage. Ford began by reaffirming his personal moral opposition to blanket amnesty: "As minority leader of the House and recently as Vice President, I stated my strong conviction that unconditional, blanket amnesty for anyone who illegally evaded or fled military service is wrong. It *is* wrong" (1974e, p. 24). This paragraph drew upon the common ground established in his introduction, affirmed his link to Nixon's policy, and laid the foundation for a treatise on semantic distinctions.

Ford went on to differentiate his personal beliefs from his presidential responsibility, and to emphasize divine rather than public accountability. Said Ford, "Yet, in my first words as President of all the people, I acknowledged a Power, higher than the people, Who commands not only righteousness but love, not only justice but mercy" (p. 24). Ford's change in position was, therefore, to be understood neither as a personal change of heart nor as a matter of political expedience. Rather, it was the result of his ascension to higher, transcendent responsibilities. Although presidents frequently invoke divine authority when announcing unpopular measures, this case seems something more than that. This question truly was a matter of conscience for Ford.

As his stunned audience waited for the next grenade to land, Ford quickly invoked Presidents Lincoln and Truman, the American system of justice, the all-volunteer army, and "the urgent problem of how to bind up the Nation's wounds"—a metaphor that could not have been more appropriate for his audience of war veterans.

But if Ford was responding to a Power higher than the people, that Power had not told him how to implement a program. He therefore explained that he had asked the attorney general, the secretary of defense, and other government officials to report "the full spectrum of American opinion . . . consolidating the known facts and legal precedents." After this review Ford himself would decide "how best to deal with the different kinds of cases—and there are differences" (1974e, p. 25). The latter phrase was a gamble.

Unlike Nixon, who had lumped all cases of desertion and evasion together, Ford acknowledged differences among individual cases. General Benade's testimony had made it clear that the Pentagon perceived differences, and Ford could have cited that testimony. But by doing so Ford would have been deferring publicly to the Pentagon's authority in this matter, and that would not have enhanced his presidential stature. By stating Pentagon reasoning as his own presidential judgment, Ford enhanced his authority without fear of contradiction. Veterans protesting his plan would get little help from General Benade's office.

The theme of "differences" operated on two levels. First, it permitted Ford to announce his intentions during this scheduled speech and to avoid a universal policy that would generate controversial exceptions, because "only a fraction of such cases . . . relate directly to Vietnam" (1974e, p. 25). Second, it invited Americans to differentiate Ford from advocates of unconditional amnesty as well as from Nixon.

Nixon had said repeatedly that no amnesty would be possible until all Americans returned from Vietnam, and Ford extended Nixon's point for his VFW audience. He observed that "the last combatant was withdrawn [from Vietnam] over a year ago by President Nixon. But all, in a sense, are casualties, still abroad or absent without leave from the real America." In this scenario Ford's willingness to bring back some of the deserters and evaders was a logical extension of Nixon's effort to bring the war to an end. "I want them to come home," said Ford "if they want to *work* their way back" (1974e, p. 25).

It remained for Ford to justify desertion and evasion to those whose loved ones had been killed in combat, and he did so masterfully. He recalled presenting fourteen Congressional Medals of Honor to parents, widows, and children:

As I studied their records of supreme sacrifice, I kept thinking how young they were. The few citizens of our country who, in my judgment, committed the supreme folly of shirking their duty at the expense of others, were also very young. All of us who served in one war or another know very well that all wars are the glory of the young. In my judgment, these young Americans should have a second chance to contribute their fair share to the rebuilding of peace among ourselves and with all nations. (1974e, p. 25)

This brief passage united Ford, the VFW membership, the Vietnam heroes, and the offenders in a recollection of youth.

All of the conventioneers were there because they still shared memories from their younger days. Many had been seriously injured, and all had had, or dreamed of, second chances to rebuild their lives after extended absences. Ford's remarks invited them, perhaps for the first time, to consider the offenders as fellow casualties of war:

I ask all Americans who ever asked for goodness and mercy in their lives, who ever sought forgiveness for their trespasses, to *join in rehabilitating all the casualties* [italics added] of the tragic conflict of the past. (1974e, p. 25)

Because of his desire to rehabilitate all the casualties of the conflict, Ford announced:

I am throwing the weight of my Presidency into the scales of justice on the side of leniency. I foresee their earned re-entry—*earned re-entry*—into a new atmosphere of hope, hard work and mutual trust. . . . As I reject amnesty, so I reject revenge. (1974e, p. 25)

Ford might not have satisfied the needs of many of the relatives of those killed in the war, but his discourse made it psychologically possible for them not to oppose him.

The earned re-entry program was begun, and Ford suffered less political fallout than might reasonably have been expected. Indeed, one student of the address has concluded that "Even though the response of his immediate audience was chilly, Americans generally were pleased" (Brock, 1988, p. 230). Remarkably, Ford was asked *not one* question about the program at his first press conference—held nine days after the announcement and nineteen days before the actual program was proclaimed. Ford did experience a 15 percent drop in aggregate public approval, from +68 three days before the address to +53 some time in "early September" (King & Ragsdale, 1988). However, his initial gaudy public support margin (71% approval versus 3% disapproval) was destined to decline somewhat even if Ford had tried to say and do only politically popular things.

In this case, President Ford (1) faced supporters who were ego-involved in the issue, (2) violated their legitimate expectations of him and his predecessor, and (3) escaped with a "chilly" reaction from the immediate audience, generalized public support, and no questions from the press. Instead, the press asked six questions about Watergate and Ford's thoughts on Richard Nixon's status.

THE NIXON PARDON SPEECH OF SEPTEMBER 8, 1974

Nixon's Watergate rhetoric has been analyzed extensively (Harrell, Ware, & Linkugel, 1975; Smith, 1988), and it is discussed in Chapter 8. Our concern here is not with the Watergate morass but with Ford's attempt to sweep the whole affair into the ashcan of history.

Ford had said to the nation upon taking the oath of office that "our long national nightmare is over" (1974d, p. 2). But the memory of a nightmare lingers on into the morning, and we often hold friends accountable for offenses that we imagined in our nightmares. Much as nightmares must be shaken off in the dawn's early light, so Ford had to help Americans to shake off their national nightmare. For this task he was unprepared, and the ghosts of arguments past would haunt his presidency for the rest of its days.

After nineteen whirlwind days as president, Gerald Ford held a press conference on August 28, 1974. He prepared for questions on the economy, White House staffing and reorganization, and his foreign policy toward Cyprus, Strategic Arms Limitation Talks, and the Middle East—not to mention topics such as the Soviet Union, his personal background, and midterm congressional elections. Ford discounted the possibility that the press would ask him about Nixon, despite warnings to the contrary. Although Ford devoted considerable attention to the status of Nixon's tapes and papers, he stated that:

I hadn't given any thought to Nixon's legal status. That was in the hands of responsible authorities, and it seemed to me that it would be inappropriate for the press to ask questions about a man whose fate was up to the Special Prosecutor and the courts. *There were too many other things of vital importance to the country at home and abroad, and I was sure reporters would ask about them. I was totally wrong* [italics added]. (1979, p. 157)

Questions about Nixon dominated the press conference, and Ford considered it a disastrous turn of events.

Ford and his advisors returned to the White House discussing the half-life of the Nixon issue. "Was I going to be asked about Nixon's fate every time I met with the press?" Ford asked.

Each of them said it would continue as long as Richard Nixon's legal status and the disposition of the papers and tapes remain unclarified. Their scenario was discouraging. I'd been hoping to have press conferences every two or three weeks. I realized now that I'd be questioned repeatedly about him and his many legal problems. Worse, I recognized that the responses I'd already given could—and probably would—be variously interpreted. . . . All this forced me to address the issue squarely for the first time. I had to get the monkey off my back. (1979, pp. 158–159)

But how?

President Ford unexpectedly took to the airwaves at 11:05 Sunday morning, September 8, 1974, to announce "a full, free and absolute pardon unto Richard Nixon for all offenses against the United States which he, Richard Nixon, has committed or may have committed or taken part in during the period [of his Presidency]" (1974b, p. 104). It was, of course, Ford's presidential prerogative to pardon Nixon or anyone else. But this was not a postwar pardon with precedents like the actions of Lincoln, Wilson, and Truman. This was a unique case, and it required of Ford an adroit rhetorical strategy. Specifically, Ford needed to retain the support of the Nixon holdovers in his administration and of Republicans who had supported Nixon, without appearing to Democrats and others to be part of the Watergate conspiracy.

Ford's pardon of Nixon was unusual, in part, because the reasons given for the pardon vary: from the Pardon Proclamation itself, to his remarks explaining it, to Ford's testimony before the Hungate Committee, to his memoirs, and to the reasons reported by his advisors. The official proclamation provided four reasons for granting the pardon:

[1] a trial could not fairly begin until a year or more has elapsed, [2] In the meantime, the tranquillity to which this nation has been restored . . . could be irreparably lost [3] by the prospects of bringing to trial a former President of the United States, thereby [4] exposing to further punishment and degradation

a man who has already paid the unprecedented penalty of relinquishing the highest elective office of the United States. (Ford, 1974b, p. 104)

The phrasing of the Pardon Proclamation was clearly friendly to Nixon's point of view. The proclamation could have highlighted Nixon's offenses even as it pardoned them to make Nixon's acceptance of the pardon unpleasant and to satisfy his adversaries, but it did not do so. In short, the phrasing of the official pardon was adapted to Nixon and his supporters.

But Ford's remarks to the nation justifying the pardon invoked four additional reasons for his decision. These included (1) the absence of precedent for Nixon's situation—not to mention Ford's, (2) the possibility that Nixon "would be cruelly and excessively penalized either in preserving the presumption of his innocence or in obtaining a speedy determination of his guilt," and (3) the possibility that "[in] the end, the courts might well hold that [he] had been denied due process, and the verdict of history would be even more inconclusive." Moreover, (4) "My conscience tells me it is my duty, not merely to proclaim domestic tranquillity but to use every means that I have to insure it" (Ford, 1974c, pp. 102–103). Why did the reasons in the remarks differ from those in the proclamation?

The building of President Ford's coalitions required a variety of responses from diverse constituencies: Nixon, the presidential staff, Congress, the Republican Party, the press, the general public, and Democrats. Like most coalitional questions this one grew in layers, like an onion. First, Ford could ill afford to grant a pardon that Nixon would denounce—that would have been the worst of both worlds. Therefore the pardon itself had to address Nixon's own personal needs. Second, he needed to induce Nixon to accept the pardon in a way that would galvanize Republicans in general, and Nixon holdovers in particular, in support of Ford's leadership. Ford therefore needed to articulate their shared commitment to the promise and successes of the Nixon years, their subsequent sense of disappointment and betrayal, and their optimistic orientation toward the future. Third, Ford needed to galvanize that Republican support without provoking an opposition coalition. He could ill afford either to incite the House to reactivate their impeachment machinery, or to invite the press to fan the glowing embers of public cynicism.

This concatenation of audiences and responses shaped Ford's rhetorical behavior. His sets of reasons were addressed to different audiences: the proclamation spoke to Nixon and his lawyers, his remarks spoke to the public, his follow-up statements and testimony before the Hungate Committee spoke to his critics, and memoirs by Ford and his aides spoke to history.

Because an official presidential pardon constitutes a complete legal act, the proclamation *was* the pardon. Perhaps some presidents could have violated rhetorical expectations, but Gerald Ford could not do so without undermining both his, and his pardon's, credibility. He needed a proclamation that hewed to generic expectations, which meant that it could not invoke Ford's *personal* morals, beliefs, conscience, or feelings. The granting of the pardon was itself an enactment of the presidential role, but one that drew attention to Ford's tenuous grip on presidential legitimacy.

Whatever Ford said in the generic proclamation had to induce Nixon's cooperation. It could therefore cite neither the absence of precedent nor the potential dismissal of the case, lest Nixon find encouragement to fight on. Nor could he afford to grant a pardon that detailed Nixon's misdeeds lest Nixon and his supporters rebuke Ford. The proclamation therefore spoke only of "certain acts or omissions occurring before his resignation" and "offenses against the United States" by "a man who has already paid the unprecedented penalty of relinquishing the highest elective office" (Ford, 1974b, p. 104). This was a characterization of Watergate that Nixon could, and did, accept.

But Ford needed additional remarks to contextualize the Nixon-oriented proclamation for his other audiences. He did so by transcending the proclamation, both literally and figuratively. As in the VFW address, Ford wrapped the announcement in other discourse. These remarks gave his audiences five reasons that had been, at best, understated in the proclamation: the absence of precedent, the dictates of conscience, the cruel and unusual nature of this prosecution, the unlikelihood of a fair trial, and the likelihood of a mistrial. These were not reasons for Nixon to accept the pardon, they were reasons why others should acquiesce in the pardon.

Response to the Nixon pardon was quick. Nixon accepted it, but the House did not. Nixon loyalists did not defect, but Ford's press secretary denounced it and resigned. The reaction from the press and the public was such that two days later White House public relations advisor William J. Baroody, Jr., wrote that "While it is probably true that the criticism . . . will burn itself out, the incident is likely to leave a reservoir of distrust and ill feeling toward the President" (1974, p. 1). Baroody went on astutely to observe that "the decision appeared to many to have been slipped to the public suddenly on a Sunday, with little success in conveying the President's reasons to the public" (p. 1).

But Baroody also rendered the following opinion, which deserves scrutiny: "Our problem is that the President's announcement of his decision was not widely seen by the public. Had it been widely viewed, his reasons for taking the action and the spirit which motivated him would have been better understood and appreciated" (1974, p. 1). Perhaps Baroody meant to distinguish "the President's announcement" from the proclamation, believing that the arguments for acquiescence had not reached their intended audience. If so, it is curious that his memorandum proceeded to recommend two major points for the press conference, one of which was a drastic departure from anything said by Ford on Sunday morning. After observing that "Justice is not an implacable, unyielding legal machine. . . . it clearly requires taking all circumstances of a case into account," Baroody discussed an issue not yet mentioned publicly by President Ford:

Argument: The country must know the truth about Watergate—*Refutation*: The fact is that the former President will testify in the trial of his aides and, in the process, much of the additional facts about Watergate will come out. In addition his [Nixon's] tapes and other materials will be available to the courts. Would a trial, conviction and subsequent pardon add substantially to our knowledge? Or would it merely prolong and perhaps deepen the divisions in the country over Watergate? (1974, p. 2)

Baroody's argument was that the presidential pardon had precluded Nixon's ability to use self-incrimination as a shield against testifying in the trials of others.

It is unlikely that this suggestion originated with Baroody's postpardon memorandum. Baroody clearly regarded this as central to Ford's "reasons for taking the action and the spirit which motivated him." Ford concurs, although he could not say so at the time. His memoirs described as "for me the most important precedent" a 1915 case in which editor George Burdick invoked potential self-incrimination to avoid testifying. The U.S. Attorney pulled out a presidential pardon so that Burdick could not claim the protection of the Fifth Amendment. Ford realized that in the Burdick decision the Supreme Court had reaffirmed the president's power to pardon, even for a crime denied by the accused and of which the accused had yet to be convicted. Even more important to Ford, "the Justices found that a pardon 'carries an imputation of guilt, acceptance, a confession to it.' These opinions were clear and unambiguous and had remained the law of the land for nearly sixty years" (1979, pp. 163–164).

In short, the joint legal considerations that (1) acceptance of a pardon signifies both guilt and confession, and (2) a pardoned individual cannot avoid testifying against others for reasons of self-incrimination were central elements in Ford's reasoning about Nixon's legal status. Ford surely could have mollified Democrats, reporters, and many of Nixon's critics by articulating the confession and incrimination reasons. But he could not do so without both tipping his hand to Nixon—whose acceptance of the pardon would constitute a legal confession and a loss of Fifth Amendment protections—and alienating Republicans and the Nixon holdovers who were keeping his administration afloat.

The reason for issuing the pardon that would have been most persuasive to Nixon's critics was missing from both the proclamation and Ford's initial remarks. But without a coalition of support Ford could not articulate publicly those reasons lest he make the pardon unacceptable to Nixon and his loyalists in the Ford administration and the Republican Party. A president with at least one solid coalition might have risked articulating these reasons; but, then again, a president with a solid coalitional base could have relied more heavily on his legitimate claim to presidential prerogatives to weather the storm.

Instead of elaborating his legal reasons for issuing the pardon, Ford made public remarks that violated the characteristics of the pardon genre. Pardons use impersonal, legalistic, archaic, and formal language, and Ford's did. But his remarks also contained sixty-four first person singular references, all related to his personal decision making, such as the pronouns we have italicized in the following passage:

I have come to a decision which *I* felt *I* should tell you and all of *my* fellow American citizens, as soon as *I* was certain in *my* own mind and in *my* own conscience that it is the right thing to do. . . . *My* conscience tells *me* clearly and certainly that *I* cannot prolong the bad dreams that continue to reopen a chapter that is closed. *My* conscience tells *me* that only *I*, as President, have the constitutional power to firmly shut and seal this book. . . . *I* do believe that right makes might and that if *I* am wrong, 10 angels swearing *I* was right would make no difference. (Ford, 1974c, pp. 102–103)

The remarks enabled Ford to personally enact the power of the presidency and to contrast his concern for principle with the amoral pragmatism of the previous administration. But he unnecessarily and unwisely invested his personal credibility in the Nixon pardon without revealing the legal reasons that warranted his moral act. It is not unrealistic to suggest that Ford could have mitigated the damage to his personal reputation caused by this flood of personal pronouns. He might better have said something like:

Clearly and certainly *we as a nation* cannot prolong the bad dreams that continue to reopen a chapter that is closed. Only *I,* as President, have the constitutional power *and therefore the obligation* to firmly shut and seal this book. . . . *As Americans we all* believe that right makes might and that if *it is* wrong, 10 angels swearing *it* was right would make no difference.

This revision reduces from sixteen to none the number of times Ford puts his own neck on the block, it twice invokes the nation as a unified whole, it shifts attention from the rightness of Gerald Ford to the rightness of the pardon, and it presents Ford as a servant obligated to act in the national interest. Perhaps most important, it seems more faithful to Ford's position as revealed in his memoirs and official presidential papers.

CONCLUSIONS

Gerald Ford faced the problems of his first thirty days with neither an electoral nor a governing coalition. He chose to heal the country by using his power to pardon both draft evaders and Richard Nixon. But his efforts to do so were complicated by a series of dilemmas emanating from his coalitional crisis. Bluntly, Ford proclaimed reasonably justifiable pardons in two speeches; one nearly perfect, the other disastrous.

Ford's rhetorical choices in the VFW and Nixon addresses were remarkably different. He entered the VFW lion's den, but he used Sunday morning television to discuss Nixon. The VFW speech was long, but the Nixon speech was brief. The VFW speech built credibility, the Nixon speech spent it. The VFW speech announced his intent to formulate a plan, the Nixon speech announced a fait accompli. The VFW speech explained its reasons, the Nixon speech advanced two sets of reasons but withheld two of the most important. Not surprisingly, then, reaction to the VFW address was moderate and manageable, but reaction to the Nixon pardon dogged him for years.

Beyond these differences is the philosophical core of Gerald Ford. In both cases he asserted the president's constitutional and moral power to pardon. In both cases he recognized an obligation to use that power to secure domestic tranquillity. In both cases he recognized both serious offenses against the United States and a transcendent need to heal the nation and to move ahead. In both cases he thought the offenders should pay a price for their offenses. In both cases his pardon presumed guilt and confession, and it offered only relief from penalties. Nevertheless, Ford himself denied seeing any similarities between the cases.

The difference between Ford's policy choices was to be found on the scales of justice: Nixon had a record of significant public service to offset his disservice, the draft evaders and deserters had none. Indeed, Ford's earned pardon program created a mechanism for the exiles to perform public service sufficient to counterbalance their transgressions. Ford's resolution of the two pardon issues was remarkably logical, consistent, and nonpartisan. It was his rhetoric that let him down.

The Nixon pardon remarks have been widely judged a failure (Brock, 1988; Campbell & Jamieson, 1990; Klumpp & Lukehart, 1978). Ford later wrote, "I have to confess that my televised talk failed to emphasize adequately that I wanted to give my full attention to grave economic and policy matters. Nor did I explain as fully as I should have the strong judicial underpinnings, in particular, the Supreme Court's ruling that acceptance of a pardon means admission of guilt" (1979, p. 179). Perhaps the surest measure of the speech's failure is that Ford (1979) credits Hartmann with its authorship, while Hartmann (1980) credits Ford (although they agree that Ford inserted the reference to Nixon's health).

Nevertheless, some criticism of the Nixon remarks failed to acknowledge either the complexity of Ford's crisis or the inexperience of Ford and his aides. Brock (1988), for example, would have had Ford announce both pardons in the same address, but Ford did not plan to have anything to do with a Nixon pardon until nine days after the VFW address. Campbell and Jamieson's (1990) critique underplays Ford's need to retain the active support of Nixon holdovers in his administration and in the party. Their critiques failed to give adequate consideration to the crisis in Ford's coalitionless presidency—to the political situation that invited and constrained the rhetoric. Ford could have provided less support for the Nixon perspective in his address, but then who would have served in his administration? The only people in the White House who were familiar with the policy apparatus were Nixon holdovers. Neither Brock nor Campbell and Jamieson were wrong in their appraisals, but they did underestimate the difficulty of Ford's coalitional situation, and consequently they misread his decisions.

Ford lost the 1976 election when Jimmy Carter parlayed a 1,682,790 plurality into a 57 electoral vote advantage. The election was so close that Ford could have won by drawing another 0.21 percent of the vote in Ohio and an extra 1.61 percent of the vote in Wisconsin. Exit polls indicated that Carter voters cited Ford's Nixon pardon more frequently than any other reason for preferring Carter. Perhaps they should have cited Ford's pardon *rhetoric*, instead.

Ironically, Ford himself became the vehicle for America's redemption. Because the pardons did not forgive, guilt and rancor were unresolved. Because he dramatically and personally pardoned unpopular people who had committed offenses against the United States, Ford shared in their guilt. The final irony is that by following his conscience and avoiding political expedience, Gerald Ford became the last victim of Watergate.

Gerald Ford rightly perceived his presidency as "a time to heal" and he used his pardoning power for that purpose. It is important to realize that Ford had an alternative rhetorical strategy available to him: the rhetoric of polarization. This surely would have been the order of the day had Spiro Agnew been Nixon's successor. Indeed, Agnew was the early Nixon administration's prime polarizer and vilifier (King & Anderson, 1971). By the end of the Nixon era public frustration with assassinations, Vietnam, and Watergate invited sacrificial victims. Nixon's successor could rather easily have forged a governing coalition by heaping blame on vulnerable parties such as Nixon or the draft resisters and then driving them from the system, thereby "purifying" America. But Ford, to his everlasting credit, chose to build public trust by forgiving and healing. Through presidential compassion he sought to nurture what might have been called a kinder, gentler America.

But the president who spoke of his hope for a kinder and gentler America, George Bush, relied heavily on the politics of division to attain it. The political implication of that rhetorical choice is the subject of Chapter 4.

REFERENCES

Bailey, K. R. (1974). Memorandum. Lt. Kenneth R. Bailey to Commander Howard Kerr, 3/5/74, folder "1974/08/09 — Veterans of Foreign Wars, Chicago, IL, (2),"

Box 1, Files of Robert T. Hartmann, Counselor to the President, Gerald R. Ford Library.

Baroody, W. J. (1974). Responses to critics of the Nixon pardon. William J. Baroody, Jr., for Robert T. Hartmann, 9/10/74, folder "9-24-74 Nixon Pardon (2)," Box 1, Files of Paul Miltich, Assistant Press Secretary, Gerald R. Ford Library.

Brock, B. L. (1988). Gerald R. Ford encounters Richard Nixon's legacy: On amnesty and the pardon. In H. R. Ryan (Ed.), *Oratorical encounters: Selected studies and sources of twentieth-century political accusations and apologia* (pp. 227–240). Westport, CT: Greenwood.

Buchen, P. W. (1989). The making of an unscheduled presidential transition. In J. P. Pfiffner and R. G. Hoxie (Eds.), *The presidency in transition* (pp. 65–73). New York: Center for the Study of the Presidency.

Campbell, K. K., & Jamieson, K. H. (1990). *Deeds done in words: Presidential rhetoric and the genres of governance.* Chicago: University of Chicago Press.

Ford, G. R. [1974a]. Memorandum for the heads of departments and agencies, August 10. *Public papers of the president* (pp. 4–5). Washington, DC: U.S. Government Printing Office.

Ford, G. R. [1974b]. Proclamation 4311, granting pardon to Richard Nixon, September 8. *Public papers of the president* (pp. 103–104). Washington, DC: U.S. Government Printing Office.

Ford, G. R. [1974c]. Remarks on signing a proclamation granting pardon to Richard Nixon, September 8. *Public papers of the president* (pp. 101–103). Washington, DC: U.S. Government Printing Office.

Ford, G. R. [1974d]. Remarks on taking the oath of office, August 9. *Public papers of the president* (pp. 1–2). Washington, DC: U.S. Government Printing Office.

Ford, G. R. [1974e]. Remarks to the Veterans of Foreign Wars annual convention, Chicago, Illinois. August 19. *Public papers of the president* (pp. 22–28). Washington, DC: U.S. Government Printing Office.

Ford, G. R. (1979). *A time to heal: The autobiography of Gerald R. Ford.* New York: Harper and Row.

Harrell, J., Ware, B. L., & Linkugel, W. A. (1975). Failure of apology in American politics: Nixon and Watergate. *Speech Monographs, 42,* 245–261.

Hartmann, R. T. (1980). *Palace politics: An inside account of the Ford years.* New York: McGraw-Hill.

Hunter, M. (1974, August 8). Vice president shuns transition talk, but says he's ready. *New York Times,* p. 7.

King, A. A., & Anderson, F. D. (1971). Nixon, Agnew, and the "silent majority": A case study in the rhetoric of polarization. *Western Speech, 34,* 243–255.

King, G., & Ragsdale, L., comps. (1988). *The elusive executive: Discovering statistical patterns in the presidency.* Washington, DC: Congressional Quarterly.

Klumpp, J. F., & Lukehart, J. K. (1978). The pardoning of Richard Nixon: A failure in motivational strategy. *Western Journal of Speech Communication, 41,* 116–123.

Koenig, L. W. (1986). *The chief executive* (5th ed.). New York: Harcourt Brace Jovanovich.

Memo. (1974). White House press secretary to White House staff, August 9. Transition File, Box 168, Seidman Files, Gerald R. Ford Library.

Move is surprise. (1973, October 13). *New York Times.*

Nixon, R. M. (1974). Photocopy of a letter. Richard Nixon to VFW Commander Ray Soden, 1/23/74, included in Bailey's (1974) memorandum, Hartmann files, Gerald R. Ford Library.

Nixon, R. M. [1975]. Address to the nation announcing decision to resign the office of president of the United States. *Public papers of the president* (p. 627). Washington, DC: U.S. Government Printing Office.

Smith, C. A. (1988). Richard M. Nixon and the Watergate scandal. In H. R. Ryan (Ed.), *Oratorical encounters: Selected studies and sources of twentieth-century political accusations and apologia* (pp. 201–226). Westport, CT: Greenwood.

4

The Politics of Division

"Divide and conquer," "with us or against us," and "as different as night and day" are all common expressions that use divergence to make sense of the world. We define ourselves by what we are and by what we are not. Politicians need to differentiate themselves from one another in ways that are meaningful and important to the citizenry. Voters are mobilized to prefer candidates and to support or oppose presidents. In both cases, the key element is the development of a rhetoric that enables disparate interpretive communities to prefer in concert.

This chapter is about convergence through divergence. Because identification and division are interrelated, polarization can be a deliberate strategy to build membership in an interpretive coalition. The politics of division is characterized by a rhetoric of polarization in which differences are stressed, similarities are downplayed, and derogatory language is developed to characterize the opposition.

In this chapter we examine the Bush years, from 1988 to 1992, to study the politics of division as opposed to inclusion. There are times when polarization functions to strengthen a group, and there are other times when polarization proves ineffectual. The Bush years provide examples of both the successes and failures of the politics of division.

SUCCESSFUL AND UNSUCCESSFUL POLARIZATION

An effective divisive strategy has six traits. First, a speaker must evoke existing or latent prejudices among members of a community.

The key is to identify carefully the prejudices or divergences that already exist and then address them. To foment new prejudices in the community is both difficult and risky. Second, the president must be identified exclusively with one group rather than another. He must be seen as a pure example of one of the groups, not as a fence straddler between the two polarizing camps. Third, the president must identify with the dominant group. If polarization is going to work to the president's advantage, it must activate communities that account for significant political resources. The wrong calculation will unite still more powerful communities against the president.

Fourth, in effective polarization the "bad group" must be linked plausibly to one or more serious societal problems. If the speaker ties the stigmatized group to a societal problem in a manner that strikes the audience as incongruous, the speaker's credibility will suffer and the polarization strategy will fail. Fifth, the president's image must not be undercut by the strategy of division. If the president is personally associated with actions that foster divisions within the community, his personal reputation and presidential legitimacy will be tarnished. It is far better for the president to have surrogates such as the vice president, members of the president's family, or administration officials make the harsh polarizing charges. This provides the president with a bit of rhetorical distance when the negative reactions splash the White House.

Finally, for a divisive strategy to be successful the "good group" must be associated with higher societal values, culture, and tradition. To be associated with the "good group" is to be a part of the uplifting moral climate of the nation. The divisive strategy seeks to encourage the feeling that it is a positive experience to be a member of the new group. Members of this new group live on a higher plane. Even when the strategy appears negative or dirty, the members can feel confident and superior by being associated with the administration's principles as defined by the president and his surrogates.

But divisive strategies often fail. Indeed, divisive strategies tend to fail for one or more of the following six reasons. First, overlapping memberships can make divisions unacceptable to the audience. If the division used by the speaker does not articulate public needs, reasons, or preferences, audiences may distance themselves from the president's position. For example, the North versus South division in the United States provides familiar distinctions between geographic areas and cultural milieux. But it is a division that has become more and more difficult for politicians to use because American society is increasingly composed of families with members living in different parts of the country. Social mobility has made the division of North versus South much less useful as a strategy of division.

Second, division will not be successful if the president or speaker is not solely associated with one group or side of the issue. Differences are the key to the divergence of groups, and the presence of any similarity between the president and the out-group complicates the argument. Past membership in the out-group, however, may increase the speaker's credibility. This occurred with the conversion of Eldridge Cleaver from the black revolutionary of the 1960s to the Christian speaker of the 1980s. The repentant soul's conversion serves to highlight the unsavory nature of the old, abandoned group and to enhance the credibility of rhetorical depictions of the "bad" group.

Third, the divisive strategy will fail if the divisions it promotes are perceived as outdated or not reflective of the general community's concerns. For example, an effort to blame social ills on liquor would seem outdated, out of touch, and ineffectual as a way of building support with American audiences of the 1990s. But blaming those same ills on drugs or homosexuality could prove quite persuasive.

The fourth strategic problem occurs when the president is associated personally with the divisive strategy. If his personal involvement is perceived as self-promotion, his reputation for presidential leadership could be irreparably damaged. Because speaker credibility is a crucial variable in persuasion, the president's persuasiveness would be compromised.

A fifth problem arises if the logical link of the stigmatized group to societal problems is not accepted by the audience. For example, in the late 1980s and early 1990s America's economic woes were often blamed on Japan. But despite latent vestiges of anti-Japanese sentiment lingering from World War II, the "Japan did it" theme did not sell as a viable division. It failed, in part, because many Americans recognized that our lack of productivity and other problems stemmed from other problems in the American culture and economy. The linking of Japan to our chain of economic woes simply did not help a majority of the American people to "make sense" of their problems.

Finally, a divisive strategy fails when it activates the "bad" groups to join protective coalitions and to establish their own dominance. Someone trying to mobilize traditional homemakers, for example, could alienate and politically activate working mothers who are the numerical majority in the country today. In this scenario, polarization would actually weaken the traditional group by activating otherwise unorganized citizens.

A divisive strategy, therefore, has six factors that encourage its success, and six factors that lead to its failure. Let us now examine how divisive strategies were used by George Bush and his surrogates from 1988 to 1992.

THE BUSH EXPERIENCE

President Bush used the politics of division to win the American presidency in 1988. He then used the politics of division to govern between 1988 and 1992, but with only mixed results. Finally, he used the politics of division without success in his campaign for re-election in 1992. The case of President Bush suggests that the variable potency of the strategy of division is not to be found in studies of the speaker alone, because the speaker, in this case, remained constant. Three variables did change: (1) the situation in which the divisive strategies were applied, (2) the execution of the rhetoric of polarization, and (3) the susceptibility of the voters, the mass media, and the candidates to the charms of divisive rhetoric. Let us turn first to the successful 1988 campaign to evaluate Bush's use of division.

Polarization during the 1988 Campaign

The 1988 campaign, in which George Bush ran against Michael Dukakis, became noteworthy for its negative tone and divisiveness (McWilliams, 1989; Polsby & Wildavsky, 1991). The Bush campaign turned to seasoned professional campaign strategists Roger Ailes and Lee Atwater. Their focus group research with samples of Reagan Democrats and Dukakis supporters suggested to them that two "hot button" social issues could change these voters' preferences from Dukakis to Bush. These two wedge issues were the prison furlough program and the Pledge of Allegiance.

The prison furlough issue raised charges that crimes were being committed by prisoners who were on furlough from prisons. The charges invited voters to infer that such furlough programs were (1) a Dukakis innovation, (2) one of Dukakis's priority programs, and/or (3) something that Dukakis would bring to the nation if elected president (Jamieson, 1989). But Dukakis had curtailed the Massachusetts furlough program begun by his predecessor, it was not related to any of his key issues, and the federal furlough program predated the Massachusetts program. However unfair the charge may have been, the Bush campaign found in the prison furlough program its first wedge to separate voters from Dukakis.

The Bush campaigners did not develop new prejudices during the campaign, but they skillfully highlighted the old ones. The "Willie Horton" spot, paid for not by the Bush campaign but by some independent supporters, invited racial divergence without mentioning race anywhere in the spot. Pictures of menacing black convict Willie Horton, who had committed rape and murder while on furlough from a Massachusetts prison, were shown on national television. The images evoked in many white citizens the fearsome stereotypes of black violence against whites (Hershey, 1989). The furlough issue successfully condensed race and crime into the symbol of Willie Horton, and voters began to perceive Dukakis as softer on crime than Bush and the majority of law-abiding Americans.

Although the Bush campaign neither paid for nor authorized the Horton ad, it satisfied their strategic needs. The independent expenditure featuring Willie Horton framed news coverage and subsequent discussion of the prison furlough issue to the extent that many viewers perceptually merged the Horton ad with the Bush "Revolving Door" prison ad—an ad that neither showed nor mentioned Horton (Jamieson, 1989).

These lines of division were not new with the Bush forces; they simply tapped into latent fears and prejudices and brought them to an emotional peak that polarized citizens and activated voters. In this case, the politics of division worked very well for the Bush campaign by allowing its supporters to associate themselves with order and against disreputable members of society, whom they linked to Dukakis.

The second division exploited by the Bush campaign of 1988 concerned the Pledge of Allegiance. Briefly, the Pledge controversy centered around Governor Dukakis's veto of a bill that would have required Massachusetts teachers to have their students say the Pledge daily. The Massachusetts attorney general had convinced Dukakis that this bill was unconstitutional. They based the veto on the case of *West Virginia State Board of Education v. Barnette* (1943), which had dealt with Jehovah's Witnesses. The Court held in that case that citizens could not be compelled to swear any oath of allegiance, because an oath must be voluntary if it is to be a meaningful affirmation. To coerce an oath, the Court said, is potentially to violate the citizen's freedoms of speech and religion.

The Pledge issue functioned as an attack on Dukakis's patriotism. It was criticized even by relatively conservative writers such as William Safire, who said that Bush was throwing "red meat to the yahoos" (Hershey, 1989, p. 86). Dukakis was peculiarly vulnerable to this kind of attack on his patriotism because he, himself, continually emphasized his ethnic heritage. For example, Neil Diamond's song "The Immigrant" became Dukakis's campaign song, and he laced his speeches with references to Greece, coming to America, and learning to love America from the outsider's perspective. The Pledge of Allegiance issue invited a divergent interpretation of Dukakis's Americanism.

Meanwhile, Bush spoke at the nation's largest flag-making company in what may have been the most fertile photo opportunity of 1988. He also ended his nomination acceptance address at the Republican convention with an invitation for delegates to say the Pledge of Allegiance (Kessel, 1992). Both rhetorical choices invited Americans to associate the Bush campaign, and only the Bush campaign, with patriotism.

The third division drawn in 1988 was between investors and spenders. Investors were portrayed in the rhetoric of the Bush campaign as the builders of America, whereas the spenders were portrayed as those who take money from the investors and workers, use the money to help those who do not work, and thereby destroy the country. In this argument the economic divisions of rich versus poor were fused with the issue of working and not working.

The fourth division used in the 1988 Bush campaign was the line drawn between liberals and everybody else (Pomper, 1989). This division was one that Bush personally advanced as he talked about the "L" word ("liberal"). Liberal as bad, of course, implied conservative as good. This was a divisive strategy that appealed to many Americans because of the frightening narrative of liberal policy horrors that was promoted during the Reagan years. Liberal issues, according to the Bush campaign, were associated with high government spending, lack of law and order, economic degeneration, and an inability to have a strong national defense.

It is interesting that Reagan and Bush characterized Jimmy Carter, Walter Mondale, and Ted Kennedy as the prime architects of the "liberal" fiasco, rarely acknowledging the fact that the liberal Kennedy had challenged Carter and Mondale for the 1980 Democratic nomination. But political narratives are written to legitimate claims to power and to remind us of the inadequacy of those who used to hold power. The conservative narrative was politically correct in 1988, and it strengthened

Bush's claim to be the heir apparent to leadership of Reagan's interpretive coalition. At the same time it enabled them to portray Dukakis not only as weak but as a classic case of the liberal who had to be kept away from the powers of the White House.

It is important to note that Bush was not particularly conservative before 1988. Certainly he was less conservative than Reagan (whom he had challenged in 1980), Jack Kemp and Alexander Haig (who challenged him in 1988), and Pat Buchanan (who challenged him in 1992). Nor was Dukakis quite as liberal as Jesse Jackson, who battled him all the way to the convention floor. But Bush used conservative language, logic, and ideology in 1988 to reposition himself toward the right. Moreover, he took advantage of Dukakis's left-facing arguments with Jackson to pin Dukakis down, left of the mainstream.

The Bush campaign was successful in reopening the Pandora's box of Democratic liberalism. At a rally in Hampton, Georgia, for example, Bush said, "To wrap up that Democratic nomination, [Dukakis] had to stay where he's been in his entire political life, and that's on the left side of things" (Edsall, 1992, p. 201).

The 1988 Bush campaign exploited latent divisions in America. It indirectly encouraged racial division by appealing to white voters' fears of black criminals. It indirectly encouraged Americans to question Dukakis's patriotism with the Pledge of Allegiance issue. It pitted investors against spenders. It then pulled all three divisions together with the master division of liberal versus mainstream. Liberals were depicted as wasteful, lazy, criminal coddling, unpatriotic persons, most of whom were Democrats. In contrast, conservatives were depicted as hardworking investors who made the country great but who were now at the mercy of criminals, racial and ethnic minorities, and foreign countries who disliked them. These depictions gained credence when Dukakis chose to "keep out of the gutter" by ignoring most of the attacks until it was too late.

POLARIZATION DURING THE BUSH ADMINISTRATION

Following such a successful divisive campaign, President Bush began his administration in 1989 with both strategies: division and inclusion. Eight years of Reagan's presidential leadership had served to galvanize the Democrats' opposition, and Bush entered that climate of conflict (Rockman, 1991). But the divisions used in his campaign were not divisions that would work well for him to mobilize a governing coalition because the prison furlough and Pledge of Allegiance issues were not amenable to presidential action. Moreover, the polarization of the campaign had alienated parts of the electorate and Congress, and it had left the country in a temper of division rather than compromise. This made it very difficult for the new president to assume his agenda-setting role.

There were early signs of consensus building in the Bush administration. The early choice of David Souter for the U.S. Supreme Court exemplified Bush's use of coalition building and compromise in a style comfortable to Bush (Rockman, 1991). Souter was much less ideologically oriented than the recent picks by Reagan, and he was seen as a nominee who could attract support from the senators whose votes he needed for confirmation.

But this changed for President Bush's next choice for the Supreme Court. His nomination of Clarence Thomas for the vacancy created by the retirement of Thurgood Marshall was an example of the use of division in a strategically sound manner. The Thomas nomination addressed the liberal community's preference for a racially diverse Supreme Court as well as the conservative community's preference for an ideological conservative. Thomas garnered some initial support from black and white liberals, but his conservative judicial holdings began to alienate many of them. Liberal interest groups mounted a public relations campaign to block the nomination that enabled Bush and Thomas's supporters to denounce the liberals' campaign and to defend Thomas. The divisiveness increased further with Anita Hill's charge that Thomas had sexually harassed her. For days the confirmation hearings turned into a sordid melodrama that further polarized the country along gender lines. The more heated the charges became, the more they invited Republicans and conservatives to defend Thomas even as they contributed to his public humiliation. When Thomas was confirmed despite what seemed to feminists to be clear evidence of sexual harassment, it was the white, male, Democratic Senate from which they were polarized. This worked to the president's advantage because it undermined the liberal-moderate legislative coalition.

But the Anita Hill subplot motivated many women to run for national office in 1992, and the election of Democrats Barbara Boxer, Carol Moseley-Braun, Dianne Feinstein, and Patty Murray to the Senate tripled the number of female senators. In the end, the politics of division allowed President Bush to splinter his opponents' coalition and to show that a president can divide and conquer, but it also resulted in a Senate that moved away from Bush's perspective.

A second part of Bush's agenda had to do with abortion. Abortion reform has long been a divisive and polarizing issue, and it was a continuing administration concern because compromises satisfy neither interpretive community. President Bush, who had changed his stand on abortion during his political career, took a tough pro-life stance during his presidency and furthered the very deep divisions on this issue. Unfortunately for President Bush, this was an issue on which his stance was the minority stance. In this regard President Bush identified with the minority rather than the majority stance, and the politics of division did not enhance his administrative success. However, the stance did help him with the conservative Republicans who sometimes doubted his conservative credentials.

The third example of the use of division to govern was Bush's relationship with Congress. Whether George Bush used divisive or cooperative strategies to deal with Congress during his first two years is a point of some disagreement among presidential scholars. These differing appraisals of the first half of the Bush administration are articulated by some of the contributors to *The Bush Presidency: First Appraisals* (Campbell & Rockman, 1991). George Edwards III concluded that George Bush generally practiced the politics of inclusion. He further noted that Bush "has not let space open between him and the Democrats, just the opposite of the polarizing approach of Ronald Reagan" (1991, p. 150). Paul Quirk (1991) regarded Bush as a cooperative leader who was not skillful at executing his approach. Bert Rockman (1991) discussed the apparent contradictions between Bush's personally amicable and considerate manner and his reliance on highly contentious polarizers, such as John Sununu and Boyden Gray. Colin Campbell (1991) was unsure of the cooperative nature of Bush's leadership, citing examples such as the Tower nomination, Bush's choice of advisers, and the prosecution of Panamanian strongman Manuel Noriega. But the increasingly divisive nature of the late Bush administration was unmistakable, and it culminated in his decision to run against the Democratic Congress in 1992.

Relationships among humans necessarily evolve, and President Bush's relationship with Congress evolved during his term. Beginning with his conciliatory inaugural address and continuing through his initial attempts to build a negotiated compromise on the budget, Bush revealed his skill with brokerage and conciliatory politics. In his February 9 address to the joint session of Congress he reiterated his inaugural offer of cooperation. "The hand remains extended, the sleeves are rolled up; America is waiting; and now we must produce. Together, we can build a better America" (Bush, 1989, p. 74). He went on to call for consensus, saying, "Let's not question each other's motives. Let's debate, let's negotiate; but let us solve the problem" (p. 80).

But executive-congressional problems were already evident in the 1990 State of the Union address when Bush sought to articulate the public's preference for action and to blame the inaction on Congress: "Let me say again to all the members of Congress: the American people did not send us here to bicker. There is work to do; and they sent us here to get it done" (1990b, p. 131). Bush became even more critical in a nationwide address from the House chamber on September 11, 1990, saying, "Most Americans are sick and tired of endless battles in the Congress and between the branches over budget matters" (1990a, p. 1361). On October 2, 1990, Bush went public with a national address to build public pressure for his deficit reduction agreements (1990c). Unfortunately for Bush, public pressure did not build.

During the budget hearings it became readily apparent that a reduction of the capital gains tax was so imperative to Bush that he would not consider compromising on it with the Democratic-controlled Congress. Although the 1990 budget process appeared cooperative with the summit agreement on concurrent resolutions in the spring and a bipartisan budget package in the fall, that appearance was misleading (Quirk, 1991). The process had been highly conflictive and many unresolved problems remained for future budgets.

The rocky relationship continued throughout Bush's governing years as the temptation to blame Congress publicly for inaction could no longer be resisted. There was a thinly veiled reference in Bush's June 22 radio address to the nation that Congress was derelict in its duty and not doing its job as well as the executive branch. According to Bush, "while government can't do everything it ought to do its job. So today, I urge Congress to join us in doing the nation's business" (1991, p. 834). The tone of congressional executive relations became much more divisive as the years passed.

Bush's reliance on Chief of Staff John Sununu and Presidential Counsel C. Boyden Gray as important liaison people to Congress turned out to be unfortunate. They further exacerbated the divisions within Congress along strictly partisan and/or ideological lines. This problem began early, with the nomination of John Tower for secretary of defense. In an attempt to build early support for Tower, Gray presented the confidential FBI report on Tower only to Republicans in the Senate. Unfortunately, this attempt to build in-group support alienated the majority of Democrats and led Sam Nunn, chair of the powerful

Senate Armed Services Committee, to say that he was ill disposed toward Tower on the basis of the process being used by the president even before the hearings had begun (Campbell, 1991). This example of dividing on the basis of party was certainly not unique to the Bush administration. It is a technique often applied by presidents in dealing with Congress. But Bush was using a partisan strategy from a minority position in which bipartisan support was necessary to attain his goal.

There were few examples of real domestic policy success for President Bush other than the Clean Air Act renewal of 1990. In most cases when the Bush administration raised its agenda before Congress there was a lack of compromise, an apparent inability to include rather than exclude, and an overreliance on a polarizing strategy when bipartisan cooperation was needed.

The fourth example of the use of division during Bush's administration was his relationship with Iraq. Iraq was a country portrayed by President Bush as the source of the problems facing America and the world. Iraq needed to be subjugated or, at least, its leader Saddam Hussein had to be brought within the laws of the international community. This call was shared by many world leaders, and Bush used Saddam Hussein as a vehicle for building support among the American people. He used the crisis to establish a framework through which criticism of his administration during the crisis would be construed as unpatriotic. This use of division between a foreign nation and the domestic constituency worked well for President Bush, as evidenced by his record 89 percent public approval ratings at the end of the Gulf War.

But the success of division was only temporary. Once the war ended, the usefulness of Saddam Hussein and Iraq as causes of our problems began to seem dated and, like the Congress charged, self-serving. Bush's public approval ratings began to drop even though he had led what most Americans believed to be a most successful war against Iraq.

Author and political correspondent Robert Shogan tried to debunk what he termed the myth that "Bush is a nice guy that came in first in 1988" (1992, p. 285). He characterized Bush as a "great ingratiator" who gave considerable attention to having people form a favorable impression of him. But Shogan argued that this approach only covered a personal arrogance. Spin doctors devoted considerable attention to Bush's image after his divisive 1988 campaign. His remarks against bigotry at a prayer breakfast honoring Martin Luther King's birthday, just days before the inauguration, were unlike his campaign rhetoric.

But when the Supreme Court ruled that flag burning is protected by the First Amendment, Bush returned to his 1988 campaign style and gave rallying speeches at a flag factory and in front of the Iwo Jima Memorial (Shogan, 1992). This openly hostile presidential response to the Court's decision played on emotions and divided Americans, not only from each other but from the federal government of which Bush himself was an important part.

President Bush joined Andrew Johnson and Ronald Reagan as only the third president to veto civil rights legislation. Although the president submitted his own version of a civil rights bill, his divisive language slowed passage of any bill for over a year. For example, President Bush said in Los Angeles that "I ask the Congress—they're sitting around up there now—they could pass it in twenty minutes if there was a genuine interest in civil rights and less interest in trying to embarrass the President of the United States" (1990d, p. 1466). Comments like that discouraged careful deliberation and prompted New Jersey Senator Bill Bradley to rebuke the president's approach on the floor of the Senate: "We measure our leader by what he says and what he does. If what he says and what he does are destructive of racial harmony, we must conclude that he wants to destroy racial harmony" (Shogan, 1992, p. 289). Whereas the president could have set the tone for harmonious discussions by couching his veto and counterproposal in supportive language, he instead challenged the motives of his adversaries with inflammatory language.

In sum, the politics of division provided mixed success during the administration of President George Bush. At times, such as during the Clarence Thomas hearings, there were successes in using division to achieve his goals. But in the areas of abortion, patriotism, and congressional relations, the president was much less successful in dividing interpretive coalitions so that he could control the national agenda. Finally, in the case of Iraq, polarization worked well for a brief period of time, but it did not have lasting appeal once the war ended.

THE 1992 CAMPAIGN

The third stage of Bush's presidency was his re-election campaign of 1992, in which he lost to Arkansas Governor Bill Clinton. He lost largely on the basis of the very strategy that had enabled him to defeat Michael Dukakis in 1988: the strategy of division.

First, there were the divisions wrought within the Republican Party itself. These divisions were graphically evident at the Republican convention when staunch conservatives such as Pat Buchanan, Pat Robertson, and Marilyn Quayle extolled the virtues of conservative social policies and identified the Republican Party with the conservative movement. Unfortunately for President Bush and his supporters, the positions of the Republican coalition were defined in the rhetoric of its most extreme interpretive community rather than by the president. This might have been a shrewd way to expand Bush's coalition if Buchanan's brigade had been a serious challenge, but Buchanan never got within 25 percent of Bush's vote in any primary. Thus, the divisions between moderate and conservative Republicans divided, rather than united, the Grand Old Party. These divisions plagued the Republicans by undermining their ability to launch a successful, united fight in the remaining months of the campaign and by allowing the unusually well united Democratic Party to coast to victory in November on the basis of only 43 percent of the popular vote.

Divisive issues gained prominence during the campaign. One example was the charge that Bill Clinton was less patriotic than the war hero, George Bush. Robert Dornan, a sharp-tongued conservative congressman from California, used a 1989 article from the *Arkansas Gazette* that described Clinton's college trip to Moscow to question Clinton's patriotism. Dornan's speeches to near empty House chambers became important when President Bush heard them, liked them, and adopted the charges. The morning after meeting with Dornan, Bush ignored the warnings of his staff and spread the charges to a national audience on the Larry King television talk show. Bush said that Clinton should "level with the American people on the draft, on whether he went to Moscow, how many demonstrations he led against his country from a foreign soil" (Greenwald, 1992, p. 28). Extensive investigations by the Bush staff, in the State Department and throughout the American governmental network abroad, attempted to classify Clinton not only as an antiwar advocate but as an individual who had visited Moscow to work against the interests of America. After drawing sharp criticism from the press and some Republicans, Bush backed off from his comments on the Moscow trip, but he intensified his attacks on Clinton's antiwar activities (Greenwald, 1992).

Unfortunately for President Bush, his attempt to divide pro-war "real Americans" from antiwar "unAmericans" proved to be a division that had outlasted its time. President Nixon had leveled this charge against antiwar demonstrators in the late 1960s and early 1970s, and it had hit an important emotional chord that enabled Nixon to divide the country on the basis of patriotic themes. But Vietnam has begun to pass into history, and its legacy is the realization that the divisions it brought were painful and harmful to the country. So Bush's attempt to resuscitate the notion of un-American behavior in the 1992 campaign was seen by many people as an inappropriate and desperate attempt by a falling president to win re-election.

There was an important difference between the 1988 campaign's use of the Pledge of Allegiance issue against Dukakis and the 1992 campaign's treatment of the "un-American" activities of Bill Clinton. The Pledge of Allegiance was an almost universally accepted political symbol with which virtually all Americans could identify. It was something that they valued, and it united them as a people. Therefore, to be charged with vetoing a bill to require the Pledge was to be seen by many Americans as symbolically vetoing the American way of life. But the charge that Clinton's activities during the Vietnam War were un-American was different. This was a war in which Americans had not been united behind a single vision or traditional narrative. Therefore, in highlighting Clinton's actions, the Bush charges highlighted the divisions in the country's rhetorical past: between father and son, between mother and daughter, and between brother and brother. It managed to resuscitate a divisive point on which there was still no clear consensus. The resultant confusion and dissonance did not help the Bush campaign.

The second issue used by President Bush and his surrogate, Vice President Dan Quayle, was the issue of traditional families versus alternative life-styles. The vice president delivered a major speech on family values in which he argued, in part, that popular media indirectly undermined traditional American values. In the process he referred to a television series in which Candice Bergen's "Murphy Brown" character chose to have her baby without getting married. Quayle, always a controversial vice president, was criticized for engaging a fictional character in debate and for criticizing a (fictional) character who had followed the pro-life movement's admonition to choose life rather than abortion. On the other hand, conservatives rallied around Quayle's larger message that such depictions did not foster traditional values. A close reading of the speech invites the observation that the specific reference to Murphy Brown was inserted to draw fire and, therefore, to divide.

The Murphy Brown speech and others by Quayle, which were supported by President Bush, argued that the traditional family—a working father, a mother at home, and children—is inherently superior to its alternatives. But the issue of family values was blown into an issue that made many other Americans, including working mothers, feel defensive. So, in presenting the traditional family as the best family, Bush and Quayle divided the country in a way that, again, ignored the numbers behind the activated groups. More specifically, most mothers today work, and most families therefore do not follow the traditional model that was being held up as the ideal by Vice President Quayle and the Bush administration. This divergence led to the activation of the wrong groups from the perspective of the Bush campaign.

The third point regarding Bush's losing bid for re-election involves the abortion issue, which was controversial throughout Bush's administration. The pro-life community's rhetoric has always sought to claim the moral high ground (Stewart, Smith, & Denton, 1994). But some of the actions taken by pro-life forces against personal property and, at times, even personal safety began to undermine their claim to the moral high ground. Thus, candidates running on pro-choice platforms often defeated pro-life candidates in the 1990 congressional races. One of the tactics in a successful polarization campaign is to associate with the group that is perceived to be the more moral, the more righteous, the "better" group. But President Bush found himself associating with a community whose image of rightness seemed to be eroding.

Finally, Bush argued at campaign stops across the country that Congress was to blame for the gridlock that blocked productive action. Six months before the end of his first term Bush used strong polarizing language to portray Congress as the problem institution. This doomed any lingering hope of governing by consensus in the vain hope of polarizing his way to victory. After prefacing his remarks at a Detroit dinner with the disclaimer that "I'm kind of holding back on going after the opponents until after the Republican Convention in the middle of August," Bush said this about his education proposal: "If parts of it are languishing in the House of Representatives because it has to go to some old subcommittee chairman that's been there for a thousand years and hasn't had a new thought since the day he arrived, we've got to change the Congress" (1992c, p. 1170). In the same speech Bush graphically described actions taken by congressmen on the balanced budget amendment: "Twelve Democrats who sponsored the resolution and sponsored the amendment, were taken to the woodshed by that liberal leadership of the House of Representatives, beaten over the head until they were a pulp, and they voted against their own amendment, and the amendment went down" (p. 1170). These statements were made while Bush was still "kind of holding back."

In making the charge that Congress, rather than the president, was the source of national problems, Bush characterized Congress as out of touch, inefficient, and negligent. His radio address to the nation on July 3, 1992, included Bush's charge that the news of "the failure of socialism and all its empty promises . . . hadn't seeped through the doors of the Democratic cloakrooms on Capitol Hill" (1992a, p. 1206). In fact, in Findlay, Ohio, on August 27, the president depicted the activities of one branch of Congress in the following derisive language: "The House of Representatives has not changed control in 38 years, and they spend their time debating, incredibly, issues like Vanna White and the 'Wheel of Fortune' while neglecting the business of the Nation" (1992d, p. 1527). To rousing cheers of "clean the house" at a rally in Canton, Michigan, Bush responded, "Get them out of there. We have been trying and trying to move this country forward, blocked by this gridlocked Congress. And I am tired of it" (1992b, p. 1508).

Congress as a body has drawn public ire at least since the days of Mark Twain. But most Americans support their own representatives even while they castigate the institution. Thus, Bush's attempt to depict Congress as the "bad guys" backfired. Even with the House banking scandal to fuel public outcries of inefficiency and corruption, President Bush was still unable to convince the American people that the inaction on the economy and other social issues was purely the fault of Congress. One of the reasons for his lack of success was that people could rail against "Congress" and "government" in the abstract, but they could not vote against Congress; they could only vote against their own incumbent representative who articulated the needs and preferences of their local community. Another reason for the failure of this tactic was that President Bush was seen as self-serving in his criticism of Congress. He used the divisive strategy of Congress versus president at a time when his own personal public opinion ratings were very low, and dropping. He was, therefore, arguing from a position of weakness rather than strength in claiming that gridlock was not an executive problem.

Far from appearing selfless and acting in the public interest, President Bush appeared selfish in his motives in attacking another legitimate branch of the American government, and the politics of division did not work. In fact, when asked how they could break the gridlock, most American voters apparently preferred to remove the president rather than their own representative in Congress. So, the 1992 campaign for re-election used the politics of division. But in this case the politics of division did not work to President Bush's advantage.

CONCLUSIONS

On the basis of these three divisions of Bush's presidential career, some conclusions may be drawn. During the campaign for election in 1988, Bush was successful in using the politics of division to win the presidency. The traits of a successful polarization campaign can be applied to the Bush campaign of 1988 to draw the following points. Bush was successful in his campaign because of his ability to identify and to highlight latent but powerful prejudices in the population—racial and ethnic prejudices, fear of crime, and nationalistic conformity—and to use them to his advantage. He chose issues that helped him to win the campaign, but issues that did not put him in a strong position to govern the country. Secondarily, the issues that Bush chose, such as being strong on defense, were helped by the actions of the Dukakis campaign. These included both his reluctance to respond to the attacks against him and strategic errors such as the film of Dukakis unconvincingly driving a tank, looking all too much like the cartoon character Snoopy. This enabled candidate Bush to portray himself as a potentially strong commander in chief and to associate himself clearly with the strong-defense community. This, in turn, enabled him to defuse the "wimp" issue that had hounded him throughout much of his political career. Bush's campaign was able to mobilize the majority necessary for victory by generating support among the Reagan Democrats, moderate Republicans, and conservative Republicans on the basis of their shared dislikes. But precisely because they preferred him on the basis of their shared dislikes, they provided him with a weak governing coalition.

The link between the "bad" group and larger societal problems was established logically in the public mind. For example, liberalism was associated with being soft on crime, with supporting excessively large government, and with supporting those who would not work in a faltering economy. Liberalism, in short, was the cause of the ills of American society. The "L" word was used in the 1988 campaign as a polarizing catchword. It exemplifies Bowers and Ochs's (1971) discussion of polarization's invention of derogatory jargon to characterize the outgroup, and it induced many Americans to prefer the more conservative candidate.

In addition, Bush was careful not to personally associate himself with some of the more mean-spirited aspects of the campaign, such as the Willie Horton ad. The campaign spot was produced and aired by people unaffiliated with his campaign organization, and this allowed him to distance himself from the negative reactions while reaping the benefits of a classic attack ad. Bush was able to articulate and to reinforce the conservative community's belief that they were the guardians of the American way of life. But if they really were the people needed to protect America from the near revolutionary liberal changes, then they were bound to be disappointed with the presidential leadership of George Bush.

The divisions that worked for President Bush were economic and racial, rather than primarily partisan or ideological. The 1988 campaign was not a campaign of big ideas, and therefore it was fertile ground for symbolic appeals and innuendoes (Rockman, 1991). Amid the rhetoric of liberal and conservative, little time was devoted to a full discussion of those larger ideologies, or even to a discussion of specific policies that would implement shared policy preferences.

During his administration President Bush used the politics of division. In the Clarence Thomas hearings it worked by splintering the liberal-moderate legislative coalition to allow the conservatives to win. These divisions were not purely ideological because they had strong crosscurrents of racial and sexual issues as well, with the result that particular interpretive communities construed the nomination in accordance with their own needs. Bush also used, with less success, the governing issues that dealt more purely with ideology: the anti-Congress charges of big government versus small government and the issues of abortion and moral values. One problem was that Bush identified himself personally with these causes rather than taking the higher presidential plane. Another problem was that the issues he chose for division lost much of their salience and appeal as the severe national economic problems developed.

Bush himself was clearly in one group and separated from the other when he made his anti-Congress charges at the end of his administration. But it was not entirely clear to many citizens which institution was the problem. Because many Americans construed Washington's big government to include both Congress and the president, his charges of gridlock had the potential to undercut their perception of the president's ability to lead. These concerns combined to make the politics of division less than successful during Bush's administration.

In 1992 the politics of division proved dysfunctional for President Bush. Bush personally associated himself with divisions fostered during the campaign. In discussing Bush's attacks on Clinton's antiwar record, Ed Rollins, a past Republican strategist, said, "This kind of attack makes Bush look more strident and less presidential. Unless

Bush does something that suddenly convinces voters he would be a different president in his second term, Clinton could win with a landslide" (Greenwald, 1992, p. 29). Rollins was not the only Republican strategist to sit out the re-election campaign, but he was the only one to head Ross Perot's presidential campaign.

Additionally, the issues that were chosen for division were more often ideological than economic or racial. For an example of the ideological stance, we return to our discussion of abortion, family values, and un-American activities as important components of that campaign. Unfortunately for President Bush, these divisions were salient only to a small number of Americans insufficient to form the majority coalition necessary to win re-election. Because he associated himself with the charges, he did not allow his administration to take the loftier plane during the campaign. Instead, the campaign was regarded by pundits and academics alike as a mean-spirited and desperate final attempt by a flailing president to hold on to his faltering grip on the reins of presidential power.

Race, sex, and income were issues that divided people in a way that had helped Bush throughout his public career. But during the discussion of traditional values he found that something had happened to those divisions. Specifically, the traditional values discussion activated Americans in a way that cut across economic and racial lines. The new majority that was diverging against Quayle was mobilizing against President Bush. Therefore, by encouraging Americans to construe traditional values as the important division within the community, he encouraged other groups to coalesce in a way that they had not previously done. This is always a danger in a divisive or polarization strategy: in the process of mobilizing and activating your group, you may be more effective in alienating and mobilizing communities on the opposite side of an issue.

In sum, the politics of division is a potent strategy that has long been used to realign communities, to build coalitions, and to produce desired behavioral changes. In the case of George Bush, we see examples of successes and failures of this strategy. In these examples we see how the language and logic of an interpretive vision can lead to political success or failure, even when the speaker remains the same. A divisive strategy functions to change sympathizers into supporters, to build strength in one's own group, and to expand one's coalition on the basis of shared disbeliefs. But as is the case with many rhetorical strategies, what works in one situation may fail in another. Therefore, the skillful use of the politics of division requires an astute knowledge of the audiences to which it is being addressed, and an appreciation of the dangers inherent in dividing a population in order to win a temporary victory. Even though the electoral victory may be won, the ability to govern by moving that divided population in the desired direction may be severely jeopardized by the divisions. We know who we are by looking at what we are not. But as a nation, there are times when we experience our collective identity by what we share.

The sense of national convergence and divergence, of coalitional comings and goings, also permeates our conceptions of history. The next chapter explores the nature of narrative conflict in the debate over the 1978 Panama Canal treaties.

REFERENCES

Bowers, J. W., & Ochs, D. (1971). *The rhetoric of agitation and control.* Prospect Heights, IL: Waveland Press.

Bush, G. [1989]. Address on administration goals before a joint session of Congress, February 9. *Public papers of the president* (pp. 74–81). Washington DC: U.S. Government Printing Office.

Bush, G. (1990a). Address before a joint session of the Congress on the Persian Gulf crisis and the federal budget deficit, September 11. *Weekly Compilation of Presidential Documents, 26,* 1358–1363.

Bush, G. [1990b]. Address before a joint session of the Congress on the state of the union, January 31. *Public papers of the president* (pp. 129–134). Washington DC: U.S. Government Printing Office.

Bush, G. (1990c). Address to the nation on the federal budget agreement, October 2. *Weekly Compilation of Presidential Documents, 26,* 1511–1515.

Bush, G. [1990d]. Remarks at a campaign rally for gubernatorial candidate Pete Wilson in Los Angeles, October 26. *Public papers of the president* (pp. 1465–1468). Washington, DC: U.S. Government Printing Office.

Bush, G. (1991). Radio address to the nation on the administration's domestic agenda, June 22. *Weekly Compilation of Presidential Documents, 27,* 833–834.

Bush, G. (1992a). Radio address to the nation on health care reform, July 3. *Weekly Compilation of Presidential Documents, 28,* 1206.

Bush, G. (1992b). Remarks at a Bush-Quayle rally in Canton, Michigan, August 25. *Weekly Compilation of Presidential Documents, 28,* 1506–1509.

Bush, G. (1992c). Remarks at the victory '92 fundraising dinner in Detroit, June 29. *Weekly Compilation of Presidential Documents, 28,* 1168–1172.

Bush, G. (1992d). Remarks to Findlay Machine and Tool employees in Findlay, Ohio, August 27. *Weekly Compilation of Presidential Documents, 28,* 1524–1527.

Campbell, C. (1991). The White House and Cabinet under the "let's deal" presidency. In C. Campbell & B. Rockman (Eds.), *The Bush presidency: First appraisals* (pp. 185–222). Chatham, NJ: Chatham House.

Campbell, C., & Rockman, B. (Eds.). (1991). *The Bush presidency: First appraisals.* Chatham, NJ: Chatham House.

Edsall, T. B. (1992). Why Bush accentuates the negative. In S. J. Wayne and C. Wilcox (Eds.), *The quest for national office* (pp. 200–204). New York: St. Martin's Press.

Edwards, G. C., III. (1991). George Bush and the public presidency: The politics of inclusion. In C. Campbell & B. Rockman (Eds.), *The Bush presidency: First appraisals* (pp. 129–154). Chatham, NJ: Chatham House.

Greenwald, J. (1992, October 19). Anatomy of a smear. *Time*, pp. 28–29.

Hahn, D. F., & Gustainis, J. J. (1987). Defensive tactics in presidential rhetoric: Contemporary topic. In T. Windt and B. Ingold (Eds.), *Essays in presidential rhetoric* (2nd ed.), (pp. 43–75). Dubuque, IA: Kendall/Hunt.

Hershey, M. R. (1989). The campaign and the media. In Gerald M. Pomper (Ed.), *The election of 1988: Reports and interpretations* (pp. 73–102). Chatham, NJ: Chatham House.

Jamieson, K. H. (1989). Remarks. *Ripon College ethics and public policy conference*, October 20. West Lafayette, IN: Public Affairs Video Archives.

Kessel, J. H. (1992). *Presidential campaign politics* (4th ed.). Pacific Grove, CA: Brooks Cole.

McWilliams, W. C. (1989). The meaning of the election. In G. M. Pomper (Ed.), *The election of 1988: Reports and interpretations* (pp. 177–206). Chatham, NJ: Chatham House.

Polsby, N. W., & Wildavsky, A. (1991). *Presidential elections* (8th ed.). New York: Free Press.

Pomper, G. M. (1989). The presidential election. In G. M. Pomper (Ed.), *The election of 1988: Reports and interpretations* (pp. 129–152). Chatham, NJ: Chatham House.

Quirk, P. J. (1991). Domestic policy: Divided government and cooperative presidential leadership. In C. Campbell & B. Rockman (Eds.), *The Bush presidency: First appraisals* (pp. 69–92). Chatham, NJ: Chatham House.

Rockman, B. A. (1991). The leadership style of George Bush. In C. Campbell & B. Rockman (Eds.), *The Bush presidency: First appraisals* (pp. 1–36). Chatham, NJ: Chatham House.

Shogan, R. (1992). *The riddle of power: Presidential leadership from Truman to Bush.* New York: Plume Book.

Stewart, C. J., Smith, C. A., & Denton, R. E. (1994). *Persuasion and social movements* (3rd ed.). Prospect Heights, IL: Waveland.

West Virginia State Board of Education v. Barnette, 319 U.S. 624 (1943).

5

Narrative Conflict and
the Panama Canal Treaties

In this era of opinion polls and market research, a president may be able to predict where the public is headed, get there first, and egg them on as though it had been his initiative. But a real leader must do more than adapt to followers' wishes. Real leaders must be able to reorient their followers on matters crucial to their communities. This is rarely as easy as it might seem because they must ground the new orientation in their followers' existing needs, preferences, and reasons.

The importance of a mutually acceptable orientation is implicit, if not explicit, in most studies of leadership. It is central to James Mac-Gregor Burns's conception of leadership as "leaders *inducing followers to act for certain goals* [italics added] that represent the values and motivations—the wants and needs, the aspirations and expectations—*of both leaders and followers*" (1978, p. 19). Indeed, "The essence of leadership," wrote Senator Nancy Landon Kassabaum in her essay on leadership, "is the identification of mutual values, needs and goals" (1979, p. 239). Senator Kassabaum's exuberance notwithstanding, a leader must do more than "identify" mutual values, needs, and goals; the leader must construct and share a coherent explanation or justification that speaks to those mutual values, needs, and goals. Nicholas Berry (1981) recognized this when he suggested that after identifying "the group's morals, values, and interests," two additional tasks await presidential leaders: "The second task revolves around convincing the group that the desired goals are possible. . . . The third task entails outlining a program of action or strategy which utilizes available resources, first circumstances, and explains why a certain sequence of actions will result in the goal" (p. 99). In short, a leader's (re)orientation of the group or society requires effective persuasion.

But presidents face a serious rhetorical dilemma if they try to usher in new orientations with propositional logic. One horn of the dilemma invites the president to use the familiar language, logic, and ideology to argue that the familiar orientation must be discarded. The other horn of the dilemma invites the president to step outside the prevailing orientation and to use language, logic, and ideology that have yet to be widely accepted. Both approaches court delay, criticism, and disfavor. Nevertheless, propositional arguments have long been the stock and trade of presidential speechwriters.

The alternative to propositional logic is the narrative logic of standard story-telling. It is the logic of choice for presidents who value critical turning points, heroes and villains, human interest, anecdotal data, and dramatic reasoning. Narrative logic can transcend world views because it depends less on factual premises than on its potential for dramatizing mutual values and goals in a compelling story that may, or may not, be propositionally valid.

As we explained in Chapter 2, our interpretive systems model suggests that a society encompasses an array of interpretive visions: an established prevailing vision that orients society, and one or more challenging visions. It is the prevailing vision that provides the tools for categorical and propositional arguments. But the prevailing vision is frequently challenged, requiring the president either to defend it or to help the country move toward a new prevailing vision.

In this chapter we explore the political implications of conflicting interpretive visions by comparing the narratives offered to Americans during the 1970s by advocates and opponents of the 1978 Panama Canal treaties. Specifically, we examine the Ford administration's unwillingness or inability to justify its renegotiation of the existing Canal treaty, the subsequent development of a compelling narrative by the "New Right," and the Carter administration's mix of propositional and narrative logics to win ratification without refuting the New Right's narrative.

PHASE I: FORD'S AVOIDANCE
VERSUS REAGAN'S "GIVEAWAY"

President Lyndon Johnson responded to 1964 Panamanian protests by initiating a re-examination of the treaties that governed ownership and use of the Canal. The process continued under President Nixon, to whom Congressman Daniel Flood (R-PA) wrote several times, warning of threats to America's navigational freedom. Flood's letter of June 3, 1974, for example, warned that "a line must be drawn somewhere and I can think of no better place to do so than at Panama where Soviet agents are already ensconced in its government" (Flood, 1974). Nixon responded:

at stake is not just our control of the canal—vital as that may be—but relations with the Republic of Panama, the nations of the Caribbean and Latin America, and by extension with much of the Third World, all of which feel a concern and involvement in the resolution of this matter. (Nixon, 1974)

Flood and Nixon here expressed the core themes of a controversy that would climax four years and two presidents later: drawing a line versus nurturing good relations with smaller nations.

When Gerald Ford succeeded Nixon, Henry Kissinger remained as secretary of state and his people continued to negotiate. But as we discussed in Chapter 3, Nixon holdovers had little respect for the newcomers and Ford's loyalists mistrusted both the holdovers and those whom they suspected of jockeying for the 1976 presidential nomination. In this atmosphere White House staffers avoided controversy by sidestepping questions, keeping few informal memoranda, and avoiding explanations.

One exchange of letters illustrates the administration's caution and its impact on the Canal controversy. William Douglas Pawley of Miami, a former ambassador to Peru and Brazil, wrote to President Ford in opposition to the negotiations. The letter went from the White House to the National Security Council to the State Department for a draft reply, then back to the National Security Council, which returned it to White House Director of Correspondence Roland Elliott. Elliott's reply to Ambassador Pawley said in part:

[our] interest in the Panama Canal, therefore, is that it continue to be efficiently operated on a nondiscriminatory basis and that it be secure. . . . The achievement of a cooperative relationship with Panama would constitute neither a surrender nor an apology to it, but rather would strengthen the mutual interests of both countries in maintaining a well run canal. (1975)

But Elliott's letter omitted major portions of the State Department's draft that would have illuminated the administration's thinking. For example, the ambassador did *not* get to read the following portions of the State Department's draft letter to him (with italics added):

In this new treaty relationship we are seeking the specific treaty rights which *allow the United States to operate and defend the canal effectively for an extended period of time and the option to expand canal capacity* either by enlarging the current canal or constructing a new sea level canal. *We believe that a new treaty* embodying . . . such rights *will fulfill our most basic interest in the Panama Canal and at the same time satisfy Panamanian aspirations* for full sovereignty over their territory and for increased participation in the Canal's operation and defense. (Elliott, 1975)

In this and other letters to influential citizens the Ford administration withheld its reasons and thereby avoided important opportunities to explain the logic in which treaty negotiations furthered the national interests of the United States.

Consequently, few Americans learned much about the treaty negotiations and rumors ran rampant. The Veterans of Foreign Wars charged that "The Battle is now clearly joined between those who would cede our Canal to the Panamanians and those who would not" without even pondering the administration's reasons for "ceding our Canal" (Jones, 1975). Senator Jesse Helms of North Carolina characterized Secretary of State Kissinger as a diplomatic Santa Claus: "After having given away our nuclear superiority, our wheat, our technology, our production capacity, and our money, Secretary Kissinger has now graduated to giving away our territory itself. The Panama Canal Zone is ours, bought and paid for as indisputably as the Louisiana Purchase, or California or Alaska" (Jones, 1975). And Phillip Harman of the American Education League railed in a mimeographed pamphlet that "It is hardly the hallmark of diplomatic genius to consider surrendering our canal lifeline— vital for our national defense and economic health—to the specious claims of an unstable, totalitarian government closely tied to history's most dangerous tyranny" (Harman, 1975).

These and similar statements chained out among conservatives because they enacted conservative recollections and fantasies about Soviet influence, military security, insecure Third World countries, public demonstrations, disrespect for the law, and the old McCarthy/John Birch Society suspicions that the American foreign policy establishment was under communist influence. The Ford administration preferred to handle renegotiation as an administrative, rather than as a political, issue. The alarmist theme therefore flourished more than it might have because it had no competing narrative from the president.

In 1976, Republicans coalesced around the candidacies of Gerald Ford and Ronald Reagan. Nowhere are their contrasting styles more evident than in their handling of Harman and the American Education League. Robert McFarlane of Ford's National Security Council scrawled "Don't answer it" on Harman's (1975) letter, but candidate Reagan made Harman his advisor on the Panama Canal and Central America.

Conservatives and Republicans were not united in their concern about the treaties. As influential a conservative as Senator Barry Goldwater found himself becoming less opposed to the new treaties. He had told the *Arizona Republic* in December 1975 that "there is peril in refusing to look ahead to eventual relinquishment" of the Canal, and the following March he wrote that "I have not firmly made up my mind on this and I am open to suggestions from the public (Goldwater, 1976). Goldwater's reservations were quite specific: "I'm cosponsoring a Senate resolution that takes a stand against relinquishing any U.S. *right or jurisdiction* [italics added] over the Canal Zone without a treaty agreed to by the Senate, and *I feel certain the matter will be presented in the form of a treaty* [italics added]" (1976). Goldwater sought to protect America's "right or jurisdiction" rather than sovereignty, and he regarded an acceptable treaty not as the problem but as the solution.

But Ronald Reagan's position diverged from that of Ford and Goldwater. Reagan's moment came in North Carolina, where he used the Canal issue to help him win the primary in Jesse Helms's state. Ford answered Canal questions from reporters but continued to avoid a major speech on the Canal treaties, perhaps because he realized that it might alienate still further the conservative wing of his party.

Reagan's problem was that most Americans were unconcerned in 1976 about Panama, the Canal, or anything else in the world at large. When asked if America should "keep" the Canal, Americans agreed with the Reagan-Helms-Harman position by a 76 to 16 percent margin. But Gallup's "most important issue" poll for May 1976 showed that Americans were concerned about the economy (62%), government dishonesty (13%), and crime (8%); only 5 percent regarded foreign policy issues most important (Channock, 1976). In short, Reagan beat Ford on the Canal issue but only 5 percent of the public cared. However, Reagan's effective use of the issue in the North Carolina primary suggested its rhetorical potential for rallying conservatives.

There were some who urged President Ford to take charge of the Canal issue. Aide Terry O'Donnell (1976), for example, suggested a National Security Council paper on the Canal "so we can catch Reagan in the midst of his lie." A newspaper publisher urged the president "to explode Ronald Reagan's campaign myths about the Panama Canal in a nationwide television address" (Rose, 1976).

One letter urging Ford to respond to Reagan was particularly significant, because it introduced what was to become a crucial semantic wedge. Godfrey Harriss of Harriss-Ragan Management, consultants to Panama, suggested that the president point out to Reagan that the existing treaty had not granted America sovereignty over the Canal Zone, it had granted America all rights *as if* we had sovereignty (Harriss, 1976). Ford's staff, already wary of critics, recognized the delicacy of even seeming to take advice from a consultant to Panama. They simply expressed their appreciation for the spirit of the offer.

Robert Pastor explained the "as if we had sovereignty" clause of the original treaty in an article for *Harvard Magazine*, published in June 1976. Pastor wrote:

Conservatives have called "the retention of sovereignty" America's primary interest in the Canal. But sovereignty is a means, not an end. Our objectives will be met only if the Canal remains open and efficiently operated. From 1903 until now, the means by which this objective has been met has been the United States' exercise of power as "if it were sovereign." Because this is no longer acceptable to Panama, or to the rest of the world, the instrument—the 1903 treaty—threatens to become an impediment to the United States' achieving its objectives. (1976, p. 43)

The Harriss letter and the Pastor article directed the administration's attention toward a literal reading of the original treaty, with two important ramifications. First, it complicated any attempt by the Ford administration to compromise with the Reagan-Helms camp. Second, it provided the administration with a stronger counterargument to treaty opponents' "giveaway" argument. But the Ford administration responded with administrative rhetoric rather than public appeals. The treaties would be ratified not by public referendum but by the Senate and, because some property would be affected, by the House. Kissinger and Ford believed that these were delicate matters for skilled negotiators, not fodder for public campaigning.

Although Reagan garnered considerable support among conservatives with the Canal issue, Ford won the 1976 Republican nomination comfortably. The Canal did not become an issue in the general election campaign because Ford and Carter were in agreement and the public was largely apathetic.

The first phase of the Panama Canal controversy was characterized by presidential avoidance. Although Presidents Nixon and Ford both supported renegotiation, neither made a vigorous attempt to persuade the public. Neither Nixon nor Ford found himself with secure governing or electoral coalitions, and each recognized his need for conservative Republican support. Antitreaty appeals from Jesse Helms, Ronald Reagan, Phillip Harman, and others evoked recollections and fantasies felt keenly by many conservatives; and although Barry Goldwater eased his opposition, Reagan and Helms discovered the persuasive potential of the Canal issue in the 1976 North Carolina primary.

With Ford and Nixon out of the White House it fell to President Jimmy Carter and the Democrats to advocate ratification. Conservatives prepared to lead the fight against the treaties and, in the process, to wrest control of the Republican Party from the Nixon-Ford-Kissinger-Rockefeller wing.

PHASE II: THE "NEW RIGHT"

Richard Viguerie exulted in 1981 that "No political issue in the last 25 years so clearly divided the American establishment from the American people as the Panama Canal treaties." The proposed treaties were supported by four presidents, the Democratic leadership in Congress, the Joint Chiefs of Staff, "Big Labor, Big Business, Big Media, the big international banks, and just about every liberal political and cultural star you could name" (1981, p. 65). Opposed to the treaties were "the American people—about 70% of them . . . probably 85% of registered Republicans" and a team of conservative spokespersons who would become known as the "New Right": Senators Paul Laxalt, Jake Garn, and Bill Scott; Congressmen Philip Crane, Larry McDonald, and Mickey Edwards; and organizers Paul Weyrich, Howard Phillips, William Rhatican, Terry Dolan, and Viguerie himself (1981, pp. 66–67).

The New Right gradually began to oppose the treaties with narrative, rather than propositional, logic. Their articulation of a dramatic vision reaped rewards far more important than ratification. As Viguerie explained:

Our campaign to save the Canal gained conservative converts around the country—added more than 400,000 new names to our [mailing] lists—encouraged many of the movement's leading figures . . . to run for public office—and produced significant liberal defeats [by defeating twenty treaty supporters while losing only one treaty opponent]. The New Right came out of the Panama Canal fight with no casualties, not even a scar. Because of Panama we are better organized. We developed a great deal of confidence in ourselves, and our opponents became weaker. That November [1978] the New Right really came of age. (pp. 70–71)

Whether or not the New Right's campaign accomplished *all* of this, it is notable that Viguerie and others *believed* that it did.

To defeat the treaties and/or mobilize a new conservative majority, the New Right needed a rhetoric that would appeal to a variety of interpretive communities. Specifically, the New Right needed to meet four rhetorical goals. First, they needed to incorporate the enduring symbols and beliefs of foreign policy conservatives (many of them Democrats) as the core of the antitreaty coalition. Second, they needed to enhance Americans' recollections of the Panama Canal. Third, they needed to dramatize latent fantasies about the perilous world to keep Americans from trusting other nations. Finally, and most delicate, they had to link the Ford-Kissinger-Rockefeller-Nixon wing of the Republican Party with Carter and the Democrats while linking together the Republican Party, treaty opposition, the New Right, and public opinion.

Reagan's success in North Carolina had shown the way, and he continued to be a prominent antitreaty voice. Although he was a private citizen in August 1977, Reagan received a private fifty-minute briefing from the chief American negotiators (Pace, 1977). Reagan was unconvinced by that briefing, and he told the biennial convention of the Young Americans for Freedom that the treaties "would eliminate the rights of sovereignty we acquired in the original treaty. . . . Without these rights we must ask what is to prevent a Panamanian regime one day from simply nationalizing the canal and demanding our immediate withdrawal. . . . Secrecy, of course, is no longer the issue. Security is" (Pace, 1977). Here Reagan replaced the State Department's legal "as if we had sovereignty" premise with the simple and familiar "actual sovereignty" premise. He then adroitly shifted from propositional argument to a narrative structure that invited his young, unbriefed, conservative listeners to fantasize. Instead of telling them what he had learned from the negotiators, Reagan asked them to allay *his* fears: How can America prevent a hostile takeover? But Reagan, who had already been briefed on the treaties, knew the explicit provisions for defending the Canal and did not share them with his young listeners.

Reagan's campaign against the treaties continued into the fall of 1977. An antitreaty letter in Reagan's name was sent out on Republican National Committee letterhead in late October. The letter advanced nine propositions:

1. In the process of giving up our Canal, Mr. Carter has also surrendered our rights to build a new one if needed.

2. There's no guarantee our Naval Fleet will have the right of priority passage in time of war.

3. The U.S. does NOT have the right to intervene to defend the Canal.

4. We must close down 10 of our military bases, Americans in the Zone will be under Panamanian rule, and we must pay Torrijos millions more each year for the Canal.

5. These treaties could cost Americans hundreds of millions. . . . Plus we'll pay higher prices. . . . [Torrijos] maintains close ties with Fidel Castro and the Soviet Union.

6. [Torrijos] seized power by gunpoint . . . [and] controls the press, he's outlawed all political parties but the Marxist Party and he controls the military.

7. Once we pull out, what's to stop Torrijos or his successor from nationalizing the Canal and ordering us out at once?

8. Panama is one of the most unstable countries in Latin America.

9. From the beginning, Mr. Carter negotiated this treaty without consulting Congressional leaders. (Wayne, 1977)

It is difficult to imagine the Republican National Committee sponsoring this same mailing if Ford had won. Indeed, five of the nine statements refer explicitly to Carter, and none mention that Republicans Ford and Nixon supported the same treaties. But by coming out so strongly against the treaties the Republican National Committee significantly disadvantaged the future prospects of Republican treaty supporters such as Ford.

The Reagan letter represents the New Right's first major victory in its effort to link its arguments with mainstream Republican opposition to the Carter administration. The Republican leadership had supported the Ford administration's position on the treaties, but they had signifi-

cant political and organizational needs, and these provided incentives
for opposing the treaty position now being supported by Democrats.

Nevertheless, the Reagan letter was flawed because it was a propositional rather than narrative argument. By detailing nine propositions
Reagan invited refutation, and this he received from many quarters
because many Republican conservatives had not yet taken a stand on
the treaties.

The most trenchant response to Reagan's letter came in a remarkable letter from none other than actor John Wayne, an icon of American
patriotism and military heroism. Wayne's personal cover letter to "Ron-
nie" expressed his regrets: "If you had given time and thought on this
issue, your attitude would have gained you the image of leadership that
I wished for you, rather than, in the long run, a realization by the public
that you are merely making statements for political expediency"
(Wayne, 1977). He told Reagan that "I'll show you point by God damn
point in the Treaty where you are misinforming people." Wayne then
gave Reagan an important warning: "If you continue these erroneous
remarks, someone will publicize your letter to prove that you are not as
thorough in your reviewing of the Treaty as you say or are damned
obtuse when it comes to reading the English language" (Wayne, 1977).
Attached to the cover letter was a four page "cut and paste" summary
of Reagan's nine points under the title "SCARE LETTER FROM THE
HONORABLE RONALD REAGAN" along with Wayne's quite specific and technical responses. His responses were replete with phrases
like "the *truth* is," "completely misleading," "complete untruth," and
"How dare you continue to make these statements."

Wayne's conclusion spoke directly to Reagan's use of the Canal as
a vehicle for fundraising. "Quite obviously," said Wayne, "you are
using . . . [the Panama Canal Treaty] as a teaser to attract contributions
to our Party. I know of our Party's need for money; but if your attitude
in order to get it is as untruthful and misleading as your letter, we
haven't a chance" (Wayne, 1977). The tone of Wayne's letter may seem
surprising in the post-Reagan era. But it must be read in the context of
1977: the treaties had been supported by Presidents Nixon, Ford, and
the Joint Chiefs of Staff, and Senator Goldwater was moving toward
support.

John Wayne's letter highlights the rhetorical dilemmas facing the
New Right in late 1977. Reagan was their best prospect for winning the
presidency in 1980, and the Panama Canal Treaty was their best issue
for mobilizing support. But Reagan's propositional arguments against
the treaties might well destroy his credibility in the process. It is there-

fore noteworthy that rhetorical leadership of the antitreaty forces passed from Reagan to Illinois Congressman Phillip Crane, a historian by profession, in January 1978.

This case study illustrates the importance of nonpresidential rhetors to presidential leadership. Two presidents' political and rhetorical options were constrained by the caliber of their opponents, particularly Reagan and Crane. Without them, antitreaty sentiment might have simmered along as it had from 1964 until 1976. But Reagan and Crane focused the arguments, addressed them to people's core needs and values, and presented them well. As a result of their heat, the renegotiation issue boiled into a near crisis for President Carter.

Crane's book, *Surrender in Panama* (1978), set forth a coherent narrative faithful to his audience's experiences because it evoked the ghosts of isthmus past, present, and future. By advancing Reagan's arguments in narrative, rather than propositional, form, Crane complicated the task of refutation and established the basis for a debate between two narrative visions of history. Moreover, Crane's narrative spared Reagan the kind of embarrassment of which Wayne had warned. Crane's narrative addressed the New Right's four strategic objectives by depicting the past, the present, and the future.

Crane's Past: America's Claim to Sovereignty over the Canal

Crane's narrative recounted the story of America's legal claim to the Canal. Crane maintained that it derived from a good treaty that reflected our shrewdness and opportunism. He quoted a letter from Secretary of State John Hay, who had negotiated the Hay-Bunau-Varilla Treaty, to the effect that failure to ratify it could have meant the end of any American Canal effort because it was:

a treaty in the main very satisfactory, vastly advantageous to the United States . . . not so advantageous to Panama. If we amend the treaty and send it back there . . . the period of enthusiastic unanimity which . . . comes only once in the lifetime of a revolution, will have passed away, and they will have entered on the new fields of politics and dispute. (p. 38)

But neither Crane nor Hay argued that our claim to the Canal derived from an *equitable* treaty. Both said that the treaty would likely have been rejected by Panama upon reconsideration. Crane's narrative emphasized the ethics of self-interest: the treaty was unfair only

because Panama's negotiators had been less skillful than ours at fulfilling their moral obligation to serve national interests. Indeed, the original treaty's unfairness constituted a major argument against
renegotiation.

The nature of Panama's complaint can be seen in the evolution of
treaties. Article IV of the 1903 Hay-Herran Treaty between the United
States and Colombia had stipulated that the treaty "shall not affect" the
Colombian sovereignty and that the "United States freely acknowledges
and recognizes this sovereignty and disavows any intention to impair it
in any way whatever" (p. 121). But when Panama seceded from
Colombia, the operative 1903 Hay-Bunau-Varilla Treaty was signed
with the United States. Article III conveyed to the United States:

all the rights, power and authority within the zone mentioned and described in
Article II of this agreement and within the limits of all auxiliary lands and
waters mentioned and described in said Article II which the United States
would possess and exercise if it were the sovereign of the territory . . . to the
entire exclusion of the exercise by the Republic of Panama on any such
sovereign rights, power or authority. (p. 136)

Crane interpreted this to mean that Panama had *ceded all sovereignty*
over the Canal Zone to the United States, and he cited a 1904 memorandum from the Panamanian secretary of government to the effect that
Panama believed that its jurisdiction ceased with ratification on February 26, 1904 (p. 36). He cited Kissinger's pro-treaty references to
"restoring Panamanian sovereignty" and several examples of American
acts usually associated with sovereignty as proof that "the United States
has full control—de facto sovereignty—in the first place" (p. 37).

What, then, is the reader supposed to make of the treaty provisions
and the acts of de facto sovereignty?

Crane's attempt to establish America's sovereignty over the Canal
on the basis of acts generally associated with sovereignty was, at best,
fallacious. No act associated *with* sovereign power can help us to discern whether a nation had *absolute* sovereignty or all the rights, power,
and authority it would possess *if* it had absolute sovereignty. The "all/as
if" construction had opened a semantic gap that Crane needed to close.
Proof of actions *inconsistent* with sovereignty can be taken as proof of
the distinction, but proof of actions *consistent* with sovereign power
can be used equally well to support either position. When presented in
propositional form, as in Reagan's letter, such a claim invites refutation.
But as part of a narrative it invites each reader to accept it as part of the

narrative flow. Thus, Crane's reliance on appearances and de facto sovereignty evaded the fundamental issue and misrepresented the contents of the treaties as they appeared in his own book's appendices.

Crane's stronger argument would have been to focus on America's changing position on sovereignty. When compared directly, the two treaties suggest a significant diminution of our concern for the sovereignty of others. Gone are the statements that the United States "freely acknowledges and recognizes this sovereignty," that it "disavows any intention to impair it in any way whatever," and gone is the pledge not to increase our territory at the expense of any Central or South American republics. Thus, Crane could have argued that the United States had developed grave doubts about Panamanian sovereignty and that *we* would have rejected any treaty that provided us with less than full sovereignty. But such an argument would have required Crane to imply that America might have been willing to not build the Canal—a concession that would have complicated his argument that the Canal has always been crucial to America's strength.

In Crane's narrative, then, our shrewd use of the diplomatic ethics of self-interest had produced an unusually good treaty for us. It gave us absolute sovereignty over the Canal Zone and enabled us to gain Panamanian independence from Columbia, to rid their country of disease, to build a canal for their economy, and to subsidize their government. It evoked memories of Teddy Roosevelt and the Rough Riders, manifest destiny, and the Monroe Doctrine. It reminded its readers of an era in which America proudly tried to make over the world in our image.

Crane's Present: An Unstable, Marxist, Banana Republic

Crane described contemporary Panama as a poverty-stricken "banana republic" dominated by "forty influential families" where Torrijos runs the "corrupt, vicious police state" he built with help from his "Marxist allies" (pp. 56–57), and which avoided bankruptcy only because of the international banking community. But how could a country receiving so much from the United States turn out so badly? Crane's narrative found explanation in two themes dear to the hearts of his conservative readers: strict paternalism and the communist menace.

Crane's perspective on Pan-American relations was distinctly paternalistic. In seventy years Panama had grown from birth to adolescence. But because the young country had been given so much by her rich Uncle Sam, she took her good fortune for granted. By 1977 Uncle Sam realized that he had bestowed countless favors upon young Panama, only to be resented. Crane described Panama's childish ingratitude with a self-congratulatory parental sniff:

To the extent that Panama exists and is a viable state today, it is because a strong America, which could have taken what it wanted without giving anything in return, has been a generous friend of Panama from the moment of ratification of the 1903 treaty. But . . . gratitude soon grows old. All of us know . . . [people] who find it harder to forgive a favor than an injustice. (p. 41)

His account provided his conservative audience with one more example of the problems attendant to parental generosity and permissiveness.

Teenagers are not only ungrateful, they also hang out with an unsavory crowd. Crane showed that Panama had been smoking ideological cigars with Fidel Castro and his Soviet benefactors and warned that it would be a "criminal blunder" to turn the Canal Zone over to a "corrupt dictator" (p. 82). Not surprisingly, Panamanian leaders had begun to ape those bad influences. General Omar Torrijos might even seize the Canal, according to Crane. Indeed, he warned that Torrijos's inflammatory rhetoric had incited rioters who might well riot again.

In short, Crane depicted Panama as an ungrateful, impressionable, and rebellious teenager. He described a ruthless and corrupt dictator facing national bankruptcy, encouraged by Marxists, threatening to humiliate America and destroy our international prestige. His diagnosis of the problem led directly to his prescription.

Crane's Future: The Perils of Change

The key to dealing properly with Panama was familiar to Crane's conservative audience: spare the rod and spoil the child. Riots are to be expected especially in the face of a "passive, docile America" (p. 93) that yielded to threats. Instead of yielding to adolescent demands for premature adulthood, America needed to remain firm because we knew best. Riots, like tantrums, are distressing. But Crane's readers understood that the real danger would arise after the departure of the parental security forces (p. 102).

A surrender in Panama would be "one more crucial American step in a descent into ignominy—to the end of America's credibility as a world power and a deterrent to aggression" (p. 113). For the world outside is a perilous place, a jungle. And the law of the jungle is "fear or be feared." Therefore, the central issues at stake in Panama were weakness and cowardice, and the treaty "would appear as not a noble act of magnanimity, but as the cowardly retreat of a tired, toothless paper tiger" (p. 112). Lest his readers fail to realize that Crane's world was more perilous than President Carter's, he warned bluntly that the world was not a "Sunday school classroom in Plains, Georgia" but "a violent, conflict-ridden place. . . . Peace comes only to the prepared and security only to the strong" (pp. 113–114). That peace and security could only be protected by holding on to the Canal no matter what the costs.

Summary

Congressman Phillip Crane advanced the New Right's case against the proposed Canal treaties in narrative rather than propositional form. The forces of Good in his story dramatized the ethics of self-interest, the can-do spirit, selfless generosity, and firm parental discipline. The forces of Evil in his story dramatized diplomatic incompetence, the character-deflating effect of government handouts, parental permissiveness, the menace of communism, adolescent rebellion, Central American instability, and the perils of the world.

It is also noteworthy that the narrative has many of the features associated with the authoritarian personality type (Maslow, 1943; Stewart, Smith & Denton, 1994): the world as a jungle, a hierarchical view of the world, and a preoccupation with dominance and submission. This narrative speaks to the psychological needs of a particular personality type quite apart from Crane's objections to the Canal treaties, and it enabled Crane to advance a narrative that contrasted sharply with the positions of Presidents Ford and Carter.

PHASE III: CARTER'S RESPONSE

As a graduate of the Naval Academy, an engineer, and a politician, President Carter was almost uniquely qualified to appreciate the national security, technical, and political dimensions of the Canal question. But he may have learned too well the tragic lesson taught to Woodrow Wilson, the prototypical rhetorical president, who alienated moderate senators by whistlestopping the country to mobilize public support for the Treaty of Versailles. Wilson campaigned when he should have been negotiating fine points of the treaty with the Senate moderates whose votes proved decisive. Unlike Wilson, Carter focused most of his attention on the Senate. Carter took his case to the public, but it was more a defensive attempt to diffuse opposition than a Wilsonian effort to create a groundswell of support for his vision.

During the 1976 presidential campaign Carter's critics had accused him of waffling on the issues. But his position paper on the Canal had been finalized by February 28, 1976. It said that America's strategic needs had changed: "Now, for those naval fleets in which aircraft carriers are integral parts, the Canal is too small; obviously our strategic missile system has no use for the Canal; and even troops during the Vietnam War were transported by plane, not ship" (Carter, 1976). Perhaps anticipating a campaign against Reagan rather than Ford, Carter continued:

There are some who pretend that the world has not changed or that American power can hold back these important changes. But there is a deceptive security in the status quo, and those people who do not recognize the important changes in the world will find themselves engulfed by them. (Carter, 1976)

But by 1980, when Carter needed to campaign against Reagan, the treaties had been ratified and the Iranian hostage crisis had found a ready explanation in the New Right's narrative.

The president set his speechwriting staff in motion about a month before negotiators reached final agreement on the treaties. On July 12, speechwriter Jim Fallows sent a memo that the president "has decided to talk about the canal" in his July 21 speech to the Southern Legislative Conference in Charleston, South Carolina. He mentioned that (National Security Advisor Zbigniew) Brzezinski was "drawing up some plan for how to talk about the Canal" (Fallows, 1977b). But Carter's Charleston address concerned the principles governing his foreign policy toward the Soviet Union, not the Panama Canal. The Fallows memo suggests that Brzezinski had decided to use the Charleston address to establish the administration's foreign policy principles with reference to long-standing and familiar Cold War concerns, principles that would later be used to warrant ratification of the Panama Canal treaties.

The Charleston address was not billed as a watershed in foreign policy, nor did Carter list his foreign policy principles. Instead it used classic problem-solution form. The problem for Carter was that changes in the world required the superpowers to move beyond their decades-old preoccupation with military competition to "accept the new responsibilities imposed on us by the changing nature of international relations" (Carter, 1977b, p. 1311). The solution is to approach foreign policy with "a vision of a gentler, freer, and more bountiful world . . . [with] no illusions about the world as it really is" (1977b, p. 1311). That new vision required that:

the agreements that we reach must be anchored on each side by enlightened self-interest—what's best for us, what's best for [them]. . . . It's not a question of "hard" policy or of a "soft" policy, but of a clear-eyed recognition of how most effectively to protect our own security and to create the kind of international order that I've just described. This is our goal. (p. 1312)

The key was to "create a relationship of cooperation that will be rooted in the national interests of both sides" (p. 1313). The familiar power politics were not to be abandoned, but "We must always combine realism with principle" (p. 1314).

President Carter's Charleston speech was a challenge to the New Right's effort to resuscitate the Cold War foreign policy rhetoric, and it threatened their cherished symbols, stories, and premises. But, for better and worse, the speech was not widely reported. Negotiators reached agreement three weeks later and the signing was scheduled for September 7 in Washington (Pace, 1977).

By late August the White House public relations effort was in high gear. By August 22 Jerry Doolittle, Joe Aragon, and Landon Butler had generated a set of themes and questions-and-answers to coordinate the administration's positions on Panama for the president's press conference the next day. The themes of foreign policy, trade, and defense all echoed Carter's Charleston speech (Doolittle, 1977a). The new treaties would remove a "long-standing barrier to closer relations" with Latin American countries and thus produce "a more friendly environment for American investment and trade." Moreover, the secretary of defense and the Joint Chiefs of Staff backed the new treaties because of two negotiated breakthroughs: joint defense of the Canal through the end of the century, and the stipulation that "we would retain forever the right to preserve the Canal's neutrality, by any means necessary" (Doolittle, 1977b).

But the key theme for the administration was the foreign policy theme. A five-sentence paragraph reiterated the Charleston principles and provided a stark contrast to the New Right's narrative. It closed with a warning:

North-South relations are likely to be as important to us in the future as East-West relations have been in the past. The Carter Administration is trying on many fronts to regain the moral high ground that the United States once had in foreign affairs. The Panama Canal issue provides this Administration with its first major chance to show that we are ready to act, not merely talk, with the maturity, confidence and generosity that befit a great power. By removing the irritant of the 1903 treaty, we remove an issue on which the third world has lined up solidly against us. *Failure to act on the new treaties would make our rhetoric sound hollow, and would severely damage a central part of the Carter Administration's foreign policy* [italics added]. (Doolittle, 1977b)

This paragraph underscored Carter's divergence from the Right in four ways.

First, foreign policy conservatives found unthinkable the notion that American foreign policy might set aside East-West concerns. Second, to act with the "confidence and generosity that befit a great power" is to act irrationally in the logic of hemispheric paternalism. Third, neither the New Right nor the Republican Party had much incentive to help this Democratic administration to modify the Nixon-Ford-Kissinger foreign policy. Finally, they worried little that their opposition might make the Carter administration's rhetoric "sound hollow."

The defensive posture of the Carter rhetoric was apparent in the questions anticipated by his staff, none of which allowed Carter to lead. The following guides to counterpunching are representative:

Q: Why should we give up a Canal we built and paid for?
A: We aren't. What we are "giving up" (although we never held sovereignty over it anyhow) are those portions of the Canal Zone which we do not need to defend and operate the Canal. . . .
Q: Still, the present treaty has worked pretty well so far, hasn't it?
A: Four Presidents of both political parties haven't thought so. . . .
Q: Why should we pay Panama good tax dollars to take over a Canal we built?
A: The financial package in the treaty calls for Panama to receive 30 cents per Panama Canal ton from tolls, plus another $10 million a year fron [sic] Canal revenues. . . . None of this is U.S. tax dollars. (Doolittle, 1977a, pp. 1, 3)

Thus, a week before Reagan addressed the Young Americans for Freedom and five months before publication of Crane's book, the writers in the Carter White House were preparing Carter to take a defensive posture on the treaties. But the president disregarded their advice.

At his August 23 press conference Carter (1977e) was neither aggressive nor defensive but magnanimous, inclusive, and understated.

The concerns raised earlier by Reagan and others "which were legitimate in the past, have now been answered successfully for our Nation" (p. 1488). When invited to call treaty opponents "not fully informed," he said that "I wouldn't want to say that anyone who disagrees with me is ignorant" (p. 1489). He concluded his support for the treaty by saying that "I'm convinced that it's advantageous. I was not convinced of this fact, say, a year ago" (p. 1489). Carter's answers reflected his decision neither to attack the New Right and divide the country over the Canal, nor to circle the wagons in defense; but to reassure the public that the treaties combined our self-interests with the principles of fairness and cooperation.

The president continued to speak frequently about the Canal, but he did not go on national television in 1977. On September 14, shortly after the signing, speechwriter Fallows wrote Chief of Staff Hamilton Jordan to urge that the president go on television for a Fireside Chat about the treaties. Fallows feared that the public would conclude that "we've abandoned the fight. We're leaving all the public argumentation to the other side," he wrote, "and by letting their crazy charges go unanswered for the moment we suggest that we don't have any answers" (Fallows, 1977c).

Fallows had written a Fireside Chat for Carter by September 19, and he preferred to err in the direction of overexposure. Fallows agreed with Harlan Strauss, legislative director of a Washington law firm, that the basic problem was "the McGuffey Reader Complex." Strauss (1977) explained that "since early this century . . . the myth that the Panama Canal and its surrounding territory was ours 'in perpetuity' was taught as a truism in the classroom and in the grammar school textbooks." Strauss's letter suggested that what the president needed to do was to re-educate "the over-50, the grade school only, and Republican" audiences about manifest destiny, the Monroe Doctrine, and the "in perpetuity" clause.

Herein lay Carter's rhetorical predicament. The New Right was busy constructing a coherent antitreaty narrative out of the recollections that older, conservative, Republican citizens had acquired early in life. Even if that narrative was as erroneous as Strauss and John Wayne had said, it was consistent with everything that this target audience had learned about the Canal, and a narrative's persuasiveness hinges largely on its fidelity to its audience's experiences (Fisher, 1987). On the other hand, the president was being advised to tell this audience that the principles of American history they had learned in grade school—principles being reinforced almost daily by the antitreaty advocates—were wrong.

To do so would be to step into the story being told by Reagan, Crane, and the others. Although Fallows agreed with Strauss's analysis, he recognized this predicament. His response to Strauss was that "It is obviously true. . . . But unless that point is made with extreme delicacy, it loses many more friends than it gains" (Fallows, 1977a).

The Fallows-Carter brand of rhetorical delicacy was largely defensive and lacking in either eloquence or creativity. David McCullough, author of a noteworthy book about the Panama Canal, wrote to the president in October to register his concern that treaty opponents seemed "full of emotion, even passion, while the arguments for the treaties, however intellectually solid, remain for many people largely an abstraction" (1977). His letter spoke of Theodore Roosevelt, the grandeur of the Canal, and the aura of power surrounding it. McCullough called on the president to argue creatively, idealistically, and eloquently for the treaties. President Carter was impressed by McCullough's letter and responded "Your letter is a beautiful expression of idealism and legitimate pride & strength" (Carter, 1977g). But his treaty rhetoric changed little.

The Fireside Chat written in September was still in limbo as Thanksgiving approached. Congressional liaison Frank Moore wanted the Chat to take place in December to prepare the public for the ratification debate. But Press Secretary Jody Powell and even Fallows, who had written the speech for September, now advised delay. "No one is interested in Panama now," they wrote to the president:

it's Christmas time, the energy bill is still pending, and between the Middle East and your trip there is all the foreign news people can handle. There is also no news hook for the speech. . . . If you give the speech, it's likely to disappear without a trace. That will do more harm than if you hadn't given it at all (Powell & Fallows, 1977)

Their arguments made good strategic sense. But Congressman Crane's book was published and widely distributed during the month they delayed.

On January 25, 1978, a revised outline for a Fireside Chat was prepared by Fallows, Powell, and the president. It was to be a short (ten- to fifteen-minute) address, "confident, positive, and forward looking" as well as "simple (7th grade this time)." But the proposed outline suggested twenty-eight points and subpoints distributed over four sections (Fallows, 1978a, 1978b). Moreover, subsequent discussions led them to add thirteen more points and to delete none: this left Fallows with an

average of fifteen to twenty seconds per point, not counting the introduction and conclusion.

Drafts of this Fireside Chat were reviewed by Pastor, Brzezinski,
Jordan, Powell, Moore, Doolittle, and Landon Butler of the speechwriting staff, negotiators Sol Linowitz and Ellsworth Bunker, Vice President Walter Mondale, and First Lady Rosalyn Carter. Butler responded
with a copy of David McCullough's recent testimony before the Senate
Foreign Relations Committee. Their advice proved to be less helpful
than it might have been. Carter's address mirrored Crane's narrative,
although his book was never mentioned anywhere in their deliberations.

Carter's Past: Panamanian Sovereignty

Where Crane used the ethics of self-interest to evaluate the original
treaty, President Carter stressed the ethics of fairness. The Panama
Canal was a source of "some continuing discontent" in Panama because
the unfair Hay-Bunau-Varilla Treaty of 1903 "was drafted here in our
country and was not signed by any Panamanian." Carter used Hay's
comment that the treaty was "vastly advantageous" to us and "not so
advantageous to Panama" (Carter, 1978, p. 258) to prove that the original treaty required renegotiation.

Carter further argued that even this unfair treaty had not given
America sovereignty over the Canal. His treatments of the sovereignty
question had previously run the gamut. They included the following
gentle answer to an "Ask President Carter" caller:

As you may or may not know, the treaty, signed when Theodore Roosevelt
was president, gave Panama sovereignty over the Panama Canal Zone itself. It
gave us control over the Panama Canal Zone *as though* we had sovereignty.
So, we've always had a legal sharing of responsibility over the Panama Canal
Zone. As far as sovereignty is concerned, I don't have any hang-up about that.
(Carter, 1977a, p. 325)

And there was the following crisp and decisive comment in Denver on
October 22 when the sovereignty question was burning: "People say we
bought it; it's ours; we ought not to give it away. We've never bought it.
It's not been ours. We are not giving it away" (Carter, 1977c, p. 1886).
But on the occasion of Carter's February 1 Fireside Chat with the
nation, his stance on sovereignty was less than assertive.

Carter might have used the Denver phrasing, but he diluted his position to "We do not own the Panama Canal Zone. We have never had

sovereignty over it. We have only had the right to use it" (p. 260). The Denver construction was an unmistakable refutation of the New Right's position, whereas the Fireside Chat said the same thing in less assertive language and in a less assertive tone of voice.

Carter and Crane each built arguments in support of their interpretations of the sovereignty issue, but each engaged the other's argument only indirectly. Crane's list of actions consistent with sovereignty had failed to refute the "as if" position. Furthermore, the president's observation that "You do not pay rent on your own land" undermined Crane's argument that America owned the Canal. Carter had made the point even more effectively in Denver, when he said that:

We [Americans] have never owned the Panama Canal Zone. We've never had title to it. We've never had sovereignty over it. . . . People born in the Panama Canal Zone are not American citizens. We've always paid them an annual fee, since the first year of the Panama Canal Treaty that presently exists, for the use of their property. (Carter, 1977c, p. 1886)

In short, Carter argued that America's claim to the Canal never amounted to anything more than the right, derived from an unfair treaty, to build and use the Canal. The arguments were familiar, but they had been stated more cogently in Denver three months before his address to the nation.

Carter's Present: Nurturing Pan-American Relations

Carter described Panama as one of our "historic allies and friends" headed by a "stable government which has encouraged the development of free enterprise in Panama" and which will hold democratic elections to "choose members of the Panamanian Assembly" (Carter, 1978, p. 262). He referred to the Canal as "the last vestige of alleged American colonialism" (1978, pp. 258, 261).

The matter of stability was delicate because where Central America is concerned, one person's stability is another's dictatorship and one person's democracy is another's chaos. In Carter's view the threat to the Canal comes "not from any government of Panama, but from misguided persons who may try to fan the flames of dissatisfaction with the terms of the old treaty" (1978, p. 262). The obvious need was to depict the government as stable, and General Torrijos was "stable" because he had been in power for nine years and was within six months of holding elections for the Assembly, if not for the presidency. But because Carter could not pin his advocacy of long-term security on Torrijos alone, he had to argue that Panamanians would so strongly support the treaty that they would keep the Canal open forevermore.

Thus, Carter had observed on August 27, 1977, that after thirteen years of negotiations, "the expectations of Latin American people that we are going to have a resolution of this question has built up hopes of new friendship, new trade opportunities, and a new sense of commonality and equality of stature between their governments and our government that never existed before" (1977d, p. 1513). And by September 15 the president saw:

a new sense of mutual purpose. There's also a new sense that we look upon our Latin American neighbors as equals. I think there's a new sense that there is a vista of improved friendship and common purpose between us and our Latin American friends in the years to come, not based on grants or loans . . . but based on the fact that this treaty corrects a long-standing defect in our relationships with countries to the south. (1977f, p. 1597)

However, Panama's appreciation for the treaties was hardly mentioned in the Fireside Chat, perhaps because it might have invited his critics to invert Hay's letter into "a treaty in the main advantageous to Panama, and not nearly so advantageous to us." Carter spoke of the "new partnership" with Panama as a "source of national pride and self-respect" (1978, p. 262). Panama was to be transformed from "a passive and sometimes deeply resentful bystander into an active and interested partner" who will "[join] with us as brothers against a common enemy" should the Canal need military defense (1978, p. 260).

The treaties would not create a "power vacuum" but would "increase our Nation's influence in this hemisphere, . . . help to reduce any mistrust and disagreement, . . . [and] remove a major source of anti-American feeling." Indeed, Carter noted that "Between the United States and Latin America there is already a new sense of equality, a new sense of trust and mutual respect that exists because of the Panama Canal treaties" (1978, p. 261). In the Carter narrative the United States was a powerful, fair, generous neighbor ready and willing to demonstrate those admirable traits by sharing the Canal with the Panamanians.

But Carter emphasized that "Panama wants the canal open and neutral—perhaps even more than we do" because "Much of her economy flows directly or indirectly through the canal." He noted that "no Panamanian government has ever wanted to close the canal," and he suggested that for this reason "Panama would be no more likely to neglect or close the canal than we would be to close [our] Interstate Highway System" (1978, p. 262). He could have strengthened this argument by elaborating on the idea that Panama would have more to lose by closing the Canal under the new treaties because it would be getting more of the Canal's revenues. But he did not do so.

Carter's Future: The Kind of Power We Wish to Be

President Carter relied heavily on David McCullough's letter to suggest that the new treaties would demonstrate America's innate sense of fairness. "This agreement is something we [Americans] want because we know it is right," said Carter, since it "is what is right for us and what is fair to others" (1978, pp. 262–263). He also spoke of defending the Canal with the Panamanian forces "joined with us as brothers," and he eagerly anticipated this "new partnership" (1978, pp. 260, 262).

But people in his target audience were concerned, many of them deeply, by the bleak picture sketched by Crane. President Carter could have reiterated his October 22 comments about defending the Canal. On that occasion he compared defense of the Canal with the United Nations action in Korea and contrasted it with the Vietnam experience. Under the new treaties, Carter said:

if we should later have to go into Panama, it will be with the endorsement of the Panamanian Government, and the Panamanian people. It will be with the endorsement of 30 or 40 or 50 other nations who will sign the neutrality treaty going into effect after the year 2000, saying, we think that the treaty with Panama and the United States is a good one. . . . So it gives us a legitimacy and an endorsement of the rest of the world . . . to keep the canal open, well managed, and to meet the security needs, the trade needs of our own country. (1977c, p. 1888)

The crux of Carter's position was this: any attempt to defend or recapture the Canal under the existing treaty could be construed by our adversaries as a violation of Panamanian sovereignty because America had only limited rights and powers over the Canal Zone. The new treaties explicated Panama's responsibility to keep the Canal open and neutral, and they committed Panamanian sovereignty and international law to the fulfillment of that responsibility.

But in the Fireside Chat, Carter was content to read the legal language from three passages in the treaties and the statement of understanding. He concluded that "It is obvious that we can take whatever military action is necessary to make sure that the canal always remains open and safe" (1978, p. 260). Without the clarifying language of his October 22 statement, treaty opponents had no way to grasp Carter's point because they believed that the United States *already* found it obvious that "we can take whatever military action is necessary."

Borrowing heavily from McCullough, Carter turned to Theodore Roosevelt who would support the treaties "because he could see the decision as one by which we are demonstrating the kind of great power we wish to be" (1978, p. 262). Roosevelt "would join us in our pride for being a great and generous people, with the national strength and wisdom to do what is right for us and what is fair to others" (p. 262). Carter said that ratifying the treaties "will demonstrate that as a large and powerful country, we are able to deal fairly and honorably with a proud but smaller sovereign nation . . . [because] We believe in good will and fairness, as well as strength" (pp. 259, 262). But the president could have used much better material from McCullough's testimony.

Unfortunately, speechwriter Landon Butler had drawn Fallows's attention to only two passages in McCullough's Senate testimony, both of them technical and dreary. One stressed the slow transition of Canal control and the other described complex engineering features. No one brought to the president's attention the following passages from the very man who had urged Carter to be idealistic and eloquent:

one of the lessons of history, one of the fundamental lessons surely, is that times change, the world moves on. Then was then and now is now. I wonder if we can remind ourselves of that fact often enough? The era that built the Panama Canal was immensely different from our own, with different needs, different realities. . . . Inevitably there will be risks involved, there will be problems along the way. But the risks of holding fast, of trying to hang on to what has been, can not help but be far greater. (McCullough, 1978, pp. 1–2)

The speech employed neither McCullough's testimony nor his technical points that had appealed to Butler. But the last 15 percent of the speech was drawn, sometimes verbatim, from McCullough's October letter describing Theodore Roosevelt's likely endorsement of the treaties as evidence of "the kind of power we wish to be."

President Carter clearly had been influenced by David McCullough's thinking, as evidenced by the fact that it constitutes the last 15 percent of a speech that, at twenty-three minutes, was twice his targeted length. Had he used McCullough's statement to the Foreign Relations Committee, Carter might have allowed his target audience—the over-50, the grade school educated, and Republicans (Strauss, 1977)—to accept ratification with their misunderstandings of the Canal's history unthreatened. Had he done so, Crane's New Right narrative might not have caught hold.

But the Fireside Chat advanced a narrative in stark contrast to Crane's. Carter asked his target audience of old-time conservatives to act on the basis of a discrepant non-McGuffey interpretation of the old Bull Moose president. By using the portion of McCullough's testimony we have just quoted, the president could better have (1) transcended the McGuffey Reader problem noted by Strauss, (2) applied the Charleston speech principles of foreign policy, (3) enhanced the nobility and passion of his appeal, and (4) minimized his opponents' prospects for polarization. But he did not do so.

The treaties passed the Senate by a two-vote (68–32) margin despite a well-publicized resolution pledging forty senators against the treaties. President Carter worked long and hard to keep his Senate support; ratification was a considerable short-term victory for him, even though many Americans remained staunchly opposed to the treaties.

CONCLUSION

Carter and Crane advanced sharply contrasting world views. Crane saw danger, Carter security. Crane wanted superiority, Carter partnership. Crane implied force and punishment, Carter generosity and kindness. Crane thought America weak, Carter thought us strong. Crane saw shame in "surrender," Carter in continued imperialism. Each believed that the other indirectly helped America's enemies.

The Panama Canal controversy of 1976–1978 illustrates six important points about the significance of arguments between interpretive visions. First, policies are grounded in historical narratives. Carter and Crane each advocated policies consistent with his own world view. *If* America had sovereignty over the Canal, then sharing that sovereignty with Panama would have been a radical change; but if Panama had always been sovereign, then the adjustment was relatively minor. *If* Panama was a corrupt, unstable, anti-American society, then the new treaties jeopardized our access to the Canal; but if it was a progressive, stable, increasingly capitalistic and democratic nation that has been resentful of our paternalistic colonialism, then a more egalitarian approach was a wise choice. Finally, *if* we want to be feared and respected abroad, then we should have continued to dictate Canal policy at the risk of unilateral military intervention; but if we want to be liked and respected at the risk of being duped, we should have approached the Canal as a hemispheric enterprise. To choose a policy is to choose a world view, and vice versa.

Thus, the second conclusion is that policy debates, especially foreign policy debates, can be conducted between as well as within world views. The New Right could have accepted the world view advanced by Carter, Ford, Kissinger, and the Joint Chiefs of Staff and attacked the treaty's legal loopholes. When the policy choices all occur within a single interpretive vision, the specific policy choice is the only question decided and major policy shifts are rare. But when the debate is between interpretive visions, proponents of the dominant view risk losing the framework—the configuration of language, logic, and ideology —in which their entire array of policies makes sense. By using the treaties to attack the dominant orientation, the New Right encouraged public doubts about the framework of American foreign policy and provided an alternative framework through which subsequent events in Iran and Afghanistan could be interpreted.

Third, dramatic narratives that excite the imagination can be more effective than arguments that rely solely upon propositional arguments. The New Right was better able than President Carter to excite the public imagination for two reasons: they wanted to alarm the public, and they worked with recollections and fantasies long held by their target audience. Moreover, the New Right's argument fulfilled the Republican National Committee's need for an issue around which to mobilize a majority, and they sent out Reagan's letter. It was, therefore, the Panama Canal debate that enabled the New Right to win control of the Republican Party's rhetorical agenda well before the 1978 midterm elections or the 1980 primaries. Their control over the agenda made it particularly unlikely that George Bush, a foreign policy specialist steeped in the Nixon-Ford-Kissinger foreign policy, would be able to wrest the 1980 nomination from Ronald Reagan.

For his part, President Carter sought to reassure the public by presenting only "the facts." This emphasis on disseminating facts rather than dramatizing the controversy was evident in several of his public statements. In his August 23 press conference, for example, he observed that:

I think there's been a great deal of misinformation about what is being concluded in Panama, which may be one of the reasons that there is not popular
support for the Panama Canal treaty at this point. . . . But it will be a major
responsibility of my own, through my own statements and through those of
others who support the Panama Canal treaty to give the American people the
facts. I think that to a substantial degree, those who do have the facts and have
studied this situation closely concur that these two treaties are advantageous
to us. (Carter, 1977e, p. 1488)

Four days later Carter reiterated his personal responsibility to "sell" the
treaties with facts: "I have a responsibility to be sure that not only the
Members of the Senate but the American people know the facts about
the current terms of the treaty. My belief is that when the facts are
known, the opinion of the American people will change" (1977d,
p. 1514). And in the Denver briefing two months later Carter still
emphasized "clear facts." But "facts," however clear, are only the perceptual threads from which narratives are woven. Crane and Reagan
treated Carter's "facts" as misinformation, aided by the fact that many
of their prospective followers had learned oversimplified versions of
the Panama Canal story as children.

  Thus were the Carter administration and the New Right able to
achieve their objectives: the former won ratification, the latter won control of the Republican Party and, later, the White House and Senate.
The New Right's efforts generated mailing lists, campaign funds, a simple criterion for electoral targeting, and a unifying world view. It
proved to be, as Viguerie had predicted, "a no-loss issue for conservatives."

  It is tempting to conclude that Carter won the battle but lost the war.
But the treaties remained in force before, during, and after the era of
Manuel Noriega, and the New Right lost control of the Republican
Party, although it is debatable whether they lost their control with the
nomination of George Bush or during his administration.

  Fourth, members of the Carter administration made many good
rhetorical choices, they just did not make quite enough of them at the
right times. For example, the Charleston address was an excellent
opportunity for Carter to build his foreign policy coalition with southern legislators, a friendly core constituency of mildly conservative
opinion leaders. But the speech was largely ignored and its principles
were neither enumerated nor stated as principles, in contrast to Richard
Nixon's personal proclamation of "The Nixon Doctrine." Furthermore,
Carter's people came up with nice, catchy, assertive ways of making

their points, but few of their successes were reprised in the Fireside Chat—Carter's best opportunity to reach his intended audience. Finally, the president neglected to conclude his Chat with a call for action. It is easy to imagine Carter concluding his speech with something like this:

Tonight I have shared with you the facts surrounding the Panama Canal. I have found that when people learn the facts, they usually see why it is so important to us that we ratify these treaties. But there are many people who do not yet understand the facts. Most of them have been underinformed, some have been misinformed, and others—a handful, really—have tried to scare people for their own private interests. Tonight I ask you to help our country at this critical moment. When you hear someone say that we own the Canal, or that we are going to give away the Canal, or that we will not be able to defend it, or that we will be paying our tax dollars to Panama, please tell them the facts as I have shared them with you. If you do that you will help to insure that the fate of these treaties, so vital to our national security, will be decided on the basis of the actual advantages and disadvantages of the new and old treaties in an atmosphere of calm and rational deliberation.

Without such a call for action the president provided his supporters with no way to counteract the New Right's campaign of petitions, telephone banks, leaflets, and speeches.

Fifth, the Panama Canal debates illustrate how narrative visions enhance a sense of community both through the narrative itself and through the interpersonal processes of recollecting and fantasizing. Viguerie misinterpreted the Canal debates in at least one important respect. Probably because he specializes in targeted mailing lists, his account of the debate emphasized the campaign's logistical gains: mailing lists, contributions, "Truth Squad" engagements, and television programs. But all mailings do not elicit comparable contributions.

It is the substance of the mailing—the rhetorical configuration of needs, symbols, preferences, and reasons—that elicits public responses. In this instance the New Right was able to send forth a message that penetrated personal defense mechanisms that had so often found their followers labeled "crackpots" and extremists. This was no John Birch Society antifluoridation campaign that asked people to believe that subversives were contaminating the water supply. This campaign was built from familiar recollections and fantasies nurtured since grade school, advanced skillfully by historian/congressman Phillip Crane and by the well-liked and respected actor and former governor of California, Ronald Reagan.

Perhaps even more than the message itself, the interpersonal excitement generated by the campaign against the treaties provided a variety of gratifications to its members. Neither the conservatives who had supported Joe McCarthy or the John Birch Society or the Goldwater campaign, nor centrist Republicans battered by Vietnam and Watergate, had found many issues capable of recharging their batteries. The New Right's campaign against the Canal treaties tapped this latent need and made it a source of energy.

Sixth, a choice between narrative visions boils down to the question of believability: which version do you prefer to believe—or, more precisely, which version do you *need* to believe to preserve your personal interpretive processes and the utility of your social interpretive structures? People who are inclined to conceive of the world as a hostile place full of danger for America could more readily embrace Crane's world view and its consequences; people who are inclined to see a changing world of diverse, independent nations neither hostile nor subservient to the United States were more likely to accept Carter's vision and its consequences.

We began this chapter with the observation that presidents need to lead, sometimes against public opinion. This chapter has demonstrated that it is possible for a president to achieve a significant policy victory and, in the process, lose control of the ideology, the logic, and the language that had been used to frame policy making and to promote presidential leadership.

REFERENCES

Berry, N. D. (1981). The foundation of presidential leadership: Teaching. *Presidential Studies Quarterly, 11*, 99–105.

Burns, J. M. (1978). *Leadership*. New York: Harper Colophon.

Carr, D. (1986). *Time, narrative, and history*. Bloomington: Indiana University Press.

Carter, J. (1976). Position paper on the Panama Canal, February 28. Staff Office Files: Speechwriters, James Fallows, Jimmy Carter Library.

Carter, J. [1977a]. "Ask President Carter" program on CBS Radio, March 5. *Public Papers of the President* (p. 325). Washington, D.C.: U.S. Government Printing Office.

Carter, J. [1977b]. Charleston, SC, July 21. *Public Papers of the President* (pp. 1309–1315). Washington, D.C.: U.S. Government Printing Office.

Carter, J. [1977c]. Denver, Colorado, October 22. *Public Papers of the President* (pp. 1884–1893). Washington, D.C.: U.S. Government Printing Office.

Carter, J. [1977d]. Interview with the president, August 27. *Public Papers of the President* (pp. 1509–1519). Washington, D.C.: U.S. Government Printing Office.

Carter, J. [1977e]. The president's news conference, August 23. *Public Papers of the President* (pp. 1486–1495). Washington, D.C.: U.S. Government Printing Office.

Carter, J. [1977f]. Radio-Television News Directors Association, September 15. *Public Papers of the President* (pp. 1594–1602). Washington, D.C.: U.S. Government Printing Office.

Carter, J. [1977g]. Response to David McCullough, November 3. Box 19. Staff Office Files: Speechwriters, Jimmy Carter Library.

Carter, J. [1978]. Panama Canal Treaties. *Public Papers of the President* (pp. 258–263). Washington, D.C.: U.S. Government Printing Office.

Channock, F. (1976). Panama Canal strategy. Staff Office Files: White House Operations, Foster Channock Files, Gerald R. Ford Library.

Crane, P. M. (1978). *Surrender in Panama: The case against the treaty.* New York: Dale Books.

Doolittle, J. (1977a). Panama Canal questions, August 22. Staff Office Files: Speechwriters, James Fallows, Jimmy Carter Library.

Doolittle, J. (1977b). Themes for Panama Canal discussions, August 22. Staff Office Files: Speechwriters, James Fallows, Jimmy Carter Library.

Elliott, R. (1975). Memoranda and drafts for the response to letter from William Douglas Pawley, October 6. White House Central Files, Foreign Policy, Panama Canal, Gerald R. Ford Library.

Fallows, J. (1977a). Letter to Harlan Strauss, September 19. Staff Office Files: Speechwriters, James Fallows Files, Jimmy Carter Library.

Fallows, J. (1977b). Memo to Bob Pastor, July 12. Panama Canal Treaty, Box 17, Staff Office Files: Speechwriters' Chronological, Jimmy Carter Library.

Fallows, J. (1977c). Memo to Hamilton Jordan, September 14. Fireside Chat, 2-1-78, Box 17, Staff Office Files: Speechwriters' Chronological, Jimmy Carter Library.

Fallows, J. (1978a). Memo to Zbigniew Brzezinski, January 27. Fireside Chat, 2-1-78, Box 17, Staff Office Files: Speechwriters' Chronological, Jimmy Carter Library.

Fallows, J. (1978b). Suggested outline: Panama Canal speech, 1/25/78. Staff Office Files: Speechwriters' Chronological, Box 17, Fireside Chat, 2-1-78. Jimmy Carter Library.

Fisher, W. R. (1987). *Human communication as narration: Toward a philosophy of reason, value, and action.* Columbia: University of South Carolina Press.

Flood, D. J. (1974). Letter to President Richard M. Nixon. White House Central Files, Foreign Policy, Panama Canal, Gerald R. Ford Library.

Goldwater, B. (1976). Letter to Robert Pastor, March 12. Staff Office Files: Speechwriters' Office, James Fallows Files, Jimmy Carter Library.

Harman, P. (1975). Our Panama Canal: A vital asset (mimeographed flier), December 16. White House Central Files, Foreign Policy, Panama Canal, Gerald R. Ford Library.

Harriss, G. (1976). Correspondence with John Marsh, May 5. White House Central Files, Foreign Policy, Panama Canal, Gerald R. Ford Library.

Jones, Col. F. P., (Ret.). (1975). The United States Canal on the Isthmus of Panama: The showdown of approaches (Official memorandum to officers and publications of the Veterans of Foreign Wars), September 25. White House Central Files, Foreign Policy, Panama Canal, Gerald R. Ford Library.

Kassabaum, N. L. (1979). The essence of leadership. *Presidential Studies Quarterly, 9,* 239–242.

Maslow, A. (1943). The authoritarian character structure. *Journal of Social Psychology*, *18*, 401–411.

McCullough, D. (1977). Letter to the president, October 21. Fireside Chat, 2-1-78, Box 17, Staff Office Files: Speechwriters' Chronological, Jimmy Carter Library.

McCullough, D. (1978). Manuscript for statement to the Senate Committee on Foreign Relations, January 19. Staff Office Files: Speechwriters' Chronological, Box 17, Fireside Chat, 2-1-78, Jimmy Carter Library.

Nixon, R. M. (1974). Response to Congressman Flood, May 29. White House Central Files, Foreign Policy, Panama Canal, Gerald R. Ford Library.

O'Donnell, T. (1976). Memorandum to Jerry Jones, May 5. White House Central Files, Foreign Policy, Panama Canal, Gerald R. Ford Library.

Pace, E. (1977, August 26). Reagan declares Canal treaties should be rejected by the Senate. *New York Times*, pp. 1, 6.

Pastor, R. (1976, June). In the Canal Zone: Who should be sovereign? *Harvard Magazine*, pp. 38–43.

Powell, J., & Fallows, J. (1977). Memorandum to the president, November 29. Fireside Chat, 2-1-78, Box 17, Staff Office Files: Speechwriters' Chronological, Jimmy Carter Library.

Rose, S. (1976). Copy of telegram to Senator Robert Dole. White House Central Files, Foreign Policy, Panama Canal, Gerald R. Ford Library.

Stewart, C. J., Smith, C. A., & Denton, R. E., Jr. (1994). *Persuasion and social movements* (3rd ed.). Prospect Heights, IL: Waveland.

Strauss, H. J. (1977). Letter to Jim Fallows, September 6. Staff Office Files: Speechwriters, James Fallows Files, Jimmy Carter Library.

Viguerie, R. A. (1981). *The New Right: We're ready to lead.* Falls Church, VA: The Viguerie Company.

Wayne, J. (1977). SCARE LETTER FROM THE HONORABLE RONALD REAGAN, November 11. Fireside Chat, 2-1-78, Box 17, Staff Office Files: Speechwriters' Chronological, Jimmy Carter Library.

6

Political Jeremiads from the Bully Pulpit

Theodore Roosevelt's characterization of the American presidency as a "bully pulpit" has become an annoying cliché in the literature on presidential speaking. It is typically invoked as expert testimony on the nature of presidential leadership since the turn of the century. This is ironic because the presidency that Roosevelt assumed upon the death of McKinley was hardly any sort of pulpit at all, bully or otherwise. True, his predecessors did deliver ceremonial addresses. But that sort of presidential rhetoric differs markedly from the policy advocacy that marked the rhetorical presidency begun by Woodrow Wilson (Tulis, 1987).

Most writers have construed the "bully pulpit" figuratively rather than literally, thereby undervaluing the sermonic nature of much of the twentieth century's presidential rhetoric. But a sizable body of recent literature has emerged that treats presidential addresses as sermonic applications of "The American Civil Religion" (Bellah, 1967) and the American jeremiad (Johannesen, 1986; Ritter, 1993; Ritter & Henry, 1992).

This chapter explores the political implications of presidential jeremiads. It contends that presidential jeremiads generally function to enhance social cohesion, to impose a sense of rhetorical order on social and economic chaos, to justify moderate changes, to elevate the presidency, and to enhance national pride. However, presidential jeremiads also confound practical problem solving, reify the Founders, inhibit discussion of fundamental principles and institutions, deny the concatenated nature of the postmodern presidency, subvert constitutional principles such as the checks on executive power, and undermine the prospects for successful presidential leadership.

THE AMERICAN JEREMIAD

The jeremiad is a rhetorical form that frames troublesome social problems in the logic of God's covenant with a chosen people. Students of jeremiads have used the term in somewhat different ways to illuminate the biblical prophecies of Jeremiah (Zulick, 1992), the political sermons of the Puritans' errand into the wilderness (Bercovitch, 1978; Miller, 1953), early American reform rhetoric (Bercovitch, 1978; Bormann, 1985; Ritter, 1979), and contemporary political rhetoric (Johannesen, 1986; Murphy, 1990; Ritter, 1980). In their most inclusive sense, jeremiads depict a people chosen by God who formed a covenant to undertake a sacred mission or errand. The serious problems afflicting the chosen people are attributed to their special stature, either as punishment for straying from their mission and covenant or as divine tests of their worthiness.

The Puritan jeremiad was the first uniquely American literary genre (Miller, 1953), but the Puritan sense of religious mission could not withstand the religious diversity of a changing America. Rather than disappearing altogether, Puritan values and forms diffused as themes in America's cultural tradition (Bercovitch, 1978; Bormann, 1985). The Puritan jeremiad evolved into the contemporary secular jeremiad, in which the American civil religion of the American dream replaced religious doctrine (Johannesen, 1986). In contemporary political jeremiads the sacred errand remains John Winthrop's command to create a shining city on a hill to serve as an example to the world. The Founders' subsequent covenant is recorded in sacred documents such as the Declaration of Independence, the U.S. Constitution, the Federalist Papers, and the pronouncements of various presidents.

Modern jeremiads evaluate our individual and societal progress in terms of our attainment of the American dream. That dream, according to Walter Fisher (1973), joins together the *moralistic dimension* of life, liberty, and the pursuit of happiness with the *materialistic dimension* of the work ethic, individual initiative, and the free market. Three centuries after the Puritan landing, American jeremiads continue to feature a special people chosen by God who can grow from their adversity and attain a better future simply by conducting themselves in accordance with the covenant and the dream.

More Logic than Language

Our discussion of the evolving American jeremiad has emphasized jeremiadic logic, as opposed to jeremiadic language; it is a distinction that merits explication. Ritter and Henry (1992) invoke Garry Wills's judgment that the jeremiad is "less a genre of oratory than a style of thought" (Wills, 1987, p. 68). Jeremiadic logic is the culturally acceptable mode of reasoning that enables the organization of the premises of a chosen people, divine sanctions, and ultimate success into the narrative form recognizable as a jeremiad. These narratives have traditionally been told in vivid language by prophets and Puritan preachers, such as Jeremiah himself and Jonathan Edwards, who typically depicted graphically the dangers facing their societies. Jeremiah 4:13, for example, warned:

> Look! Like the clouds he goes up,
> Like the cyclone his chariots,
> Swifter than eagles his horses—
> Woe to us for we are undone!

And Jonathan Edwards concluded his sermon "Sinners in the Hands of an Angry God" with the words:

Therefore let every one that is out of Christ now awake and fly from the wrath to come. The wrath of Almighty God is now undoubtedly hanging over a great part of this congregation. Let every one fly out of Sodom. *"Haste and escape for your lives, look not behind you, escape to the mountain, lest ye be consumed."* (1741, p. 32)

But vivid, apocalyptic language can be used to tell nonjeremiadic stories, and jeremiadic logic can be conveyed in dispassionate, if nonetheless disquieting, language. Indeed, the use of graphic language is not generally considered a defining characteristic of jeremiads (Bercovitch, 1978; Bormann, 1985; Miller, 1953; Murphy, 1990; Ritter & Henry, 1992).

What, then, are the sources of the modern jeremiad's rhetorical power? First, the modern jeremiad—unlike its Puritan forebear—reinforces the chosen people's sense of exceptionalism while enabling them to escape direct blame for their problems. This is possible because of the pluralistic nature of our contemporary democratic and rhetorical order, which is a sharp contrast to Puritan rhetorical hegemony. Nowadays jeremiads tell of chosen people led astray by false prophets who are to blame for our tribulations. The "led astray" theme became both possible and necessary because of popular sovereignty; possible because of the growing multitude of prophetic voices, and necessary as a psychological escape clause that explains regretted preferences. The change implies a crucial distinction between "the people" and "the *chosen* people." Rarely are the people castigated sharply for following false prophets (some of whom used jeremiads of their own), because the people vote. Rather, the essential goodness and wisdom of the *chosen* people function as proof of the false prophets' wickedness and deception.

A second source of jeremiadic cogency lies in its transcendence of contradictions (Bercovitch, 1978). Without jeremiadic logic to guide them, most rational people would regard as illogical most, if not all, of the following claims: (1) God's chosen people will suffer adversity, (2) hard times warrant optimism, and (3) future success requires a return to the past. Each of these statements pairs unpleasant but undeniable empirical observations (adversity, hard times, and an uncertain future) with psychologically necessary reassurances (ego-support, optimism, and past glories) and fuses them with the fire of the jeremiadic Truth. The modern Jeremiah climbs to a different logical vantage point from which the apparent contradiction is no contradiction at all, but a validation of all that the chosen people need to believe during times of trouble. By transcending these seeming contradictions the jeremiad fetches optimism out of pessimism, good out of evil, hope out of despair, the future out of the past, certainty out of uncertainty, stability out of instability, and continuity out of change (Bercovitch, 1978; Bormann, 1977; Murphy, 1990).

A third source of persuasiveness can be found in the jeremiad's ability to stimulate and to validate shared fantasies. In Ernest Bormann's theory of symbolic convergence a "fantasy" is "the creative and imaginative [personal] interpretation of events that fulfills a psychological or rhetorical need" (Bormann, 1985, p. 5). A fantasy, in this sense, can entail actual, vicarious, or imagined persons and events. Similar scenarios or plots related to the fantasy theme constitute a "fantasy type"—"a stock scenario repeated again and again by the same characters or by similar characters" (p. 7). Bormann contends that the presence of fantasy types indicates "The emergence of a rhetorical vision that is clearly formulated and well understood by both speaker and audience" (p. 7). He continues by highlighting the relationship between rhetorical visions and the sense of community: "When a rhetorical vision emerges, the participants in the vision (those who have shared the fantasies in an appropriate way) come to form a rhetorical community" (p. 8). The jeremiad is a fantasy type comprised of the fantasy themes previously discussed (the chosen people, the mission, the divine afflictions, and the promise of ultimate reward). Membership in, and loyalty to, a rhetorical community derive both from the shared fantasies and from the emotional gratifications attendant to self-disclosure and sharing.

Fantasy themes provide discursive gratification for psychological needs, thereby stimulating emotions and providing interactants with "meanings and emotions that can be set off by a commonly agreed upon cryptic symbolic cue" (Bormann, 1985, p. 6). Jonathan Edwards heightened the Puritans' sense of community in his 1741 jeremiad by describing the angry God's state of mind and the kinds of people who typically anger Him in vivid, concrete language that intensified emotions by emphasizing the proximity of His wrath (Smith & Hyde, 1991). Thus, jeremiads evoke emotional responses through the use of fantasy themes that provide rhetorical gratification for psychological needs and by increasing the perceived proximity of the sanctioning agent and dangers.

In summary, the secular jeremiad is an important element of America's rhetorical culture. It is a particular narrative logic that recounts the history of chosen people who as the heirs to a unique covenant between God and the Founders are destined to attain both the moralistic and materialistic dimensions of the American dream. Whenever the chosen people have violated the spirit of their covenant they have been beset by social, economic, and political crises that cannot be alleviated by social, economic, or political changes alone, because those tribulations are divine sanctions. Instead, repentance and restoration of the ancient truths are necessary, perhaps even sufficient, to resolve the crises. Jeremiads persist because they are persuasive; and they are persuasive because they enable the chosen people to avoid blame for their society's problems, they transcend apparent contradictions, and they provide emotional and psychological gratifications.

Jeremiads and American Political Leadership

A jeremiad can neatly account for America's tribulations. But which tribulations are divine opportunities for growth? Which tribulations are punishments for abandoning the covenant? And which tribulations are unrelated to divine concerns? Such questions invite the political discourse of leadership. Because jeremiadic logic presumes divine interest in the lives of Americans without presuming that each American receives direct, personal divine guidance, that logic demands

prophetic leaders. Emergent leaders who cast their messages in jeremiadic logic simultaneously tap into community logic and don the vestments of secular prophets.

Sacred prophets lambasted their congregations as wicked and sinful, a reasonable approach in a theocracy. But in a pluralistic democracy it is imprudent for elected officials to blame social problems on the
wicked, corrupt, selfish, and sinful citizens whose votes they need.
Instead, they echo Jeremiah's warnings of false prophets: crises
occurred because the chosen people were led astray by false prophets
who must be renounced and replaced by the new prophet, who will help
them to restore the covenant. Not surprisingly, jeremiads abound in the
corpus of presidential nomination acceptance addresses, as the emergent prophet unifies his chosen people around their sacred missions of
wresting power from the false prophets and then enabling America to
live up to the promise of the American dream (Ritter, 1980).

The jeremiad's need for prophetic leadership and the bully pulpit of
the American presidency were made for one another. There is no comparable political pulpit from which to summon the chosen people, to
warn them of their peril, or to direct their behavior. Nor is there a comparable rhetorical form through which a president can find optimism in
pessimism, a bright future in a proud heritage, order in chaos, peace in
war, or secular advice in sacred writings—all while reinforcing the
claim to prophetic leadership. Although most presidents probably
would eschew the label of prophet, twentieth-century presidents have
readily taken on the role of interpreting political realities and redirect-
ing public behavior (Tulis, 1987).

Let us turn now to a consideration of specific presidential jeremiads. We shall discuss speeches of two types—inaugural addresses and
policy addresses—to suggest the political and rhetorical potentialities
of the form.

INAUGURAL JEREMIADS

If emerging leaders use jeremiads to summon the chosen people,
and if presidential candidates use jeremiads to rally their people against
the false prophets (Ritter, 1980), then it is not unreasonable to expect
some of those same candidates to use jeremiadic logic to inaugurate
their presidencies. Indeed, a jeremiad can help the president-elect to
perform the rhetorical tasks required by the inaugural genre.

Karlyn Kohrs Campbell and Kathleen Hall Jamieson (1990) explained that presidential inaugural addresses function to invest the president-elect with the powers of the office and to facilitate governmental continuity. They summarized the rhetorical properties of presidential inaugurals as follows:

From a generic perspective, then, a presidential inaugural [1] reconstitutes the people as an audience that can witness the rite of investiture. [2] It rehearses communal values from the past, [3] sets forth the political principles that will guide the new administration, and demonstrates that the president can enact the presidential persona appropriately. Still more generally, the presidential inaugural address is [4] an epideictic ritual that is formal, unifying, abstract, and eloquent; at the core of this ritual lies timelessness—[5] the fusion of the past and future of the nation in an eternal present in which we reaffirm what Franklin Roosevelt called "our covenant with ourselves," *a covenant* between the executive and the nation *that is the essence of democratic government* [italics added]. (p. 36)

Jeremiadic logic facilitates the reconstitution of the people through the fantasy theme of the chosen people witnessing a ritual of the civil religion. The fantasy theme of the covenant and the mission rehearses communal values from the past. The sermonic form of the jeremiad is itself formal, unifying, and abstract, while the fantasy themes of the people, the tribulations, and the promise invite eloquent language. Finally, the jeremiad is suited, almost uniquely, to the reaffirmation of the democratic covenant. In short, presidential use of a jeremiad can facilitate performance of the basic functions of inaugural addresses.

Kurt Ritter's (1993) analysis of Lyndon Johnson's 1965 inaugural address reveals its jeremiadic structure. His examination of the speech drafts revealed that the jeremiadic themes were used in the introduction to the speech through the first two drafts and were moved to the conclusion only after the body of the speech had taken shape. Johnson described a covenant of justice, liberty, and union "with God, with earlier generations, and with the land." The former schoolteacher then outlined tests by which Americans could judge their progress: justice would be measured by progress on civil rights, liberty would be measured by global progress toward individual freedom, and union would be measured by our sense of national community. Johnson advised his students to prepare for their tests: "You must look within your own hearts to the old promises and the old dreams" (Ritter, 1993).

Ritter contends that Johnson's speechwriters wanted a domestic jeremiad but found that the logical structure of the speech (the jeremiad) required that the foreign policy material on liberty be incorporated into the mission. Indirectly, Ritter argues, jeremiadic logic committed Johnson's presidency to progress on civil rights, victory in Vietnam, and a stronger sense of community at home—three goals that came into conflict, perhaps because Johnson's jeremiad made it impossible for him to prioritize those goals.

But Johnson's inaugural has not been the only inaugural jeremiad. Let us examine more closely two significant inaugurals that mirror one another—the Roosevelt and Reagan inaugurals. Their first inaugural addresses both used economic crises to break with the values and priorities of the outgoing administrations.

Franklin D. Roosevelt's First Inaugural

During the seventy-two years following Abraham Lincoln's inauguration only Grover Cleveland and Woodrow Wilson had been able to break the Republicans' grip on the White House. The uncertainty of Democratic hegemony, the enormity of Roosevelt's landslide, and the political realities of the Depression all invited Roosevelt to signal decisive changes in his 1933 inaugural, and he used the jeremiad to do so.

Roosevelt's jeremiad emphasized the unselfish "interdependence of the various elements . . . [of] the United States . . . [as a] permanently important manifestation of the American spirit of the pioneer" ([1933], p. 22). He idealized the "neighbor who respects his obligations and respects the sanctity of his agreements in and with a world of neighbors" (p. 22). For such neighbors the pursuit of happiness "lies in the joy of achievement, [and] the thrill of creative effort" rather than in "the mere possession of money" (p. 20). The secular covenant "thrives only on honesty, on honor, on the sacredness of obligations, on faithful protection, on unselfish performance" (p. 20).

Roosevelt partitioned America into the people, the rulers of the exchange, and the government. When the people work because they find it stimulating to do so, they reap modest economic rewards. But when the rulers of the exchange tempt them to work selfishly for profit, and when the government guided by Republican false prophets encourages such selfishness, severe moral decay is inevitable. Thus, Roosevelt attributed the Depression to the "lure of profit" and the "false leadership" of the "rulers of the exchange of mankind's goods" and to "the unscrupulous money changers" who knew "only the rules of a generation of self-seekers" (p. 20). A Puritan jeremiad would have chastised the chosen people for their transgression, but this was a modern jeremiad. The chosen people and Roosevelt had contracted on election day to undertake the recovery. They were not at fault, except insofar as they had previously followed the leadership of false prophets. Neighbors should not have sought to profit at the expense of other neighbors; but, tempted by the false prophets of profit, they forgot the ancient truths and devoted their energies to "the mad chase of evanescent profits" (p. 20).

Because Americans are a chosen people amenable to reform, God punished their selfishness with a material adversity detailed by Roosevelt:

Values have shrunken to fantastic levels; taxes have risen; our ability to pay has fallen; government of all kinds is faced by serious curtailment of income; the means of exchange are frozen in the currents of trade; the withered leaves of industrial enterprise lie on every side; farmers find no markets for their produce; the savings of many years in thousands of families are gone. More important, a host of unemployed citizens face the grim problem of existence, and an equally great number toil with little return. (p. 19)

The chosen people's transgression was moral but their tribulations were not. The punishments for straying from the ancient truths were to "concern, thank God, only material things" (p. 20).

It was Roosevelt's sermon itself that began the national recovery. It was he who announced that "The money changers have fled from their high seats in the temple of our civilization." It was he who proclaimed that "We may now restore that temple to the ancient truths." And it was he who warned that "The measure of the restoration lies in the extent to which we apply social values more noble than mere monetary profit" (p. 20).

The restoration of noble values required a change from passivity to action, but whose action was it to be? Having dismissed the self-seekers from "the temple of our civilization," Roosevelt invested government with the authority selflessly and aggressively to cultivate conditions hospitable to the ancient truths. Hoover's quiet inaction was thus replaced with Roosevelt's willingness "to speak the truth . . . frankly and boldly" (p. 19), to "assume unhesitatingly the leadership of this great army of our people dedicated to a disciplined attack upon our common problems" (p. 22), and, if necessary, to "ask the Congress for . . . broad Executive power to wage a war against the emergency, as great as the power that would be given to me if we were in fact invaded by a foreign foe" (p. 23).

Selflessness and action were fused in the New Deal. "Our greatest primary task is to put [the other chosen] people to work," and it was Roosevelt who would do the putting, through "direct recruiting by the [now active] Government itself" (p. 21). By personally putting the chosen people back to work Roosevelt's government would enable them to experience "the joy of achievement, . . . the thrill of creative effort, . . . the moral stimulation of work" and, almost incidentally, "the mere possession of money" (p. 20), all the while "accomplishing greatly needed projects" (p. 21). The moral dimensions of the economic crisis were so central, and recovery through the reaffirmation of selfless interdependence so certain, that "These dark days will be worth all they cost us if they teach us that our true destiny is not to be ministered unto but to minister to ourselves and to our fellow men" (p. 20).

In Roosevelt's view, overemphasis on the material dimension of the American dream had undermined the moral dimension. Only through a return to a less materialistic conception of the pursuit of happiness could material prosperity be restored. To reinstate morality it was necessary, first, to drive the evil moneychangers from the temples of civilization; second, to recognize the falsity of material wealth as the standard of success; and third, to "act wisely and courageously . . . to stimulate and reorganize the use of natural resources" even if less morally courageous persons would counsel patience or raise constitutional questions.

Jeremiadic logic allowed Roosevelt to contrast two visions of government—the Democrats' selfless activism and the Republicans' passive selfishness—and to identify the former as the ancient truth on which America had been built. This enabled Roosevelt to blame the Republicans for the nation's economic and moral collapse, thereby encouraging public support for values rather than evanescent policies or persons. The jeremiad enabled Roosevelt personally to take command of the economic recovery, to disadvantage his critics, to set aside prosperity as the measure of economic recovery, and to inaugurate his presidency without tying himself to his rejected predecessor.

But the jeremiad committed Roosevelt to success, lest America fail to achieve its destiny. He called, appropriately, for prompt congressional support for his programs. But jeremiadic logic compelled Roosevelt to pledge independent personal action should Congress fail to act. His jeremiad provided the rationale for the accumulation of unprecedented presidential power in the name of the Founders' ancient truths.

Ronald Reagan's First Inaugural

Jeremiads abound in the rhetoric of Ronald Reagan (Erickson, 1985; Johannesen, 1986), and Ritter and Henry (1992) used the jeremiad as a framework for analyzing his rhetorical career. Reagan's crucial first inaugural address to his people, to history, and to the world exhibited all the elements of the jeremiad; indeed, it inaugurated a jeremiadic administration. This occurred largely because of Reagan's idolization of Roosevelt's leadership, and it made this speech the antithesis of Roosevelt's first inaugural.

Reagan was a New Deal liberal until about 1948, when, he is fond of saying, the Democratic Party left him. Greenstein (1983) described Roosevelt as Reagan's "idol of the Depression years and the model for his political style of reaching out rhetorically to the American people through the electronic media" (p. 9). Roosevelt loomed large in Reagan's 1980 campaign for the presidency:

"We have to be willing to be Roosevelt," asserted Reagan's adviser Richard Whalen during the 1980 campaign. Quoting FDR twice in his speech accepting the presidential nomination, Reagan cloaked himself in Roosevelt's mantle. At a time of economic and spiritual crisis comparable to the Great Depression, Reagan promised to restore the old Roosevelt coalition of middle-class, blue-collar, ethnic, and southern white Protestant voters and renew confidence in America. (Rogin, 1987, p. 33)

But Reagan's electoral coalition had questions about his presidency.

The softness of Reagan's mandate has been largely forgotten with the passage of time. The customary reliance on national voter surveys accurately predicted a close popular vote. But Reagan parlayed 50.7 percent of the popular vote into 91 percent of the electoral votes, thereby winning the right to claim a mandate, even if the mandate was primarily a repudiation of the Carter presidency. Compared to his seven predecessors, Reagan took office with the lowest initial public approval rating (51%), with disapproval ratings (14%) second only to Harry Truman, and tied with Richard Nixon for the largest percentage of nonopinionated constituents (36%). The four elected presidents preceding Reagan (Eisenhower, Kennedy, Nixon, and Carter) were inaugurated with approval ratings that averaged sixty points higher than their disapproval ratings; Reagan's margin was but 37 points (King & Ragsdale, 1988).

Here we find the kinds of contradictions that confound nonjeremiadic logic: a conservative Republican modeling a liberal Democrat, soft public approval following an electoral college landslide, and an approach to the 1980s grounded in the 1930s. It was just the sort of rhetorical task that invited a jeremiad. Moreover, Reagan was well versed in FDR's speech—he had memorized portions of it during the 1950s and could impersonate Roosevelt's delivery (Rogin, 1987). Although his ideas had changed, Reagan approached his inauguration still under the influence of Roosevelt's jeremiad and its style of thought.

Reagan's covenant was more traditionally jeremiadic than Roosevelt's. "God intended us to be free" ([1981], p. 38), said Reagan, largely because we have a political system that "guarantees individual liberty to a greater degree than any other" (p. 33). Indeed, we "prospered as no other people on Earth, . . . [because] we unleashed the energy and individual genius of man to a greater extent than has ever been done before" (p. 35). In short, God blessed America with prosperity in exchange for creating a place for individuals to be free.

America's support of individual liberty "makes us special among the nations of the Earth" (p. 35). It is the "citizens of this blessed land" (p. 36) who are the chosen people. They are the "men and women who raise our food, patrol our streets, man our mines and factories, teach our children, keep our homes, and heal us when we're sick—professionals, industrialists, shopkeepers, clerks, cabbies, and truck drivers. They are, in short, 'We the people' this breed called Americans" (p. 34). Simply, Americans—all Americans—are heroes.

But unlike Roosevelt's neighbors, Reagan's heroes could profit from their neighbors:

You meet heroes across a counter, and they're on both sides of that counter. *There are entrepreneurs* [italics added] with faith in themselves and faith in an idea who create new jobs, new wealth and opportunity. They're individuals and families whose taxes support the government and whose voluntary gifts support church, charity, culture, art and education. Their patriotism is quiet, but deep. *Their values sustain our national life* [italics added]. (p. 36)

These chosen people faced the world armed with a unique moral power because "no arsenal or weapon in the arsenals of the world is so formidable as the will and moral courage of free men and women. It is a weapon that our adversaries in today's world do not have. It is a weapon that we as Americans do have" (p. 37).

But if all Americans were chosen people, working hard and valuing freedom, how did America go astray? Reagan's answer lay neither in sinful citizens nor in false prophets, but in "government," an impersonal, runaway truck of a thing that had careened out of the chosen people's control. The "troubles parallel and are proportionate to the intervention and intrusion in our lives that result from unnecessary and excessive growth of government" (p. 35). This reversed almost perfectly Roosevelt's diagnosis of financial greed and prescription of government intervention. Implicit in Reagan's analysis was the equation of government intrusion with government spending. According to Reagan:

For decades we have piled deficit upon deficit, mortgaging our future and our children's future for the temporary convenience of the present. . . . You and I, as individuals, can, by borrowing, live beyond our means, but only for a limited period of time. Why, then, should we think that collectively, as a nation, we're not bound by that same limitation? (p. 34)

Government intrusion stifled individual liberty and betrayed the covenant, while government spending sought even greater prosperity than God saw fit to provide under the terms of our covenant. Punishment must surely follow.

By betraying the covenant the chosen people were "confronted with an economic affliction of great proportions." Reagan continued:

We suffer from the longest and one of the worst sustained inflations in our national history. It distorts our economic decisions, penalizes thrift, and crushes the struggling young and fixed-income elderly, alike. It threatens to shatter the lives of millions of our people. (p. 33)
Idle industries have cast workers into unemployment, human misery, and personal indignity. Those who do work are denied a fair return for their labor by a tax system which penalizes successful achievement and keeps us from maintaining full productivity. (p. 34)

There was no mention of these tribulations being "only material," because material success was, in the Puritan tradition, a divine sign of morally correct conduct.

The key to restoration of the American dream, in Reagan's analysis, was action by the chosen people to get government under their control. Because the covenant promised prosperity in return for the protection of individual liberty, and because government intrusion/spending had led the chosen people to betray that covenant, Reagan urged the chosen people toward "a healthy, vigorous, growing economy that provides equal opportunities for all Americans" without government intrusion. Thus, "It is time to check and reverse the growth of government" (p. 35) because "In this present crisis, government is not the solution to our problem; government is the problem" (p. 34).

Specifically, Reagan intended "to curb the size and influence of the Federal establishment and to demand recognition of the distinction between the powers granted to the Federal Government and those reserved to the States or to the people." Government was put to work for business: "Government can and must provide opportunity, not smother it; foster productivity, not stifle it" (p. 35).

America was assured of salvation if it would return to the covenant's emphasis on individual liberty. Reagan explained that:

The economic ills we suffer . . . will not go away in days, weeks, or months, but they will go away. They will go away because we as Americans have the capacity now, as we've had in the past, to do whatever needs to be done to preserve this last and greatest bastion of freedom. (p. 34)

Reagan told Americans that, "Progress may be slow, measured in inches and feet, not miles, but we will progress" (p. 36). To triumph against these economic woes Americans would need to muster our moral qualities—"all the creative energy at our command . . . and renew our determination, our courage, . . . our strength . . . our faith and our hope" (p. 36).

But who would make this renewal happen? Reagan's depiction was deceptively subtle. Notice, for example, the evolution in the italicized portions of the following passage:

In the days ahead *I will propose* removing the roadblocks that have slowed our economy and reduced productivity. . . . *Steps will be taken.* . . . These will be *our priorities.* . . . [One] of the greatest among the Founding Fathers . . . said . . . "*On you depend the fortunes* of America. *You are to decide* the important questions. . . . *Act worthy of yourselves.*" (p. 37)

Reagan here depicted a solution in which *he proposed* steps but in which the chosen *people would be responsible* for the success of those steps. Their prosperity would be restored by believing in freedom, by acquiescing to Reagan's diminution of the federal establishment, and by working individually rather than cooperatively or collectively.

Reagan's inaugural affirmed a sacred covenant that guaranteed economic prosperity as a reward for the advancement of individual liberty. The intrusion of the federal government into both social life and the money markets had undermined the covenant by stifling initiative. Economic renewal would come only when the heroic chosen people freed themselves from government and unleashed their individual talents, inducing God to again bless them with prosperity.

Jeremiadic logic enabled Ronald Reagan simultaneously to establish the centrality of his personal presidency and to cut back the federal government. The logic of the address, as opposed to its language, established the speaker as a prophet relative to his audience. As a unique interpreter of the ancient truths, the speaker as prophet transcended the occasion and commanded respect. Although soapbox jeremiads can be dismissed as crackpot ramblings, presidential legitimacy and jeremiadic logic make a powerful combination. Indeed, it is difficult to imagine any other way in which a president could argue for both enhanced presidential authority and diminished federal government without inviting charges of inconsistency or arrogance.

Reagan's inaugural mirrored Roosevelt's in many ways. Roosevelt sanctified selflessness, Reagan exalted individualism. Roosevelt's chosen people worked for moral stimulation, Reagan's worked for profit. Roosevelt's people had been led astray by the entrepreneurs' lure of profit, Reagan's had been corrupted by government largesse and the stifling of initiative. Roosevelt's federal government could save people from the entrepreneurs, Reagan's entrepreneurs could save people from government. Both Roosevelt and Reagan announced moralistic reaffirmation as the answer to economic problems, and both prescribed support for their presidential initiatives.

In summary, jeremiads have provided a rhetorical form through which presidents have satisfied the generic requirements of the inaugural address. They are especially useful for presidents like Roosevelt, Reagan, and Bill Clinton, who must establish continuity in the wake of discredited presidencies because jeremiads ground the new presidency in ancient truths. Moreover, inaugurals are opportune moments for jeremiads because the new president cannot yet be held responsible for the nation's problems. But different dynamics are at work when sitting presidents use policy jeremiads during their administrations.

POLICY JEREMIADS

If presidents are to lead they must periodically tackle vexing problems, and the most vexing problems for elected leaders are those that require voters to change their personal interpretive processes and conduct. In some of these situations presidents chastise their congregations in the process of advocating policy changes. This is a delicate task, since voters can reject the sermon and blame the nation's problems on the president's failure to lead. Two important policy addresses merit analysis as jeremiads: John Kennedy's June 11, 1963, address on civil rights and Jimmy Carter's "crisis of confidence" speech of July 15, 1979.

Kennedy on Civil Rights

Until June 1963 American presidents dealt with civil rights only as a legal issue, if at all. On September 24, 1957, President Eisenhower had urged the people of Little Rock to accept lawful integration of Central High School because "A foundation of our American way of life is our national respect for law" ([1957], p. 195). The Kennedy administration continued in this vein, lending little rhetorical assistance to civil rights demonstrators. Then, on June 11, 1963, Alabama Governor George Wallace stood in the "Schoolhouse Door" at the University of Alabama to forestall its integration. In remarks prior to his removal by federal authorities, Wallace argued against the federal government's legal authority to override state laws.

After two years of reluctance, President Kennedy chose to address the nation on television with a jeremiad that transformed civil rights from a legal issue to a moral one. Because events in Alabama had unfolded quickly, Kennedy speechwriter Theodore Sorensen had time to prepare only one draft of the address prior to the reading copy that was completed shortly before air time, and the president freely extemporized the conclusion (Windt, 1990). This jeremiad was understandably unpolished and the themes weave in and out, but the jeremiadic logic is unmistakable.

Kennedy's ancient truth was America's covenant to follow the Golden Rule. "This Nation was founded," said Kennedy, "on the principle that all men are created equal, and that the rights of every man are diminished when the rights of one man are threatened" ([1963], p. 197). As a corollary of that covenant:

It ought to be possible . . . for every American to enjoy the privileges of being American without regard to his race or his color. In short, every American ought to have the right to be treated as he would wish to be treated, as one would wish his children to be treated. But, this is not the case. (p. 198)

When chosen people stray from their covenant tribulations afflict them, and Kennedy described two kinds of affliction. First, he detailed the plight of American citizens who happened not to be Caucasian:

The Negro baby born in America today, regardless of the section of the Nation in which he was born, has about one-half as much chance of completing a high school as a white baby born in the same place on the same day, one-third as much chance of completing college, one-third as much chance of becoming a professional man, twice as much chance of becoming unemployed, about one-seventh as much chance of earning $10,000 a year, a life expectancy which is 7 years shorter, and the prospects of earning only half as much. (p. 198)

Lest his audience be unable to empathize with "the Negro's" plight, Kennedy invoked the Golden Rule:

If an American, because his skin is dark, cannot eat lunch in a restaurant open to the public, if he cannot send his children to the best public schools available, if he cannot vote for the public officials who represent him, if, in short, he cannot enjoy the full and free life which all of us want, then who among us would be content to have the color of his skin changed and stand in his place? Who among us would then be content with the counsels of patience and delay? (p. 198)

Kennedy castigated his people for forgetting the Golden Rule, thereby denying the American dream to millions of American citizens.

But even as Kennedy spoke for the disenfranchised and oppressed, his language perpetuated the underlying problem. While lamenting racial distinctions, he nevertheless addressed whites as "we" and "us" and described blacks in the third person. Moreover, the objects of his concern, regardless of their race, were males. Consequently, his call to recognize blacks as full-fledged American citizens is coupled with his implicit reinforcement of white males as the chosen people who must rectify the situation. Kennedy's call for change was not radical, but progressive.

Kennedy's progressive stance was also evident in his moderating of the language of Sorensen's draft. For example, "*The cesspools* of segregation and discrimination" became "*Difficulties,*" "A *social revolution* is at hand" became "a *great change,*" "This *is* an elementary right" became "This *seems to me,*" the "*shamefully* slow" pace of desegregation became the "*very*" slow pace. Even Sorensen's call for Congress "to act, *boldly*" to "give the *enforceable* right to be served in facilities which are open to the public" became Kennedy's call for Congress "to *act*" to "*give*" the right, a construction that changed Sorensen's call for protection of inalienable rights into the president's call for Congress to *give* those rights to black Americans (Sorensen, 1963).

Yet progress in civil rights had been delayed for centuries, and the chosen people had failed to recognize the urgency of reform. Kennedy, therefore, tackled the question of time by tying it to America's mission:

One hundred years of delay have passed since President Lincoln freed the slaves, yet their heirs, their grandsons, are not fully free. They are not yet freed from the bonds of injustice. They are not yet freed from social and economic oppression. And this Nation, for all its hopes and all its boasts, will not be fully free until all its citizens are free. (p. 199)

Lest the positive motivation of fulfilling America's destiny prove inadequate to the task at hand, Kennedy invoked powerful images of danger and destruction as negative sanctions: "The fires of frustration and discord are burning in every city, North and South, where legal remedies are not at hand. Redress is sought in the streets, in demonstrations, parades, and protests which create tensions and threaten violence and threaten lives" (p. 199). How, then, could the chosen people restore the Golden Rule, fulfill their destiny, and extinguish the fires of frustration?

"We face," said Kennedy, "a moral crisis as a country and as a people . . . that cannot be met by repressive police action, . . . by increased demonstrations in the streets, . . . [or] by token moves or talk" (p. 199); nor is it enough to "pin the blame on others." Instead, he said, "It is a time to act in the Congress, in your State and local legislative body *and, above all, in all of our daily lives* [italics added]. . . . Those who do nothing are inviting shame as well as violence. Those who act boldly are recognizing right as well as reality" (p. 199).

Nevertheless, Kennedy stopped short of endorsing, or even defending, the courageous Americans whose understanding of this covenant preceded his own (Miroff, 1976). Instead, he addressed the "parades and demonstrations" from the perspective of the inconvenienced white majority, saying that "We have a right to expect that the Negro community will be responsible, will uphold the law, but they have a right to expect that the law will be fair, that the Constitution will be color blind" (p. 202).

Kennedy proposed legislation to desegregate public establishments, to facilitate class action litigation, and to protect—but not to extend— voting rights. By coupling his call for moral reform with a legislative package he made civil rights into an agenda item that would later appeal to Lyndon Johnson, legislator extraordinaire.

President Kennedy took great pains to pre-empt the argument that segregation was a sectional issue. He raised the sectional concern three separate times. The third time he tied unity to the covenant, saying, "This is one country. It has become one country because all of us and all the people who came here had an equal chance to develop their talents" (p. 201). If Americans heeded Kennedy's call to live up to the Golden Rule, then black Americans would live better lives, the fires of frustration would subside, America would fulfill its destiny, and peace and freedom would be extended around the world.

Kennedy's civil rights jeremiad was an appropriate use of the Puritan form. He used it to stop sinful behavior and to return his followers to an ancient truth. But in the process he moderated social change by linguistically perpetuating white male dominance.

Carter's Crisis of Confidence

Jimmy Carter's most memorable speech may have been his "energy sermon" of July 15, 1979 (Hahn, 1980). The energy crisis first identified by President Nixon peaked during the summer of 1979 with a severe gasoline shortage that led many states to institute alternate-day gasoline-buying programs. An economically conservative Democrat, Carter found himself caught between liberal Democrats calling for gas rationing and more conservative Republicans who wanted market forces to control consumption. Worse, he found himself caught between his media advisor, his pollster, his domestic policy advisor, and his speechwriters.

Today few Americans recall the enthusiasm with which they greeted the Carter presidency. From January through March 1977 his approval ratings were above 70 percent—sustained ratings comparable to those of Kennedy, Johnson, and Reagan and higher than those of Truman, Eisenhower, Nixon, Ford, Bush, and Clinton. But approval of Carter's leadership began a steady twenty-seven month slide that bottomed out at 28 percent in late June 1979—an approval rating comparable to those of Nixon's final days (King & Ragsdale, 1988).

By July 1, 1979, President Carter faced three severe problems: (1) the energy crisis, (2) declining public confidence in his leadership, and (3) divisions among his advisors. The first two were the subject of his jeremiad, which was complicated by the discord among his advisors who provided Carter with four different interpretations of "his problem."

In February 1979, media advisor Gerald Rafshoon advised Carter to correct the operational deficiencies in his administration. "There is no hierarchy," wrote Rafshoon. "No one seems to be in charge. . . . Cabinet members contradict one another on major policy and it is never made clear who is speaking for the administration. People get reprimanded from time to time, but *no one ever gets fired*" (quoted by Holland, 1990, p. 65). As the time for the speech drew near, Rafshoon urged Carter toward bold language and personal accountability to rectify this operational deficiency:

a. Rather than saying . . . that we may make mistakes, I suggest you only emphasize boldness and innovation.
b. The section needs *either* a series of brief, clear specific directions and proposals ("I will propose . . ." "I will direct . . .") or a non-explicit summary of categories of effort to be outlined the next day, e.g., "I will propose . . ." (Rafshoon, 1979, p. 1)

It was Rafshoon's desire to have Carter personally take charge.

The second interpretation of "the problem" came from pollster Patrick Caddell. Caddell's polls told him that Americans were beset by a "crisis of confidence marked by a dwindling faith in the future" (Holland, 1990, p.65). Caddell urged Carter to project confidence and optimism to inspire people, and to frame the country's problems as opportunities. His advice to Carter about meeting with several governors illustrated this view: "It is important that you underscore your concern, your determination, and to some extent the burden of your responsibility. . . . Also, that you feel you're on the right track, you feel good about it, that you are confident" (Caddell, 1979, p. 2). Caddell worried that the country had a pervasive sense of malaise that undermined confidence in Carter's leadership. He was especially concerned that this diffuse demoralization would eventually be attributed to Carter's leadership. Thus he advised Carter to radiate confidence, optimism, and a readiness to face the energy challenge (Holland, 1990).

The third interpretation came from the speechwriting staff. They sent a stinging memo to Rafshoon that stressed the need for action. It said, in part, that

the country does not want or need another energy speech. It wants and needs energy actions. . . . The first priority is to let people know something is being done. . . . If "war" is the analogy we use for energy, then we have to fight the problem *like* a war with clear targets and victories—not like some complicated seven year lawsuit. . . . [W]e need the broadest based, broadest minded course of action that is specific and visionary. We can announce it anytime, anyplace. After we have decided to act. (Speechwriting Staff, 1979)

This memo may have influenced Rafshoon to urge Carter to take personal action. But if it did, Rafshoon's advice failed to convey fully the speechwriters' strong preference for policies.

The fourth interpretation of the problem came from domestic policy advisor Stuart Eizenstadt. It was Eizenstadt who urged Carter to skip his Hawaiian vacation after the Tokyo summit to meet with people about the crisis facing his administration. He also suggested that Carter engage in a polarizing effort with the Organization of Petroleum Exporting Countries (OPEC) as the villain (Holland, 1990). This strategy had the potential to unite the American people behind Carter's leadership, to attribute the economic and energy problems to OPEC, and to undermine his domestic critics' ability to attack him.

The president was scheduled to address the nation on July 5, 1979, and he was given a speech draft prior to his departure for Camp David on July 3. The speech planned for July 5 was stark in its presentation of three themes. The first part was Eizenstadt's message that OPEC was to blame for the energy and economic problems. The second section presented specific policy steps, as advocated by the speechwriters, to be undertaken personally by Carter, as Rafshoon had urged. The final portion introduced Caddell's crisis of confidence theme and pledged the president to address the public more frequently "not about false hopes or the painless solutions, but about the hard facts of our problems, and of how, if we work together as one nation, we will prevail" (Hertzberg,

Rafshoon & Eizenstadt, 1979). The draft was a clear, powerful narrative that merged the nation's problems into one, attributing them to a foreign cartel of which the president was not a part. It invited Americans to follow his lead, and it offered reasons and policies capable of satisfying the public's need for direction, optimism, confidence, and policy directing. But President Carter canceled the speech and set in motion the "crisis of confidence" speech of July 15.

In Carter's jeremiad of July 15 the chosen people faced Caddell's "crisis of confidence." In Carter's analysis,

The confidence that we have always had as a people is not simply some romantic dream or a proverb in a dusty book that we read just on the Fourth of July. It is the idea which founded our Nation and has guided our development as a people. Confidence in the future has supported everything else. . . . Confidence has defined our course and has served as a link between generations. We've always believed in something called progress. We've always had faith that the days of our children would be better than our own. ([1979], pp. 258–259)

That traditional confidence grew out of our sense of divine mission, because "We always believed that we were part of a great movement of humanity itself called democracy, involved in the search for freedom and that belief has always strengthened us in our purpose" (p. 259).

Like Roosevelt and Reagan, Carter observed that the "changes did not happen overnight" (p. 259). They had come upon us gradually over the last generation, "years that were filled with shocks and tragedy" including the murders of John Kennedy, Robert Kennedy, and Martin Luther King, Jr., as well as Vietnam, Watergate, and "a growing dependence on foreign oil" (pp. 259–260).

Fortunately, chosen people who have lost faith in their sense of purpose are sometimes given divine opportunities to test their mettle. In Carter's hands the energy crisis provided just such a test of faith. "So, the solution of our energy crisis can also help us to conquer the crisis of the spirit in our country," said Carter. "It can rekindle our sense of unity, our confidence in the future, and give our Nation and all of us individually a new sense of purpose" (pp. 263–264). A people less fortunate would not be blessed with such a challenge. But "On the battlefield of energy . . . we can seize control again of our common destiny" (p. 261).

How should America respond to gas shortages? Carter went against the advice of his speechwriters, who had called for clear, coherent policies. Instead, Carter said, the answer was faith. Note Carter's use of "faith," italicized four times in this brief passage:

First of all, we must face the truth, and then we can change our course. We simply must have *faith* in each other, *faith* in our ability to govern ourselves, and *faith* in the future of this Nation. Restoring that *faith* and that confidence to America is now the most important task we face. (p. 260)

Only when Americans faced the truth and regained their faith and confidence would gasoline pour from the pumps.

The jeremiad casts its speaker as prophet, enhancing that prophet's prospects for credit and blame as others decide whether he is a true prophet or a false prophet. Carter's jeremiad had the potential to assert his moral leadership while delegating to others the practical political problems. But Carter characteristically took personal responsibility for both moral leadership and practical problem solving. This was a bold but unwise decision, because prophets win followers with their visions; few have been admired for their practical problem-solving abilities.

Carter made his own personal leadership central to his jeremiad, using "I" six times as often as "we." This is especially ironic because he said that a visitor to Camp David had told him that "The strength we need will not come from the White House, but from every house in America" (pp. 260–261). Nevertheless, after asking what *we* could do, he explained what *he* would do. Notice the fourteen italicized self-references in the following passage:

I am tonight setting a clear goal for the energy policy of the United States. . . . *I* will use *my* Presidential authority to set import quotas. *I'm* announcing tonight that for 1979 and 1980, *I* will forbid the entry into this country of one drop of foreign oil more than these goals allow. . . . *I* am asking for the most massive peacetime commitment of funds and resources in our Nation's history. . . . *I* propose the creation of an energy security corporation to . . . issue up to $5 billion in energy bonds, and *I* especially want them to be in small denominations. . . . Moreover, *I* will soon submit legislation [to] Congress . . . *I'm* asking Congress to mandate . . . *I* will urge Congress to create an energy mobilization board . . . *I'm* proposing a bold conservation program . . . *I* ask Congress to give me authority . . . *I'm* proposing tonight an extra $10 billion dollars to issue bonds. (pp. 262–263)

In short, Carter asked to sit in the hot seat. That had been Rafshoon's advice, and Caddell's fear.

Carter compounded his problems when he discussed the certainty of the chosen people's inevitable triumph. Predictably, "we" were destined to win. But here we see Caddell's optimism combine with Rafshoon's self-references: "You know we can do it. We have the resources. We have more oil in our shale alone than several Saudi Arabias. We have more coal than any nation on Earth. We have the world's highest level of technology. We have the most skilled work force, with innovative genius" (p. 264). Why, then, was the prophet so measured in his enthusiasm and so personal in his distribution of responsibility, as indicated by the seven italicized "I"s in the following paragraph?

I do not promise you that this struggle for freedom will be easy. *I* do not promise a quick way out of our Nation's problems, when the truth is that the only way out is an all-out effort. What *I* do promise you is that *I* will lead our fight, and *I* will enforce fairness in our struggle, and *I* will ensure honesty. And above all, *I* will act [all italics added]. (p. 264)

Perhaps his lack of confidence in the chosen people was related to their lack of confidence in his leadership. More likely it was Rafshoon's preference for "a harsh warning in the harshest of terms" (Rafshoon, 1979, p. 2).

Contradictions abound in this speech because it was written by advisors in conflict with one another. If confidence is the key to the future, why does Carter propose so many policy changes? If *our* lack of faith is the problem, why is *he* the prime mover? If our individual households have the key, why is the White House acting? If confidence in Carter's leadership is so important, why does he begin the speech with six biting indictments of that leadership such as "Mr. President, you are not leading this Nation—you're just managing the Government" (p. 257)? If he has led so poorly, why should we support his new personal initiatives? And if we are destined to win with or without confidence that we will win, why is Carter so measured in his enthusiasm? Is he more lacking in confidence than are his people?

A large part of the problem was that Jimmy Carter compromised the rhetorical advantages provided him by jeremiadic logic. The July 5 address could have united Americans behind Carter by polarizing them against OPEC (Eizenstadt's view), but the president canceled it. The replacement speech was a jeremiad. This had considerable potential because jeremiads cast their speakers as prophets who admonish the chosen people to end their tribulations by mending their ways (Caddell's view). A clear advantage of that strategy, here, is that it would have absolved the prophet from practical responsibility for the problems. But after doing so, Carter explicitly reclaimed personal practical leadership and all the risks of personal accountability (Rafshoon's view).

By reclaiming personal responsibility Carter created a dilemma for his presidency. If the energy crisis truly was a crisis of confidence amenable to solution only through reaffirmation of faith, then the practical steps Carter advocated were neither necessary nor sufficient to end the tribulations. But if Carter could not ascertain whether the energy crisis was a divine challenge or a practical policy problem, he could not expect to nurture either public faith or confidence in his prophetic leadership.

Presidential approval polls are an imperfect measure of rhetorical success because individual speeches are but one variable in citizens' perception of the president's success. Carter's April 5 address had delivered bad news about energy, and his public approval dropped below 30 percent (King & Ragsdale, 1988, p. 304). It stayed below 30 percent until the Crisis of Confidence jeremiad of July 15 provided an 11 percent boost. It looked as though Carter had begun to turn the corner, and his subsequent addresses in Kansas City and Detroit were well received. Then, four days later, attention turned to Carter's dramatic overhaul of his administration. This purge of his core governing coalition was remarkably like Nixon's disastrous housecleaning the morning after his re-election victory (Nixon, 1978), and it was the kind of change that Ford managed to avoid with his pardoning rhetoric. The move undermined Carter's effort to inspire confidence in his leadership, and he finished July with just 3 percent higher approval ratings than he had received before the speech. Moreover, he remained in the low 30 percent approval range until four months later, when the Iranian hostage crisis gave him a twenty-point lift.

Those disapproving of Carter's leadership continued to outnumber his supporters by a 5-3 ratio, and they seized on the mistakes in his jeremiad to advance their critique. For them, the reorganization illustrated the dark side of Carter's message—admitting a lack of leadership, blaming the chosen people for the country's problems, and lacking faith in America. All these problems can be traced to mishandled elements of his energy jeremiad, a speech mishandled because it was, literally, never made clear who was speaking for the White House.

POLITICAL IMPLICATIONS OF PRESIDENTIAL JEREMIADS

The jeremiad is an archetypal form in American rhetoric that takes on significant political repercussions when used by presidents. The cases of Roosevelt, Reagan, Kennedy, and Carter suggest that presidential jeremiads are both politically functional and dysfunctional.

Positive Functions of Presidential Jeremiads

Jeremiadic logic can facilitate the accomplishment of four political functions. First, jeremiads have the potential to enhance social cohesion by invoking Americans' sense of exceptionalism, by addressing them as a chosen people, by framing immediate problems with "Ancient Truths," and by invoking tenets of the American civil religion. This can be especially helpful in times of disorientation and political gridlock, because jeremiads transcend immediate differences by discussing fundamental truths that unify: our willingness to work hard, our resentment of government intrusion, our commitment to the Golden Rule, and our national self-confidence. Jeremiadic logic enables a rhetor to meet contradictions head-on and then to transcend them with a restoration of ancient American truths.

Second, jeremiads have the potential to provide a sense of order and security among disparate phenomena by linking current problems to a glorious past and a bright future. All four presidents spoke during periods of confusion, doubt, and uncertainty. Roosevelt and Reagan each executed an appropriate jeremiad that provided a parsimonious explanation for his chosen people's economic problems. Kennedy used America's institutionalization of the Golden Rule to pre-empt segregationists' use of regionalism and states' rights as counterarguments. Carter attributed the energy crisis to America's loss of confidence, but he sent conflicting signals about the means of restoring that confidence. Every jeremiad provides a source of order for a confused community, because its essential logic is that Americans' problems result from a lack of commitment to their divine mission. Therefore, the greater the chaos and the more abundant the contradictions, the more powerful is the logic of jeremiadic order.

Third, jeremiads can justify change in society. They provide a familiar logic through which presidents call for changes when the "real problems" have been misunderstood. This is important because the constraints of legislative debate make incremental decision making the norm in American politics. This, in turn, means that presidents normally choose either to tie new policies to existing rationales or to find new rationales for existing policies. But jeremiads enable presidents to advocate more new policies tied to new analyses, because it roots them both in ancient, enduring American truths. Roosevelt could lasso the free marketers and Reagan could reign in government because both presidents were restoring the ancient truths on which business and government in America were founded. Kennedy could propose legislation that governed human relations because of the Golden Rule, and Carter could propose energy policies to restore our faith in ourselves.

Fourth, jeremiads cast their speakers as prophets such that presidential jeremiads elevate the president relative to other political actors. Jeremiads cast presidents as ordained interpreters of the national covenant while casting everyone else as either members of the congregation or false prophets. Any president, with the possible exception of the unelected Gerald Ford, possesses power resources by virtue of popular sovereignty, constitutional authority, and role expectations. By speaking to the nation in jeremiads, presidents don the vestments of divine sovereignty as well. Tulis (1987) observed that nineteenth-century presidents spoke rarely and sought constitutional authority for their positions and that twentieth-century presidents speak frequently with reference to moral, rather than constitutional, authority. Presidential jeremiads are an important facet of this increasingly sermonic presidency.

Political Dysfunctions of Presidential Jeremiads

Jeremiads are not, however, always beneficial. First, presidential jeremiads mystify practical problem solving by disconnecting problems from solutions. Let us be clear: jeremiads are appropriate when, but only when, societal tribulations really are divine sanctions for inattention to a covenant. But surely some of America's problems result from our incessant tinkering with matters unrelated to the covenant. Moreover, problems arise when the policies proposed to restore the covenant are implemented: How heavily do God and the Founders want us to tax capital gains? Do God and the Founders want us to maintain 150,000 troops in post–Cold War Europe or bring 50,000 of them home to face unemployment? Of the four jeremiads studied, only Kennedy's treatment of civil rights seems to address issues of truly spiritual import. The other three presidents disconnected economic problems from their economic causes and, therefore, from their economic solutions the better to solidify their claims to presidential authority. Indeed, all four presidents quickly proposed legislative packages to address these allegedly spiritual problems.

Second, jeremiads both reify and distort the American covenant. Federalist writers and Alexis de Tocqueville are widely used as sages on the proper meaning of the covenant. Yet implicit in the Constitution is the importance of flexibility. The Framers' interpretations are instructive but not binding, as their staunch belief in the rationality of human beings would dictate.

Jeremiads evoke a conception of agreement among the Framers that reifies what are actually temporarily ascendant interpretations of the American dream while subverting other interpretations (Fisher, 1973). Kennedy, for example, found the rationale for integration in covenants written by slaveholders like Jefferson. In short, presidential jeremiads reify features of history by freezing them in time and ignoring the marketplace of ideas in which each feature reached its ascendancy. Moreover, the act of connecting today's problems with 200-year-old truths requires presidential speechwriters to revise those truths in fundamental ways. This leads presidential jeremiahs to wreak havoc with the Constitution.

Thus, the third dysfunction is that presidential jeremiads undermine the constitutional covenant itself. The Framers' commitment to flexibility led them to write a brief and general constitution rather than a lengthy, extended document designed to cover every eventuality. The Framers worried about a demagogue's potential to fan the flames of unreason and, thus, to slip the constraints of the delicately balanced federal system. Tulis reminded us that "The founders worried especially about the danger that a powerful executive might pose to the system if power were derived from the role of popular leader. *The Federalist* literally begins and ends with this issue" (1987, p. 27). They would not have been comforted by the prospect of presidential jeremiads.

Presidential jeremiads loosen constitutional checks on the president by reconstituting legal-political issues as tests of faith. Ironically, the presidential jeremiads that urge us to keep faith with the Framers' covenants ignore, and often circumvent, the very checks and balances that those Framers wrote into that covenant because of their mistrust of powerful executives. All the presidents discussed justified presidential activism by stressing a covenant that had actually created a more limited presidency.

The fourth political dysfunction is that jeremiads inhibit dissent and significant social change. As others have noted, social change through jeremiads consists of variations on a theme, with that theme itself insulated from scrutiny. (Bercovitch, 1978; Murphy, 1990). Precisely because presidential jeremiads justify change through a restoration of "first principles," they preclude serious examination of those first principles. At the time of Roosevelt's inaugural a variety of Americans had lost faith in capitalism and many thought that the fundamental assumptions of capitalism needed examination, but Roosevelt's address made it clear that those assumptions were not open for discussion. The problem was the moneychangers, not the system that required money changing. Reagan blamed America's economic distress not on its economic institutions but on governmental interference with those institutions. Kennedy's civil rights address assumed that the chosen white people should extend equal rights to black males, leaving unexamined the questions of inalienable rights for women.

Because jeremiads establish one interpretation and application of a particular ancient truth as pre-eminent, they undermine other interpretations and applications of ancient truths. By undermining competing analyses of the nation's problems presidential jeremiads inhibit legitimate public discussion and dissent. Few leaders worry about undermining their critics, but it is dysfunctional from the perspective of democratic theory. It is also a pragmatic dysfunction, because it complicates the task of building coalitions with political actors whose claims to morality and patriotism have been undermined.

In short, jeremiads are politically dysfunctional for constitutional democracy because they mystify practical problem solving, they reify and distort the American covenant, they undermine the constitutional covenant, and they inhibit dissent and significant social change.

CONCLUSIONS

This chapter has described the American jeremiad and the reasons for its prevalence in American rhetoric. It has examined two inaugural jeremiads and two policy jeremiads and summarized the political functions and dysfunctions of this important rhetorical form.

The Roosevelt and Reagan inaugurals were effectively executed jeremiads that mirrored each other in many respects. Taken together they illustrate that jeremiadic logic can facilitate the fulfillment of the demands of the inaugural genre. Kennedy's address on civil rights and

Carter's energy speech were policy jeremiads that combined efforts to reform public behavior with legislative initiatives. Kennedy's jeremiad marked a turning point in American history: never before had an American president publicly urged equal rights for all Americans as a moral obligation, nor has any of his successors taken issue with Kennedy's jeremiad. Carter, however, coupled a jeremiadic call for reaffirmation of faith with a complicated list of practical policy initiatives to be undertaken personally by the president and a lengthy critique of his shortcoming as a leader. Indeed, the mishandling of the jeremiad form itself explains a good deal of the public's negative reaction to the speech.

Rhetorical choices have political implications. When presidents use jeremiadic form to structure their arguments they reshape, subtly but fundamentally, the political landscape. Presidential jeremiads can enhance social cohesion, provide a sense of order and security, justify change, and elevate the presidency. But they also mystify practical problem solving, reify and distort the covenant, undermine constitutional checks and balances, and inhibit dissent and significant social change. Jeremiads are not inherently good or bad. It is the use to which they are put that determines their value.

Students of the presidency searching for factors that influence policy deliberations in a society that is long on presidential advocacy, personal adulation, and self-righteousness cannot afford to ignore the role of jeremiadic logic in the conduct of the rhetorical presidency. Many other kinds of variables contributed to the development of this presidency. But communication shapes, and is shaped by, roles and relationships. As presidents have relied more heavily on public persuasion in this century, their rhetorical choices have contributed to a redefinition of presidential leadership and its relationship to the public, the Congress, the private sector, and the Constitution.

REFERENCES

Bellah, R. N. (1967, Winter). Civil religion in America. *Daedalus, 67,* 1–21.
Bercovitch, S. (1978). *The American jeremiad.* Madison: University of Wisconsin Press.
Bormann, E. (1977). Fetching good out of evil: A rhetorical use of calamity. *Quarterly Journal of Speech, 63,* 130–139.
Bormann, E. R. (1985). *The force of fantasy: Restoring the American dream.* Carbondale: Southern Illinois University Press.

Caddell, P. H. (1979). Memorandum, "Talking points governor's meeting tonight," July 6. Box 137, Office of the staff secretary, "Camp David [1]," Jimmy Carter Library.

Campbell, K. K., & Jamieson, K. H. (1990). *Deeds done in words*. Chicago: University of Chicago Press.

Carter, J. [1979]. Energy and national malaise, July 15. In C. A. Smith & K. B. Smith (Eds.), *The president and the public: Rhetoric and national leadership* (pp. 256–265). Lanham, MD: University Press of America, 1985.

Edwards, J. (1741). Sinners in the hands of an angry God. In J. Andrews & D. Zarefsky (Eds.), *American voices: Significant speeches in American history* (pp. 21–32). New York: Longman.

Eisenhower, D. E. [1957]. The situation in Little Rock, September 24. In C. A. Smith & K. B. Smith (Eds.), *The president and the public: Rhetoric and national leadership* (pp. 192–196). Lanham, MD: University Press of America, 1985.

Erickson, P. D. (1985). *Reagan speaks: The making of an American myth*. New York: New York University Press.

Fisher, W. R. (1973). Reaffirmation and subversion of the American dream. *Quarterly Journal of Speech, 59*, 160–167.

Greenstein, F. I. (Ed.). (1983). *The Reagan presidency: An early assessment*. Baltimore: Johns Hopkins University Press.

Hahn, D. F. (1980). Flailing the profligate: Carter's energy sermon of 1979. *Presidential Studies Quarterly, 10*, 583–587.

Hertzberg, R., Rafshoon, J., & Eizenstadt, S. (1979). Memorandum and draft, "Energy speech," 7-30. Box 46, Office of the Director of Communications, "Proposed speech, 7-5-79," Jimmy Carter Library.

Holland, J. W. (1990). The great gamble: Jimmy Carter and the 1979 energy crisis. *Prologue* (Spring), 63–79.

Johannesen, R. L. (1986). Ronald Reagan's economic jeremiad. *Central States Speech Journal, 37*, 79–89.

Kennedy, J. F. [1963]. The desegregation of the University of Alabama, June 11. In C. A. Smith & K. B. Smith (Eds.), *The president and the public: Rhetoric and national leadership* (pp. 197–202). Lanham, MD: University Press of America, 1985.

King, G., & Ragsdale, L. (1988). *The elusive executive*. Washington, DC: Congressional Quarterly.

Miller, P. (1953). *The New England mind: From colony to Providence*. Cambridge, MA: Harvard University Press.

Miroff, B. (1976). *Pragmatic illusions: The presidential politics of John F. Kennedy*. New York: Longman.

Murphy, J. J. (1990). "A time of shame and sorrow": Robert F. Kennedy and the American jeremiad. *Quarterly Journal of Speech, 76*, 401–414.

Nixon, R. M. (1978). *RN: The memoirs of Richard Nixon*. New York: Grosset & Dunlop.

Rafshoon, J. (1979). Memorandum. "The speech," July 12. Box 139, Office of the staff secretary, "Camp David [2]," Jimmy Carter Library.

Reagan, R. [1981]. Inaugural address, January 20. In C. A. Smith & K. B. Smith (Eds.), *The president and the public: Rhetoric and national leadership* (pp. 33–39). Lanham, MD: University Press of America, 1985.

Ritter, K. (1979). *Significant form and rhetorical criticism: The jeremiad and the rhetoric of the American revolution*. Paper presented at the meeting of the Central States Speech Association.

Ritter, K. (1980). American political rhetoric and the jeremiad tradition: Presidential nomination acceptance addresses, 1960–76. *Central States Speech Journal, 31*, 153–171.

Ritter, K. (1993). Lyndon Johnson's inaugural address: The jeremiad and national policy. In H. R. Ryan (Ed.), *Rhetorical studies of presidential inaugural addresses* (pp. 195–208). Westport, CT: Greenwood.

Ritter, K., & Henry, D. (1992). *Ronald Reagan: The great communicator*. Westport, CT: Greenwood.

Rogin, M. (1987). *Ronald Reagan, the movie: And other episodes in political demonology*. Berkeley: University of California Press.

Roosevelt, F. D. [1933]. First inaugural address, March 4. In C. A. Smith & K. B. Smith (Eds.), *The president and the public: Rhetoric and national leadership* (pp. 19–23). Lanham, MD: University Press of America, 1985.

Smith, C. R., & Hyde, M. J. (1991). Rethinking "the public": The role of emotion in being-with-others. *Quarterly Journal of Speech, 77*, 446–466.

Sorensen, T. C. (1963). TCS—2nd draft, Radio and TV report to the American people on civil rights, June 11. Box 45, President's Office Files, Speech Files, John Fitzgerald Kennedy Library.

Speechwriting Staff (1979). Memorandum, "Energy speech," June 29. Box 46, Office of the Director of Communications, "Proposed speech, 7-5-79," Jimmy Carter Library.

Tulis, J. K. (1987). *The rhetorical presidency*. Princeton, NJ: Princeton University Press.

Wills, G. (1987). *Reagan's America: Innocents abroad*. Garden City, NY: Doubleday.

Windt, T. O. (1990). *Presidents and protesters: Political rhetoric in the 1960s*. Tuscaloosa: University of Alabama Press.

Zarefsky, D. (1986). *President Johnson's war on poverty*. Tuscaloosa: University of Alabama Press.

Zulick, M. (1992). The agony of Jeremiah: On the dialogic invention of prophetic ethos. *Quarterly Journal of Speech, 78*, 125–148.

7

Presidential Mobilization for Sacrifice

Individuals and nations periodically forego immediate need gratifications to attain a future goal. Millions of people trim their daily expenses to buy new homes, students postpone their entrance into the work force to achieve long-term professional and personal growth, and nations call on their citizens to sacrifice their personal interests for the greater good of the state.

Who "we" are as a community is determined partially by our conceptions of citizenship. The individual's relation to the state is the subject of a continuing debate in political philosophy. Individualists (Dworkin, 1977; Rawls, 1971) contend that the individual defines "self" and acts in rational ways, sometimes as part of a community. But because it is the individual's perspective that counts, it is rational for individuals to use the public arena to satisfy their personal needs and even to ignore the community's needs when they fail to address the individual's needs.

Communalists (Sandel, 1982; Taylor, 1973) respond that the individuals are defined by their relation to the state, and that community membership may be the essence of moral behavior. One communalist, David Miller (1992), argues that citizenship

is not just a matter of possessing rights, even if those are broadly interpreted. . . . [One] must act as a citizen, that is as a member of a collectivity who is committed to advancing its common good. . . . [M]oreover, he [*sic*] cannot regard politics merely as an arena in which to pursue his [*sic*] private interests. (p. 96)

The individualist and communalist camps both offer strong arguments, which is why the debate continues. Our interpretive systems model transcends the debate between individualists and communalists. Each is an academic community united by its own interactions and shared disbeliefs. Moreover, each group needs the other because neither position makes sense without the other: it is the rhetorical tension of the dialectic that sustains, verifies, and energizes them. So it is for society.

Each of us has individual needs, each of us has a sense of the shared needs of the various interpretive communities to which we belong, and each of us has a grudging respect for the reasonable needs of others. So it is that we carry on the individualist-communalist debate in our own minds. We think in arguments: sometimes we know the philosophical bases, but usually not; sometimes our symbolization of the issues is well differentiated, articulated, and integrated, but more often it is anecdotal and clumsy.

We therefore argue that there are times when the broader needs of the state take precedence over the individual needs of the citizen. The state has a right, even a moral obligation at times, to promote actions for the good of the community that cause individual discomfort and sacrifice. But the terms and specifics are always arguable, and it is the interplay of arguments that influences social change. Sacrificing entails the giving up or foregoing of something valued for the sake of something greater. Individuals ultimately determine for themselves when a sacrifice is appropriate. But they reach that decision after communicating with others and after rehearsing and sorting in private the arguments they have learned.

Who speaks for the whole nation when a societal sacrifice is required? Rejecting divine right and the rule of the jungle leaves a limited number of options. Religious leaders speak to their interpretive communities with various appeals for behavioral change and personal denial. But without an established religion we have no established clerics to speak for the nation. Yet there is the American civil religion with its "bully pulpit" of the presidency (Bellah, 1967; Fairbanks, 1981). Our democratic creed teaches us to use votes to link the governors and the governed. Federalism has created a system of regionally based constituencies, but only the president and vice president have a national constituency.

The president of the United States has the symbolic function of representing all Americans. As the sole elected official with a national constituency, he is able to articulate the dominant interpretation of the public interest and, sometimes, to establish an emerging interest as dominant. Additionally, the expanding nature of the modern presidency and the proliferation of interpretive communities have increasingly led Americans to look to the president for direction and priority setting. Indeed, that is the essence of the rhetorical presidency.

Constitutionally, the president has substantial power to direct the executive branch. But to be a national leader the president must also encourage cooperation: from the rest of government, from nongovernmental institutions, and from the people. Thus, when a national sacrifice is necessary, it is the president who is responsible for persuading citizens to act in the "public good."

This presidential responsibility occurs during peace and war. As the nation has moved from an era of gratifying abundance into a time of limited growth, some adjustments in life-style have become necessary. Government-directed alterations in individual behavior are never easy to induce, but the promotion of a nationally oriented sacrifice program is particularly difficult when people are accustomed to self-interest and advancement.

Investigations of governmental attempts to modify mass consumption patterns can help us to identify the components of successful sacrifice campaigns. Specifically, President Truman's famine emergency plan and President Carter's energy plan will be considered as attempts to persuade Americans to sacrifice with respect to their consumption of scarce commodities.

STRATEGIES FOR INDUCING SACRIFICE

Mobilizing is persuasion. The mobilizer must attract, unite, organize, and orient people toward the attainment of a goal. The president as mobilizer must find the arguments or appeals to which the appropriate individuals will respond. Presidents can try to mobilize entire interpretive communities into coalitions or they can attempt to personally rally individuals. In either case, presidents and their surrogates create a cafeteria of rhetorical appeals from which citizens can find something to satisfy their individual and community needs.

The president as mobilizer cannot settle for ordinary political acquiescence. Instead, the mobilizing president must spur individual and collective action. These actions can be induced with either compulsory or voluntary strategies, but voluntary compliance is generally to be preferred. If millions of people are to voluntarily prefer concerted action to passivity, the new action will have to fulfill one or more of their personal needs. In other words, the rhetoric of mobilization must perform an array of psychological functions for citizens so that they will perform mobilization functions for the president.

There are two basic ways in which governments can alter citizens' behavior. One is the use of coercion, or pressuring strategies (Olsen, 1978). Such strategies involve a structural approach to change. They use laws or controls to compel individuals and groups to engage in the desired activities. The rationale behind this approach is that changes in laws lead to changes in behavior, and that behavioral change will encourage the attitude change that insures continuation of the desired behavior. Two examples of coercive strategies are food rationing during World War II and the 55 MPH speed limit to conserve energy. The coercive approach is a straightforward approach to change that utilizes the state's monopoly on legitimate force, but serious dangers inhere in coercion.

First, representative democracies should rarely need to force a majority of their citizens to do what the government deems necessary. Adequate communication between governors and the governed should serve an educative role, leading people toward cooperation in most instances (Smith, 1981). But even strategically, coercion will often prove ineffective unless a substantial commitment of resources is made to vigilantly enforce the regulations. At worst, the program will fail and the government's legitimacy will be challenged as well.

The irony is that even government coercion entails persuasion. The government must inform people of the mobilization campaign and its sanctions. It must persuade them of its ability and willingness to use those sanctions, and of its ability to achieve its goal, even over their opposition. This is not always easy. The rhetorical irony of coercion is this: successful coercion requires persuasion, so if the government is going to justify coercion with persuasion, it might better use persuasion to achieve voluntary compliance.

Voluntary compliance is the second approach to mobilization. It requires that the president be rhetorically attuned to the needs of people. That task is complicated by the fact that the incongruent interpretive communities respond differently to the same discourse. Thus to mobilize, the president must build a coalition of supporters with a successful public campaign. Whether coercive or voluntary, the public campaign needs to use a blend of five strategies of persuasion. The major strategies for inducing voluntary compliance are a self-improvement strategy, an exemplification strategy, an incentive strategy, the hanging sword strategy, and a humanitarian strategy.

In the self-improvement strategy the government attempts to show how one can better fulfill one's personal needs by adopting new behaviors that, almost coincidentally, serve the public good. The needs of the individual and the community converge when understood in the new way. Such campaigns have transformed the status ascribed to driving large cars and abusing drugs; and they have emphasized the health and beauty benefits of walking to satisfy people's personal needs for fitness and attractiveness, while saving gasoline in the process. The self-improvement strategy addresses people who comply with government directives when the new behaviors provide personal need satisfactions, not because they can help other people or solve problems.

Exemplification necessitates that those who recommend a change enact it for the public. Thus, when President Truman called for a significant reduction in bread consumption, the White House reduced its own bread consumption (Lee & Cohan, 1946). The egalitarian theme in American political rhetoric makes it imprudent for leaders to ask more of their followers than they themselves are prepared to sacrifice. Furthermore, those setting the example need to publicize their actions and to indicate the continuing nature of their behavior, lest it be dismissed by the public as a token act. Those individuals and groups who follow the directives can be used as models to indicate the program's success and to stimulate a bandwagon effect and a positive spiral of public opinion (Noelle-Neumann, 1984).

The third strategy for motivating the public is to provide economic incentives to sacrifice. Pricing uses cost as an incentive to achieve compliance with desired goals (Olsen, 1978). When the cost of noncompliance with a government campaign is unacceptably high, individuals should prefer cooperation. Following this strategy the rapid increase in the cost of heating fuel and gasoline should have produced a concerted effort by consumers to lower their home thermostats and to drive less. The Federal Energy Administration's 1977 national telephone survey concluded, in part, that rising prices were not enough to change consumption patterns (Milstein, 1978), but "higher fuel rates" was, nevertheless, the most frequent reason given by those who did conserve (Olsen, 1978). The lesson is that pricing induced many Americans to conserve because it addressed their needs, but it left many other Americans' needs unmet.

Tax credits for weatherproofing and certificates of achievement for energy efficient construction are other ways of applying the incentive strategy. Basically, voluntary cooperation results from individuals believing that they can reap greater personal benefits from compliance than from ignoring the government's advice. This motivational strategy can hurt the less affluent consumers, particularly when it proves ineffective.

The fourth strategy for promoting voluntary compliance is the hanging sword strategy, so named because it portrays doom as the inevitable consequence of noncompliance. Crucial to the success of this strategy are the credibility of the president and the citizens' belief that the danger is real. President Truman was probably credible when he told the nation on April 19, 1946, that "We cannot doubt that at this moment many people in the famine-stricken homes of Europe and Asia are dying of hunger" ([1946d], p. 215). But according to a *New York Times* poll ("Survey," 1977) only half of those surveyed believed that the oil-supply situation was as serious as Carter had reported. This strategy requires either a belief in, or some visible proof of, the threatened danger and its immediacy.

The final strategy, humanitarianism, also stresses danger and depends upon the credibility of the president, but it emphasizes the need for us to sacrifice in order to help others. To be effective this strategy must convince people (1) that a real need for sacrifice exists, (2) that their personal sacrifice will help significantly to alleviate that need, and (3) that everyone in the society—individuals and communities—is sharing in the sacrifice. Failure to establish any of these three arguments weakens the persuasive effort. Relieving hunger was a problem that Truman properly couched in humanitarian terms. "We would not be Americans," said Truman, "if we did not wish to share our comparative plenty with suffering people. I am sure I speak for every American when I say the United States is determined to do everything in its power to relieve the famine of half the world" ([1946d], p. 215). President Carter also used humanitarian appeals to conserve so that *all* Americans could have the energy they required. But his explanation of the program failed to meet the three criteria we have just outlined. Particularly, surveys found that many Americans believed their group would be unfairly burdened by the energy plan (Gottlieb, 1978).

In sum, the need for sacrifice campaigns occurs periodically in the nation's history. These campaigns need to be directed by the people's national spokesman, the president. Both coercive and voluntary approaches can be employed to induce these societywide changes. Voluntary compliance can be sought through the self-improvement, exemplification, incentive, hanging sword, or humanitarian strategies.

SACRIFICE CAMPAIGNS

Truman's famine relief program and Carter's energy program were chosen as examples of large-scale campaigns that asked the American people for sacrifices. The food and energy plans share at least four significant characteristics. Both programs were identified with, and personally promoted by, presidents. In both cases, the public was asked to respond immediately to the directions being issued from the Executive Office to meet an imminent threat. Both plans required a sacrifice from the American people to reach a necessary goal. Finally, although neither program relied entirely on voluntary cooperation, both stressed that success of the programs depended on the individual voluntary actions of the American people. Despite their similarities, they also have glaring differences that should be noted before we compare them.

Perhaps the greatest difference between these two programs concerns the spirit of the times in which they were implemented. Truman operated in the immediate aftermath of World War II, a time of extensive national sacrifice. People were accustomed to putting aside personal desires for public needs, and they were accustomed to presidential directives. They had seen what the concerted effort of the American people could accomplish for the war effort, and they had little reason to doubt that individual efforts would produce results in peacetime as well. They believed that their government was legitimate and truthful, and that their new president needed their support. Indeed, when we compare the public approval levels of Presidents Truman through Reagan three months into their presidencies, we find that Truman's 87 percent was the highest of the group (King & Ragsdale, 1988, p. 294). All these factors point to a population that would respond well to one more request by a president for sacrifice.

On the other hand, these postwar Americans had been sacrificing, at times severely, for four years. Their lives had been restricted by numerous government policies that were just beginning to be lifted. For some, making one more sacrifice by not eating the foods that they could only now afford was quite difficult. Furthermore, some Americans felt that Americans had already sacrificed sufficiently to help the world. "No food for Germans!" wrote a New York City woman to President Truman to complain about his call for yet another sacrifice. "Haven't we lost enuf [sic] sons without adding our money? When Americans are bankrupt, who will feed us?" (McCarthy, 1957). Even in postwar America, Truman needed to mobilize the people behind the famine emergency program, because their support was not automatic.

President Carter spoke to a society in 1977 that was not accustomed to working together for a united purpose. Public attachment to the federal government in the aftermath of Vietnam and Watergate was much lower than it had been in the early Truman years. The energy plan's appeal for conservation was addressed to a population that turned a cynical ear to the president. Thus, the times in which the famine and energy programs were promoted were distinctly different.

The two programs also differed in their substance and implementation. There are differences between reducing the consumption of food and the consumption of energy. Although food is physiologically necessary and most energy consumption is not, one food can be substituted for another whereas most energy conservation leads to physical discomfort. In addition, President Truman directed most of the famine relief effort from within the executive branch, whereas President Carter's energy plan required substantial congressional action. Comparisons of these two campaigns suggest the difficulties of presidential mobilization.

TRUMAN'S FAMINE RELIEF PROGRAM

The devastation of World War II left millions of people on the brink of starvation. President Truman responded with a nationwide famine relief program to supplement the relief efforts of the United Nations. On April 19, 1946, Truman asked the national radio audience to conserve food. This brief address included all the sacrificing strategies discussed except pricing.

The April 19 address emphasized the humanitarian theme in lines such as: "Surely we will not turn our backs on the millions of human beings begging for just a crust of bread" ([1946d], p. 215).

Truman cited the United States Government as setting a good example of exporting wheat and supporting conservation. But the hanging sword nevertheless dangled over the world. The United States was in danger because it could never be safe in an unsafe world. "Millions will surely die unless we eat less and a sound world order can never be built upon a foundation of human misery" (Truman [1946d], p. 215).

But alongside these lofty goals Truman used the self-improvement appeal. "I am glad here and now to renew an appeal which I made the other day. I said then that we would be better off, physically and spiritually, if we ate less" ([1946d], p. 215). Truman pressed on with specific suggestions for his listeners to adopt, such as consuming two days a week the amount of food eaten by "the average person in the hungry lands" and reducing "every slice of bread, ounce of fat and oil consumed" (p. 210). In sum, President Truman used a number of appeals to promote sacrifice. He emphasized not what he personally would do, but what the citizens needed to do.

The program was administered within the existing structure of the executive branch in conjunction with a series of temporary support groups. On February 27, 1946, Truman sent a telegram to twelve noted Americans that read in part, "I have directed the agencies of Government to do everything possible to this end [end famine]. But government is not enough. We cannot meet this situation without an aggressive voluntary program on the part of private citizens to reduce food consumption in this country" (1946b). This telegram invited the recipients to a Food Conference to be held at the White House the following week. The conference became the nucleus for the development of a continuing organization called the Famine Emergency Committee (FEC).

The Committee was appointed by President Truman to "1) help bring about as much voluntary conservation of food by the American people as was possible and 2) to create a 'moral climate' that would permit the Government to institute even more drastic controls" (Famine Emergency Committee, 1948). Former president Herbert Hoover was appointed Honorary Chairman with Chester Davis, president of the Federal Reserve Bank of St. Louis, serving as Chairman of the Committee. The illustrious members of the Famine Emergency Committee included representatives of businesses, universities, civic groups, and the mass media.

To achieve even broader public representation and involvement, a National Famine Emergency Council was formed at the suggestion of the FEC and the personal invitation of President Truman. His telegram to about 125 leading citizens indicated the grassroots nature of the Council. Truman wrote on March 12, 1946, that a "General meeting of the Council is not to be called but you will be asked to serve in your community and organization to further objectives of emergency food program, and to submit your suggestions and recommendations" (1946c). Those invited to join the Council included representatives from labor, business, farmers, social groups, religious groups, veterans' groups, and other assorted civic leaders.

On September 25, 1947, President Truman announced the appointment of a Citizens Food Committee "to advise on ways and means of carrying out the necessary conservation efforts." This nonpartisan committee was composed of twenty-six business, labor, and public leaders. Headed by Charles Luckman, it was called upon to "develop plans for bringing the vital problem of food conservation to the attention of every American for action" (Truman, 1947). There was no federal funding for the committee, which was intended to act quickly and then dissolve ("Food," 1947).

Within the more formal confines of the Executive Office Truman established a Cabinet Committee on Food in September 1946. The three permanent members were the Secretaries of State, Commerce, and Agriculture, with the latter serving as chair. The role of this committee was to keep abreast of the world food situation and to recommend government actions. President Truman asked that this committee develop a "coordinated information program" to keep Americans informed about the changing world food situation and the attendant actions that the government might take in the future (Anderson, 1946a). The Department of Agriculture in particular led efforts to promote, coordinate, and implement the famine relief program. Structurally, Truman's famine relief program used the existing organization of the executive branch while emphasizing the role of voluntary, nongovernmental groups in taking the program to the American people.

Some coercive strategies were applied to the growers, manufacturers, and shippers of food, but the main thrust of the appeals to the people was voluntary cooperation. Several government orders were issued to increase the supplies of wheat, corn, and oats available for export. These orders included requirements that bakers reduce the weight of bread and rolls by 10 percent, prohibitions on the manufacture of flour of less than 80 percent extraction, and tighter restrictions on the licensing of wheat exporters. But Secretary of Agriculture Clinton Anderson was quick to add that "These limitations are not a substitute for voluntary conservation efforts. On the contrary, vigorous self-rationing will continue to be necessary" (Anderson, 1946b).

All five of the previously discussed strategies for promoting voluntary cooperation—self-improvement, exemplification, incentives, the hanging sword, and humanitarianism—were employed in the famine relief program.

The self-improvement strategy was used to show the personal gains to be derived from the conservation of food. The Famine Emergency Committee suggested a number of retail advertisements geared toward personal gratification. When menswear stores promoted their lightweight summer clothes it was suggested that their customers could also eat lighter lunches—"all adding up to the formula for cool comfort" (Famine Emergency Committee, 1946). The FEC also emphasized the slimming benefits of the emergency diet. An advertisement for men's suits mentioned that "stripes will produce an optical illusion on a fat man, but less wheat and fat will produce a lasting result" (Famine Emergency Committee, 1946). Slogans such as "less bread, less spread," and "for a figure that's neat, go easy on wheat" were also promoted by the Committee.

Even a customer's complexion would be improved by the emergency diet. Cosmetic ads would sell their products along with the advice to "also live on this wonderful complexion-clearing diet that's so full of vitamins and so free of fats and starches that cloud your complexion. Pretty is as pretty eats" (Famine Emergency Committee, 1946). Thus, following the emergency diet could make one cooler, slimmer, and generally more attractive.

The exemplification approach to conservation was also employed. Through radio and newspaper coverage the famine program stressed conservation by public officials and voluntary conservation by the general public. A CBS interview revealed that the White House served only one-crust pies (less flour and fat); saved bread by serving a Truman favorite, "potato casserole"; had one breadless day per week; saved crumbs for cooking; and did not serve bread at formal White House dinners (Lee & Cohan, 1946).

Federal government cafeterias promoted the program by placing on most tables double-card posters that explained the "desperate plight of millions of starving people throughout the world," by making verbal appeals over the Muzak system, and by providing menus of the least restricted foods ("U.S. Cafeterias," 1946).

Radio stations held contests to publicize the best food conservation ideas; winners received prizes and the opportunity to have their ideas publicized by the local press in columns like "Martha Ellyn's Platter Chatter" (Ellyn, 1946). Newspapers covered neighborhood block parties and other community efforts that raised food contributions.

Even a trip to a hotel restaurant reminded Americans that others were conserving food. Menu placards often indicated that "the usual second roll or slice of bread with each meal; and extra helpings of food-fat items, salad dressings and oils will be served only if you request it" (American Hotel Association, 1946).

Some appeals were also based on providing incentives to voluntarily conserve food. Because some wartime pricing restrictions remained in effect, the cost of restricted items was not drastically increased to reduce consumption. Rather, the pricing appeal was applied to the growers and manufacturers of food items. The Department of Agriculture offered a bonus of thirty cents above the market price on the date of delivery for each bushel of corn sold to the U.S. Commodity Credit Corporation (Famine Emergency Committee, 1948). These plans were intended to provide farmers with an incentive to market their crops and not to use (or hoard) them for livestock feed.

The hanging sword appeal attempted to show the dangers of noncooperation. The Famine Emergency Committee had a media division that produced and distributed newsreels and films. One of its four-minute messages included the following:

Many are determined to forage for themselves in the sheer effort to keep alive—ready to pillage, rob and kill if necessary. How we treat these children today may determine the kind of world we live in tomorrow—a generation of peace loving people or another generation of storm troopers. The helpless of today may become the Hitlers of tomorrow. (Truman, 1946a)

The hanging sword was often found with the humanitarian appeal, as indicated by an excerpt from an address by Agriculture Secretary Clinton Anderson: "The desperate world food shortage and its consequences—hunger, misery, death and danger to the world's future—point unmistakably to the need for more effective action now" (Anderson, 1946b). Thus, the antifamine campaign highlighted the dangers to world stability and to peace for Americans if the world's need for food was not met by the United States.

Finally, the humanitarian appeal was a natural approach considering the central nature of food for human life. In his radio address to the nation, President Truman said:

It is my duty to join my voice with the voices of humanity everywhere in the behalf of the starving millions of human beings all over the world. We have a high responsibility as Americans, to go to their rescue. . . . Now we cannot ignore the cry of hungry children. . . . Once again I appeal to all Americans to sacrifice so that others may live. (1946d, p. 215)

Newspapers carried cartoons of the grim reaper checking off lives as shoppers purchased bread and fat. Members of the FEC and the Council publicly related their personal experiences with hungry victims of war throughout Europe (Fenton, 1946). Movies like "Suffer Little Children" dramatized the problem and were distributed to schools, churches, and civic groups. This appeal for voluntary cooperation stressing the benefits of conservation for others was a central part of the antifamine campaign.

In summary, the famine program utilized some governmental coercion to meet the established food quotas. But voluntary cooperation and personal sacrifice were central to the program's success. All five strategies were used to induce compliance.

CARTER'S ENERGY PROGRAM

President Carter was not the first president to address the problem of energy conservation. But he was the president who "staked his reputation on the National Energy Plan, addressing Congress and national television audiences when he introduced it, defending it vigorously (even emotionally) and dramatically postponing a foreign trip to be available" (Davis, 1979).

In his first televised address on energy policy, April 18, 1977, Carter said, "I want to have an unpleasant talk with you about a problem unprecedented in our history" ([1977a], p. 656). Few listeners flock to the prospect of an "unpleasant talk," yet so began Carter's dialogue with the American people on energy policy. Throughout the address Carter told the audience that the energy proposals would not be well received. Not content to state that "many of these proposals will be unpopular" ([1977a], p. 656), Carter said that "I'm sure that each of you will find something you don't like about the specifics of our proposal. . . . To some degree, the sacrifices will be painful— but so is any meaningful sacrifice. It will lead to some higher costs and to some greater inconvenience for everyone" (p. 661). This address ignored the humanitarian, exemplification, and self-improvement strategies and it mentioned incentives only once. Instead, it focused on the hanging sword. According to Carter, "The most important thing about these proposals is that the alternative may be a national catastrophe. Further delay can affect our strength and our power as a nation" ([1977a], p. 656). No specific suggestions for individual change are discussed in the speech.

Six months later, Carter again addressed the nation on the National Energy Plan. On November 8, 1977, the goal was to tell the American people "how serious the challenge is" ([1977c], p. 1982). Using mainly the hanging sword approach again, Carter quoted the secretary of defense's remark that "The present deficiency of assured energy sources is the single surest threat to our security and to that of our allies" ([1977c], p. 1983). In discussing the dimensions of the problem Carter spoke of how "we" are "proposing," "recommending," "using research and development projects." President Truman's "we" had connoted the unity of president and people, but Carter's "we" referred only to his administration. He further separated himself from the public by using "I" repeatedly and by asking for citizens' help only rarely. In concluding, Carter returned to the unpleasant nature of the choices: "I'm confident that we can find the wisdom and the courage to make the right decisions—even when they are unpleasant" ([1977c], p. 1987). Whereas Truman had taken an irritating everyday incident—a housewife being unable to buy bread—and interpreted it as a positive sign that the grain was helping starving people, Carter emphasized the generally negative nature of the energy proposals.

Two years later, on April 5, 1979, President Carter again addressed the nation on the energy problem. At this late date in his administration he still felt compelled to say that "the energy crisis is real" ([1979a], p. 197). His main appeal was the importance of the passage of the Windfall Profits Tax. The address asked people not to conserve but to "please let your Senator and Representatives in Congress know that you support the Windfall Profits Taxes" ([1979a], p. 612). The need for this appeal at this date was attributable to Carter's rhetorical inattention to pricing as a legitimate strategy of conservation. He also asked citizens to honor the 55 MPH speed limit and to "drive 15 miles a week fewer than you do now" ([1979a], p. 613).

The other sacrificing strategies were not used on April 5 other than as a continuation of the hanging sword approach. But the address was given by a president with very low public approval ratings on a topic that he had been addressing repeatedly with little apparent effect. It was therefore unsuccessful in persuading citizens to act. Carter's public approval dropped to 37 percent.

Almost 150 advisors came to Camp David to advise President Carter before his next address, the jeremiad of July 15. Vice President Mondale said in a subsequent interview that "I felt very strongly that the American people had to be approached in a positive, hopeful way" (Germond & Witcover, 1981, p. 31). As we discussed in Chapter 6, this good advice became a small part of the July 15, 1979, address. Carter gave the six points of his energy policy and pledged leadership, but he also lamented "a crisis of confidence that strikes at the very heart and soul and spirit of our national will" ([1979b], p. 1237).

President Carter took the high moral plane in this speech to direct the country's attention to the meaning of our nation and our heritage along with the present problems. Significantly, Carter used the self-improvement strategy for the first time in his energy addresses. A solution to the energy crisis would not only "rekindle our sense of unity but it will give our nation and all of us individually a new sense of purpose" ([1979b], p. 1240).

Carter talked about the comments of individual Americans and humanized what he had called the "invisible threat." Not only did he set out what he as president would do, but he also concluded with a specific painless request: "Whenever you have a chance, say something good about our country" ([1979b], p. 1241). This speech promoted the need for a general national unifying effort of which the energy crisis would be a test, but it requested few specific sacrifices. As we discussed in Chapter 6, the initial response to the speech was positive. It brought an eleven-point increase in Carter's approval rating and a volume of (overwhelmingly favorable) mail to the White House that was more than had been received at any time since Ford had pardoned Nixon (Germond & Witcover, 1981). But Carter did not trust the usefulness of the speech without direct action, so he collected resignations from sixteen cabinet-level officials and eighteen members of the Senior Staff of the White House. The public response turned dramatically negative.

In sum, Carter used public addresses to persuade the American people to follow his energy program. But his appeal stressed his own leadership role rather than the specific ways in which citizens could help solve the problem with voluntary conservation. Few of the sacrificing strategies were well applied to his programmatic ends. Structural and strategic problems also awaited Carter's energy campaign.

Structurally, American energy policy had been administered by the Federal Energy Office and the Federal Energy Administration prior to the Carter administration. These agencies lacked centralized direction, and they were often divided and ineffective. Soon after his election Carter appointed James Schlesinger to head an Energy Task Force in the Executive Office of the President, and this later became the leadership group in the new Department of Energy (DOE). The new cabinet-level organization was established by the Department of Energy Organization Act of August 31, 1977. A major goal of the new department was the centralization of government planning and activity in the area of energy policy.

President Carter's remarks on the establishment of the new Department of Energy foresaw the basic problem:

The creation of a Department of Energy is an important step toward dealing with our energy problems. . . . But simply creating a department will not solve our energy problems. We will never do that without a clear will among government and our people to end waste, to use energy more efficiently and to look for practical new sources of energy. ([1977f])

Three years later the "public will" was still not forthcoming, and the White House organized a communication and support plan for the DOE "Energy Conservation Visibility Program."

The White House plan outlined twenty-six major work areas to be covered by seventeen lead administration people (H. Carter, 1980b). As late as February 29, 1980, the White House plan sought to "help DOE mobilize massive grass roots participation in the President's energy conservation programs" (H. Carter, 1980a). An effort billed as "continuing" the mobilization effort of the DOE would have been a more positive sign of the conservation effort's ongoing success.

Unfortunately, the cool James Schlesinger did not become a favorite with the members of Congress who dealt with energy policy. The new department had frequent conflicts in congressional hearings over conflict of interest with their personnel, their inefficiency, and the lack of strict enforcement measures against oil executives (Mollenhoff, 1980). Secretary Schlesinger lost his position in the cabinet purge of July 1979 and was replaced by Charles Duncan, whose direct link to the White House diminished the Department of Energy's institutional initiatives. Duncan acted less as a spokesman for his department than as a presidential appointee perched on the back of a large bureaucratic organization.

Unlike Truman's vigorous attempts to involve many sectors of the society in the development of the food campaign, Schlesinger's task force on energy was secretive. Only after demanding entrance into the deliberations did representatives of the Treasury, the Office of Management and Budget, the Council of Economic Advisors, and the National Security Council see the final draft of the energy plan (Davis, 1979).

The legislative package on energy policy became the centerpiece of what Carter called "an exhaustive fight" lasting over the years of his administration (Carter, 1982). This legislative struggle reduced the number of coercive measures available to the president, although he could still issue executive orders. But it did not strike directly at the heart of the program: voluntary conservation.

Various structures were used to foster conservation, including interagency committees and White House support groups. But all such groups worked under the DOE leadership. The viability of the new department, therefore, would affect the operations of all administration conservation efforts. Thus Carter attempted to centralize the energy plan in a new department, and he relied heavily on government promotion and implementation of the conservation effort.

The self-improvement approach was rarely used by the Carter administration to promote conservation. Although the DOE published numerous pamphlets teaching consumers ways to conserve, the rationale was usually either the national interest or thrift. Little attention was given to the personal benefits to be derived from reduced energy conservation.

Ironically, the Carter White House Staff Files contain examples of advice given to the Ford administration that highlighted a personally oriented strategy. The Gallup Poll prepared a report on consumer energy conservation for the Federal Energy Administration on March 26, 1976. Based on group discussions with teenagers, the report had concluded that "Instead of the ineffective themes of self-denial, sacrifice, and patriotic duty, the positive rewards of energy conservation, that is, *the development of a satisfying life style that can be 'fun'* [italics added], might be an effective theme" (Gallup Organization, 1976). Individuals would prefer to conserve because of the personal benefits and enjoyment they might achieve.

Two and a half years after Carter's first energy address the White House staff continued to grapple with the conservation program strategy. In a Memorandum for the President on August 14, 1979, Jack Watson observed that:

We can only turn supporters into allies if we ask them to take specific, concrete actions which people believe others are also taking. This is true of both opinion leaders and the public-at-large. Giving them briefings is not enough. . . . Our energy goals should be translated into terms that better reflect the immediate concerns and daily activities of individual Americans. It's hard for people to identify with "barrels-per-day" savings. (Watson, 1979)

Unfortunately, this astute memorandum on the need for an individual benefit strategy was not well received by Carter, who wrote on the memorandum, "we seem to be going backward from more specific to generalizations. . . . Enough W.H. memos" (Watson, 1979).

From the White House Press Office came a background report promisingly entitled "Energy Conservation The Individual" [*sic*] (Office of Media Liaison, 1979). The six-page report began with one and a half pages on the reasons for conserving before discussing the many ways in which the individual could help. But even that brief justification did not follow the self-improvement strategy. Five examples explained the benefits of conserving, but every example discussed solely national, rather than individual, benefits in statistical, rather than visionary, language. The examples included: improving insulation in homes to save enough natural gas to heat an estimated four million homes; lowering household heating temperatures by six degrees over a 24-hour period to save over 570,000 barrels of oil per day; raising air-conditioning temperatures by six degrees to save the equivalent of 190,000 barrels of oil per day; doing household chores during off-peak hours to reduce public utilities' fuel use; and putting one more person in the average commuter car to save over 600,000 barrels of oil per day (Office of Media Liaison, 1979). The figures were impressive, but the strategy of emphasizing national public benefits instead of individual private benefits continued to prove uninspiring.

Conservation ideas could have been framed in a self-improvement strategy. Weatherization was promoted in order to "reduce the load on the heating and cooling equipment," but a more personal approach would have suggested the more comfortable, cozy home environment obtained by eliminating those nasty drafts of cold air. The appeal that reducing the consumption of hot water by using "half hot and half cold water for bathing . . . would save about five gallons of hot water each time" could have stressed a personal benefit by saying that the warm water would be less drying and better for one's complexion. Finally, the conservation promotion of "eliminating unnecessary car trips" by using the mail and telephones could have taken the next step of mentioning the precious time to be saved that could be used for personal enjoyment (Office of Media Liaison, 1979). A self-improvement strategy could also have emphasized the healthy effects of walking or cycling to work, or the beneficial effects of lower home temperatures on skin condition and house plants. In short, energy conservation could have been promoted as a source of numerous personal benefits for citizens.

The exemplification strategy was employed by President Carter and the executive agencies as they lowered thermostats, reduced the number of federal employees entitled to government motor vehicles, and increased the number of fuel efficient vehicles in the government motor pool. Additionally, President Carter was frequently filmed in warm attire as he performed his White House duties. His televised fireside chats showed President Carter sitting in front of a roaring fire dressed in a cardigan sweater, presumably because of the lowered thermostats in the White House. But was this Carter's normal attire, or merely a staging device? Successful exemplification requires that the audience perceive the example as normal and routine. Some praised the anti-imperial nature of the setting, but others criticized the informal nature of Carter's presidential demeanor.

Within the executive branch, the postal employees cut their gas consumption by 7 percent in 1978 by using smaller vehicles and walking more. Unfortunately, the Department of Energy itself used 29 percent more fuel during the 1976–1979 period than the agencies from which it was formed ("Energy Crisis," 1979). Despite the DOE's example, the president and his agencies generally set an example of conservation.

The incentive strategy for encouraging voluntary conservation was often cited during the energy conservation campaign. The variety of monetary assistance programs in operation was a common theme of government brochures and reports. These programs gave citizens financial incentives to weatherize their homes, to conduct energy audits, and to invest in solar or wind energy (Office of Media Liaison, 1979). Residential energy credits on federal income tax forms for the installation of approved home insulation provided another kind of pricing incentive. Separate publications on home insulation, driving techniques, and solar energy stressed the incentive to save money by conserving energy. The appeal was reinforced by continuing increases in the price of gasoline and other energy sources. By Executive Order Carter phased out controls on domestic crude oil, in 1979 allowing the prices to quickly rise. But according to energy experts, by the end of the Carter administration "the failure of price controls and other regulations was taking hold" (Basile, 1982, p. 214).

As previously discussed, the hanging sword approach to conservation was used frequently to induce cooperation with the Carter program. He appealed to Americans to view the energy problem as a "moral equivalent of war" (Carter [1977a], p. 656). The threats of worse days ahead included gasoline rationing, continued dependency upon foreign energy, and continued increases in cost. According to the president, "If we fail to act soon, we will face an economic, social, and political crisis that will threaten our free institutions" ([1977a], p. 659). Similar examples of the hanging sword approach can be found throughout the energy address. Unfortunately, the Carter team had great difficulty persuading Americans that these threats were real, significant, and amenable to change through conservation. Moreover, Carter failed to persuade the public that they were armed with the weapons needed to fight a moral equivalent of war.

Finally, humanitarian appeals to assist other people by conserving energy were not a major facet of the Carter campaign. This may seem surprising in light of the human rights theme of his administration. Actually, President Carter did discuss the humanitarian aspects of the energy crisis, as when he said, "I am even more concerned about the growing cost in human suffering that will increase if severe winter weather continues" ([1977g], p. 6). But such references were rare, and they were not pursued by the public relations arm of the energy program apparatus. The effect of energy conservation on other people is more difficult to visualize than President Truman's "saving food—saving lives." Nevertheless, this appeal would have been applicable as a national appeal when California and the Northeast were dangerously low on gasoline and/or heating oil and supplies elsewhere were adequate.

Symbolically, Carter proclaimed October 1979 as International Conservation Month and all of 1980 as the Year of Conservation to focus attention on his high priority issue of conservation. But the public perceived an abundance of words and a paucity of actions. Pollster Patrick Caddell (1979) wrote to Carter that "You are seen at the moment as someone who talks a lot about the problem. Education *is* crucial. Speaking out *is* a vital leadership component. However, too much speaking without the support of actions/accomplishments runs the risk of being seen only in a PR or campaign posture." He added, "You are seen as a president with programs that are (a) complicated, (b) long term, and (c) cause pain. What has been lacking has been an identification by [*sic*] you as being *personally concerned* with the impact of the energy situation on consumers and ordinary citizens" (Caddell, 1979).

Caddell criticized not only the president's personal stance but his coalition-building strategy as well. He described a significant problem in the conservation efforts when he wrote that "What is lacking is a sense that we need and want real *allies* as opposed to *supporters* for this program. We are briefing, we are asking for support but we have not established the programs of involvement and participation that build true allies" (1979). Caddell realized that Carter had confused mobilization with acquiescence.

In summary, the Carter energy plan worked with a new Department of Energy and less reliance on existing community groups than had the antifamine campaign. The techniques employed included both pressure tactics and appeals for voluntary compliance. But only the exemplary, incentive, and hanging sword approaches were utilized to any significant extent. The self-improvement and humanitarian strategies were largely ignored.

CONCLUSIONS

The president plays a vital role in mobilizing the American people behind national campaigns. This task is particularly difficult when people are asked to sacrifice personal benefits for the broader national good. Truman's famine program and Carter's energy program both requested such alterations in the life-styles of millions of Americans, but they met with different degrees of success.

The famine program was successful because its goals were met within the required time. Secretary of Agriculture Clinton Anderson told President Truman that:

The 400 million bushel "bread" grain commitment for the year was met by June 30. . . . The real extent of this accomplishment in grain export is brought out by the fact that the amount shipped is nearly double the original requirement for the year which was presented to the Cabinet Food Board a year ago. ("Report," 1946)

A 1948 report acknowledged that "Conservation efforts, in response to our urgent request last fall, and careful handling of our supplies made it possible to set a new record of grain exports without putting any limitations upon the use of bread and other cereal products by United States consumers" (Cabinet Committee, 1948).

President Carter's energy plan met with considerably less success. His congressional disappointments were compounded by the lack of voluntary conservation. In July 1977 Carter observed that "The public is not paying attention. . . . I would say at this point, the public has not responded well" ([1977b], p. 1391). He noted specifically that "We've had in the first half of this year a rate of importing oil—it's higher than we've ever experienced in the history of our country" ([1977e], p. 1599). This was necessary in part because "gasoline consumption was higher [in 1977] than it has ever been before" (Carter [1977d], p. 1685).

Both structural and strategic elements for a successful sacrifice campaign can be inferred from these two programs. A sacrificing campaign needs to maintain the sense of urgency established by the president's first announcement of the problem. This requires the administration to act quickly and with unity. If time is short, establishing a new cabinet-level department is rhetorically inappropriate and politically dysfunctional because of the attendant growing pains and jurisdictional battles. Formation of a new department exonerates other parts of the executive branch from their responsibility to work on the problem. Because cooperation rather than rivalry is necessary between departments, the best approach may be to include various cabinet members in a joint committee to promote the campaign.

The principle of broadening participation and committing more factions to the campaign also applies to volunteer groups. In our pluralistic society, interpretive communities are sensitive to exclusion from government deliberation and implementation. People are most susceptible to persuasion from the people with whom they have frequent, positive contact: authority figures in their interpretive communities. Therefore the president needs to reach out and pull these grass roots communities into his programs, and to build broad based interpretive coalitions. As we have seen, Truman did this effectively and Carter did not.

Strategically, presidents must sell the importance of their programs and solutions. But Carter learned that it is difficult to convince people of government's wisdom during a period of low confidence in government. This is complicated by the notion of a "spiral of silence" in which people are more likely to voice support for a president or policy that they perceive as popular (Noelle-Neumann, 1984). As his popularity declined, Carter compounded his difficulties by describing his policies as unpopular and his leadership as ineffective. A massive public relations effort was therefore needed to produce a "mood of acceptance" in the country for the specific governmental policies and regulations that Carter later issued. But Carter's rhetoric of unpopularity continued to confound his efforts. If active support cannot be mobilized, the president at least needs public acquiescence. But public acquiescence does not lower the thermostat.

Sacrificing campaigns need a coercive element to promote rapid responses and to establish the level of governmental commitment to the problem. These regulations must be perceived as scrupulously fair to all elements of society if everyone is asked to sacrifice. The energy program suffered from the charge that the program burdened the poor and middle class more than the wealthy (Gottlieb, 1978), and Carter needed their support to be re-elected.

Coercion may begin a program, but voluntary cooperation by the people is essential for its success. Of the five strategies discussed, the self-improvement approach may be the most effective for producing public compliance, because it speaks to personal, everyday needs. This conclusion is based on the success of the Truman campaign, the failure of the Carter campaign, and the temper of our times. When relatively few people can even remember a united national effort they may prefer appeals to help themselves, and if the country benefits in the process, so much the better.

The exemplification approach is necessary for any presidential campaign geared toward joint popular action. Presidents are generally expected to enact the same behaviors that they ask of their constituents. Therefore a presidential example is important whether or not it motivates people, because it protects the president from criticism. Grass roots examples of conservation are also an important component of sacrifice campaigns because they are easier to identify and may imply a groundswell of support.

The incentive approach can be useful if the benefit received for cooperation is substantially greater than the perceived sacrifice. Studies applying this to gasoline pricing found that a dramatic increase in the cost per gallon was required before most Americans preferred to alter their consumption patterns. Program goals might, therefore, be met at an unacceptably high level of personal hardship and social inequality. Additionally, people are likely to return to their prior consumption patterns when they become accustomed to the higher prices. Pricing incentives may work better for short-term changes than for long-term adjustments, but short-term dramatic price changes can have long-term economic consequences.

The hanging sword strategy will emerge in any sacrifice campaign because there should be a significant perceived danger before a president issues a call for action. But presidents need to be very cautious about overplaying this approach and losing their credibility. This is a primarily negative appeal based on fear. Short-term responses may be forthcoming, but a continued effort to sacrifice will be difficult to maintain unless the threatened danger materializes. The long-term prospects can be enhanced by framing the danger as part of a clear and coherent jeremiad, as we discussed in Chapter 6.

Finally, the humanitarian approach can be a very effective strategy if the results of one's sacrifice are readily visible, if the requested sacrifice seems justified, and if the brunt of the sacrifice is fairly shared. For example, newspaper coverage of families that need clothing or shelter generally produce an outpouring of assistance from the citizenry, often more than the family requires. People may respond voluntarily to the needs of specific persons more readily than to the more abstract concept of "the national good."

One theme runs throughout this chapter: successful national sacrifice campaigns motivate the individuals who comprise the society. They must be motivated directly, personally and truthfully. To motivate millions of people directly, personally, and truthfully, the campaign must (1) offer a blend of all five rhetorical strategies, (2) coordinate existing interpretive communities, and (3) simplify the administration of the program. The best rationale for preferring to change one's lifestyle is personal, but personal needs will vary with the times, and each president works within a unique temporal framework. Thus, successful presidential sacrifice campaigns require that the president understand both the approaches to persuasion and the mood of the people.

REFERENCES

American Hotel Association. (1946). Letter, March 29. Papers of Harry S Truman, Official File, Harry S Truman Library.

Anderson, C. P. (1946a). Letter of Secretary of Agriculture Anderson, September 23. Papers of Harry S Truman, Official File, Harry S Truman Library.

Anderson, C. P. (1946b). Radio address, April 19. Papers of Harry S Truman, Official File, Harry S Truman Library.

Basile, P. S. (1982). U.S. energy policy. In W. Kohl (Ed.), *After the second oil crisis* (pp. 195–224). Lexington, MA: Heath.

Bellah, R. N. (1967). Civil religion in America. *Daedalus, 96* (Winter), 1–21.

Cabinet Committee on World Food Programs. (1948). Report to the president by the Cabinet Committee on World Food Programs, July 1948. Papers of Harry S Truman, Official File, Harry S Truman Library.

Caddell, P. (1979). Memorandum for the president, August 7. Staff Office, Office of the Staff Secretary, Handwriting file, Jimmy Carter Library.

Carter, H. (1980a). Outline of WH communications and support plan for DOE Energy Conservation Visibility Program, February 29. Administrative Staff Office File, Jimmy Carter Library.

Carter, H. (1980b). WH support plan for DOE Conservation Visibility Program, March 1. Administrative Staff Office File, Jimmy Carter Library.

Carter, J. [1977a]. The energy problem, April 18. *Public papers of the president* (pp. 656–662). Washington, DC: U.S. Government Printing Office.

Carter, J. [1977b]. Interview with the president, July 29. *Public papers of the president* (pp. 1387–1395). Washington, DC: U.S. Government Printing Office.

Carter, J. [1977c]. National energy plan, November 8. *Public papers of the president* (pp. 1981–1987). Washington, DC: U.S. Government Printing Office.

Carter, J. [1977d]. News conference, September 29. *Public papers of the president* (pp. 1684–1693). Washington, DC: U.S. Government Printing Office.

Carter, J. [1977e]. Radio-TV news directors association: Telephone session with convention, September 15. *Public papers of the president* (pp. 1594–1600). Washington, DC: U.S. Government Printing Office.

Carter, J. (1977f). Remarks by the president on the Department of Energy, press release, September 13. Staff Office, Speechwriters' Chronological File, Jimmy Carter Library.

Carter, J. [1977g]. Statement by the president announcing initiatives to deal with the crisis, January 21. *Public papers of the president* (pp. 6–7). Washington, DC: U.S. Government Printing Office.

Carter, J. [1979a]. Energy, April 5. *Public papers of the president* (pp. 609–614). Washington, DC: U. S. Government Printing Office.

Carter, J. [1979b]. Energy and national goals, July 15. *Public papers of the president* (pp. 1235–1241). Washington, DC: U.S. Government Printing Office.

Carter, J. (1982). *Keeping the faith: Memoirs of a president.* New York: Bantam.

Davis, D. H. (1979). Pluralism and energy: Carter's national energy plan. In R. Lawrence (Ed.), *New dimensions in energy policy* (pp. 191–200). Lexington, MA: Heath.

Dworkin, R. (1977). *Taking rights seriously.* Cambridge, MA: Harvard University Press.

Ellyn, M. (1946, April 12). Martha Ellyn's Platter Chatter. *Washington Post.* Clipping file, Harry S Truman Library.

Energy crisis: Carter's hard choice (1979, July 16). *U.S. News and World Report,* p. 23.

Fairbanks, J. D. (1981). The priestly function of the presidency: A discussion of the literature on civil religion and its implications for the study of presidential leadership. *Presidential Studies Quarterly, 11* (Spring), 214–232.

Famine Emergency Committee. (1946). Memo to members of retailers division, April 23. Papers of Harry S Truman, Fleur Fenton Files, Harry S Truman Library.

Famine Emergency Committee. (1948). Summary of report. Papers of Harry S Truman, Official File, Harry S Truman Library.

Fenton, Fleur. (1946, April 24). Interview with Miss Fenton, *Home Services Daily.* Papers of Harry S Truman, Fleur Fenton Files, Harry S Truman Library.

Food problem continues in 1947. (1947, September 28). [Washington] *Sunday Star,* Clippings file, Harry S Truman Library.

Gallup Organization. (1976). Group discussion regarding consumer energy conservation, March 26. White House Staff File, Gerald Rafshoon Papers, Jimmy Carter Library.

Germond, J. W., & Witcover, J. (1981). *Blue smoke and mirrors.* New York: Viking Press.

Gottlieb, D. (1978). Texans' response to President Carter's energy proposals. In S. Warkov (Ed.), *Energy policy in the United States* (pp. 33–44). New York: Praeger.

King, G., & Ragsdale, L. (1988). *The elusive executive: Discovering statistical patterns in the presidency.* Washington, DC: Congressional Quarterly.

Lee, E., & Cohan, L. (1946). Interview under auspices of the Famine Emergency Committee, April 1. Papers of Harry S Truman, Fleur Fenton Files, Harry S Truman Library.

McCarthy, [Mrs.]. (1957). Letter of February 28. Papers of Harry S Truman, Official File, Harry S Truman Library.

Miller, D. (1992). Community and citizenship. In S. Avineri & A. DeShalit (Eds.), *Communitarianism and individualism* (pp. 85–100). Oxford: Oxford University Press.

Milstein, J. (1978). How consumers feel about energy. In S. Warkov (Ed.), *Energy policy in the United States* (pp. 79–90). New York: Praeger.

Mollenhoff, C. R. (1980). *The president who failed: Carter out of control.* New York: Macmillan.

Noelle-Neumann, E. (1984). *The spiral of silence: Public opinion—our social skin.* Chicago: University of Chicago Press.

Office of Media Liaison. (1979). Energy conservation [*sic*] the individual. Office of Assistant to Women's Affairs, Dennis Tapsak File, Jimmy Carter Library.

Olsen, M. (1978). Public acceptance of energy conservation. In S. Warkov (Ed.), *Energy policy in the United States* (pp. 91–109). New York: Praeger.

Rawls, J. (1971). *A theory of justice.* Oxford: Oxford University Press.

Report to the president on 1945–46 famine relief food shipments (July 8, 1946). Papers of Harry S Truman, Files of Dallas C. Halverstadt, Harry S Truman Library.

Sandel, M. (1982). *Liberalism and the limits of justice.* Cambridge: Cambridge University Press.

Smith, K. B. (1981). The representative role of the president. *Presidential Studies Quarterly, 11* (Spring), 203–213.

Suffer little children (pamphlet, n.d.). Papers of Harry S Truman, Official File, Harry S Truman Library.

Survey indicates president faces skepticism over energy program (1977, April 29). *New York Times*, p. 16.

Taylor, C. (1973). *Hegel and modern society.* Cambridge: Cambridge University Press.

Truman, H. S. (1946a). Draft of filmed message, "Famine," June 28. Papers of Harry S Truman, Files of Dallas C. Halverstadt, Harry S Truman Library.

Truman, H. S. (1946b). Press release of February 27. Papers of Harry S Truman, Official File, Harry S Truman Library.

Truman, H. S. (1946c). Press Release, March 12. Papers of Harry S Truman, Official File, Harry S Truman Library.

Truman, H. S. [1946d]. Radio appeal to the nation for food conservation to relieve hunger abroad, April 19. *Public papers of the president* (p. 215). Washington, DC: U.S. Government Printing Office.

Truman, H. S. (1947). Statement by the president, September 25. Papers of Harry S Truman, Files of Dallas C. Halverstadt, Harry S Truman Library.

U.S. cafeterias report saving several carloads of food. (1946, May 20). *Washington Post*, Clipping File, Harry S Truman Library.

Watson, J. (1979). Memorandum for the president, August 14. Staff Office, Office of the Staff Secretary, Handwriting File, Jimmy Carter Library.

8

The Presidency in Rhetorical Crisis

This chapter explores one of the dangers inherent in the rhetorical presidency. The rhetorical presidency generates a staggering amount of verbiage, an increasing amount of which finds its way into the public record. The sheer quantity of that talk virtually guarantees that the presidential foot will, sooner or later, find its way into the presidential mouth. Journalistic watchdogs and political adversaries routinely pounce on these errors to offset the president's rhetorical successes. Some presidential misstatements articulate underlying problems and public doubts. The resulting accusations sometimes win a sufficient number of adherents to invite a presidential defense. If the debate escalates the president can find himself in a state of rhetorical crisis, a potentially terminal affliction for a rhetorical presidency.

THREE DIMENSIONS OF RHETORICAL CRISIS

Presidents have a threefold claim to political legitimacy. From the office they derive structural legitimacy, from citizens' identification with their expressed beliefs and principles they derive ideological legitimacy, and from citizens' perceptions of their trustworthiness and competence they derive a measure of personal legitimacy (Harrell, Ware, & Linkugel, 1975). Because all three sources of legitimacy hinge on public perceptions, all three vary as citizens interpret political news.

To be regarded as a successful rhetorical president, one must nurture and sustain (1) an image of trustworthiness, (2) a reputation for managerial competence, and (3) a consistent and coherent rhetoric that coordinates the political perceptions of diverse publics. Rhetorical presidents operate in a three-dimensional space bounded by trust, competence, and consistency. Public perceptions fluctuate, and a president's position will vary within the cube. But we can reasonably expect that a president high in trust, high in competence, and relatively high in rhetorical consistency will be more successful than one who is low in one or more of these qualities.

For successful presidents trust, competence, and consistency are a troika of horses pulling together. But when one of those horses comes up lame or, worse, when two of the horses begin pulling in opposite directions, the president driving the wagon is in crisis. And presidents in rhetorical crisis face three dangers.

The first danger is that key constituencies will begin to doubt the president's professional competence. These doubts may relate to his fitness for the office, his ability to surround himself with an able staff, his ability to monitor his administration, or his ability to adjust to changing circumstances. Doubts about competence must be handled well, lest they encourage doubts about the president's intentions.

Thus the second, and more serious, danger is that key constituencies may come to doubt the president's trustworthiness. This is most obvious when the controversy centers around discrepancies between the president's words and actions. But the president is jeopardized in a far more subtle way when people realize that he has chosen strategically from among the possible ways of sharing his thoughts with them. The onset of rhetorical crisis forces constituents to step out of the president's world of words, it escorts them to a new vantage point, and it invites them to consider their president as a purveyor of policies packaged in rhetoric.

The third danger is that the president's efforts to protect his reputation for competence and trustworthiness will lead to rhetorical changes that undermine the consistency of the rhetoric that has framed the administration's choices. These flaws may derive from contradictions among the president's core principles, or his logic may seem unable to account for the flow of events. Alternatively, the crisis may exhaust the effectiveness of a previously useful rhetorical strategy. In any case, the problem undermines the consistency of the president's framework for persuading citizens, thereby weakening his ability to exercise presidential leadership.

Presidents must, therefore, decide when to ignore their critics, when to engage them, and on what argumentative grounds. No president can afford to be a public punching bag, but neither can a president afford to make a federal case out of every small error or accusation. When presidents do defend themselves against accusations they can try to defend their competence, their trustworthiness, and their rhetoric; but they will normally single out one of these as most important.

Watergate and Iran-Contra are the archetypal rhetorical crises. Presidents Nixon and Reagan were renowned for their use of televised speeches to bring public pressure to bear on the Congress, and each lost only one state and the District of Columbia in his re-election bid. Yet both were visited by disgrace, and both had significant policy initiatives thwarted as they attempted to defend themselves. At the risk of stretching the comparison, both were succeeded by their vice presidents who proved unable to fully implement their programs, and who lost the office in the subsequent election.

We shall attempt to demonstrate two propositions as we examine Watergate and Iran-Contra. First, Nixon sacrificed his rhetorical consistency and his perceived trustworthiness to salvage his perceived competence. Second, Reagan sacrificed his reputation for managerial competence and tempered his rhetoric to sustain his reputation for trustworthiness.

RICHARD NIXON AND WATERGATE

The Watergate scandal began during the night of June 17, 1972, when five men associated with the Committee to Re-elect the President (CRP) were discovered inside Democratic National Committee (DNC) headquarters in the Watergate hotel complex, apparently fixing a wiretapping device. President Nixon was concerned "more by the stupidity" of the break-in "than by its illegality" and he hoped that no White House people were involved because "it was stupid in the way it was handled" and he "could see no reason whatever" for bugging the national committee (Nixon, 1978, pp. 629, 627).

Democratic Party Chairman Lawrence F. O'Brien's phone had been the object of the break-in, and he announced a million dollar lawsuit because of CRP's "potential involvement" in the break-in and a "clear link to the White House" (Bernstein & Woodward, 1974). O'Brien's suit was risky because there was only circumstantial evidence of CRP involvement, and a decision vindicating them would have been politically damaging to the Democrats. But litigation provided several important advantages. It brought to bear on CRP the rules of civil procedure, including subpoena power and depositions. It challenged Nixon to reconcile CRP's behavior with his recurrent "Law and Order" theme. And it created a second judicial arena lest the original criminal prosecution be confined to the burglars.

Avoidance and Containment

The DNC suit and its attendant publicity lured Nixon and his aides into the controversy. Perhaps because they were cruising confidently to re-election, they made two unwise decisions. First, Nixon declared categorically that "there was no White House involvement [in the break-in] whatsoever" (Nixon, 1972a). This statement undermined his ability to differentiate between active and passive involvement by present and past employees, even though he suspected that White House Special Counsel Charles Colson had authorized the burglary to fulfill a presidential directive (Haldeman, 1978). But while denying White House complicity, Nixon shrewdly ignored the allegations against CRP because he knew that several of them had been involved (Nixon, 1978).

Nixon's more damaging mistake occurred during a morning meeting with Haldeman on June 23, 1972. Concerned that the CRP money in the burglars' possession might be traced, Nixon told Haldeman to ask General Vernon Walters of the CIA to warn acting FBI Director L. Patrick Gray that its Watergate investigation would reopen the Bay of Pigs fiasco and endanger national security (Haldeman, 1978). Nixon explained his reasoning in his memoirs:

If the CIA would deflect the FBI from Hunt, they would thereby protect us from the only White House vulnerability involving Watergate that I was worried about exposing—not the break-in, but the political activities Hunt had undertaken for Colson. *[I] did not want [the CIA] to get the idea that our concern was political—which, of course, it was* [italics added]. (1978, pp. 641–642)

The president and his associates were henceforth engaged in both a criminal conspiracy to obstruct justice and an abuse of presidential power, whether the White House had been behind the break-in or not.

Nixon's defensive strategy had jelled between the break-in and the June 23 meeting. The White House sought to minimize the political significance of the break-in, to distance the White House from the controversy, to limit investigations, and to punish only the burglars who would be paid hush money to take the blame (Dean, 1976, p. 118). Haldeman (1978) later claimed that Nixon himself had initiated the ideas of CIA intervention and financial support for the burglars as early as June 20, but his account cannot be corroborated. The defensive strategy was coordinated by White House Counsel John Dean, who later recalled that:

The "stonewall" strategy functioned from the very first episodes of the cover-up. . . . It was instinctive, from the very top of the administration to the bottom . . . developed in small reactions to the flurry of the day's events. There was not time to take stock of the whole case or to plan a careful defense. . . . Instead, we found ourselves trying to hold a line where we could. But the line could not be held. (Dean, 1976, pp. 114, 116–117)

These defensive postures dominated the summer of 1972 as Republicans renominated Nixon and Agnew, and Watergate received scant attention. With the Vietnam War nearing an end, the economy healthy, and pre-trial depositions sealed until after the election, the containment strategy had worked—in the short run.

The containment strategy made sense to Nixon because he could not imagine that the public would care about the break-in. In a June 21 tape declassified in 1993, Nixon and Haldeman talked about the political fallout. Nixon said that the charges would attract the national press, but not the public:

Most people around the country think it's probably routine, everybody's trying to bug everybody else, it's politics. . . . I don't think you're going to see a great, great uproar in the country about the Republican committee trying to bug the Democratic headquarters. (Associated Press, 1993)

Nixon needed to save face and to protect his electoral coalition. His political reasoning led him to the conclusion that the controversy would blow over, and he preferred to help it blow over by containing investigations and by paying the burglars to take the rap. His prediction was an accurate reading of the electorate in 1972.

Indeed, Watergate was only a minor national news story in 1972. But it generated interest among Washingtonians as local news. While other news organizations turned their resources elsewhere, the *Washington Post* assigned local reporters Bob Woodward and Carl Bernstein to cover it. On August 1 they reported that a check earmarked for Nixon's campaign had been deposited in a Watergate burglar's bank account. A subsequent General Accounting Office audit referred eleven possible violations of the Campaign Finance Act to the Justice Department for investigation.

President Nixon commented publicly on Watergate at his August 29 press conference. Buoyed by his large lead over McGovern, Nixon tempted fate. He went beyond his earlier condemnation of the stupidity of the break-in to urge that "the guilty should be punished." But he resisted urgings that he appoint a special prosecutor on the grounds that the FBI, the Justice Department, the Government Accounting Office, the Senate Banking and Currency Committee, the CRP, and John Dean were already investigating the case (Nixon [1972b]). Nixon's position seemed reasonable enough. He simply failed to mention that the FBI had been influenced by the CIA, that the Justice Department was reporting to the White House, that the Senate Banking and Currency Committee was unlikely to get subpoena power, or that CRP was an interested party. Indeed, as Dean later wrote:

These investigations, plus several others, were precisely the ones that I was spending most of my waking hours juggling and deflecting. . . . For a moment I wondered whether the President might not *really know* what I was doing. . . . I damn near fell off the bed at what I heard next . . . "I can say categorically that [Mr. Dean's] investigation indicates that no one in the White House staff, no one in the administration, presently employed, was involved in this very bizarre incident." . . . What a reality warp. . . . I had never heard of a "Dean investigation" much less conducted one. (Dean, 1976, pp. 124–125)

In short, Nixon called boldly for convictions that were to be brought about through investigations that he knew to be toothless.

Although the containment defense was proceeding as planned, Nixon nevertheless redefined the culpable act:

We are doing everything we can to investigate it and not to cover it up . . . [since] what really hurts in matters of this sort is not the fact that they occur, because overzealous people in campaigns do things that are wrong. *What really hurts is if you try to cover it up* [italics added]. (Nixon, 1972b, p. 828)

Nixon thus redirected attention from the issue of White House/CRP complicity in the break-in—a charge that was being contained—to the White House's commitment to investigate and to punish—a position clearly at variance with the facts. According to Nixon, any evidence of administration efforts to delay, to impede, to obstruct, or to influence investigations should be considered more serious than evidence of complicity in the break-in. This is a wise approach for a president trying honestly and aggressively to uncover misconduct in his administration, but Nixon had personally directed his aides to deflect the investigations. Clearly, this unnecessary, unwise, and, in this instance, unethical transformation of the central issue contributed directly to Nixon's eventual demise.

The Justice Department announced that the September 15, 1972, grand jury indictments of E. Howard Hunt, G. Gordon Liddy, and the burglars ended its investigation. The containment strategy had worked, or so it seemed. Woodward and Bernstein reported the indictments as but an incremental development: "Though the indictment does not touch on the central questions about the purpose or sponsorship of the alleged espionage, it alleges . . . new details" (Bernstein & Woodward, 1974, p. 72). Their anonymous source, "Deep Throat," and their relentless inquiries had led them to believe that the Watergate break-in was only one in a series of efforts by White House/CRP personnel to maximize their power illegally and unethically. Woodward and Bernstein's accusation transcended the break-in and cover-up and postulated a policy of covert domestic intelligence operations, and they elaborated their allegations during the fall of 1972. They charged that CRP had a secret fund for spying on Democrats. Then, on October 4, the *Los Angeles Times* published an interview with a CRP security guard who described the break-in and said that his wire-tap transcripts had been sent to the White House (Bernstein & Woodward, 1974).

Nixon had said that no White House personnel had been involved in the break-in; indeed, the unraveling allegations concerned only CRP personnel. But that distinction was a precarious one. John Mitchell had been attorney general, Robert Mardian had been an assistant attorney general, Maurice Stans had been commerce secretary, Jeb Magruder had worked for Chief of Staff Bob Haldeman; and Magruder, Liddy, and Hunt had all occupied White House offices. Because of the inbreeding among the administration and CRP, the ties were clear enough to undermine Nixon's technically correct denial. Asked to make a "clean breast about" Watergate at his press conference a month before the election, the president condemned the break-in as useless, relied solely on the FBI investigation and the indictments, and declined comment on cases still before the courts (Nixon, 1972c).

But as the allegations continued to broaden and the White House continued to avoid them, press coverage nurtured doubt about the scope of the criminal indictments and the campaign of political espionage. Senator Edward Kennedy, chairman of the Judiciary Subcommittee of the Senate Committee on Administrative Practices and Procedures, ordered a preliminary inquiry into the Watergate charges on October 12. By Election Day the *Post* had charged that Nixon's personal lawyer was the paymaster for the "spy-fund," and that CRP Treasurer Hugh Sloan had testified that Haldeman had had access to the secret fund (Bernstein & Woodward, 1974). But many Americans regarded the *Post* as a de facto arm of the McGovern campaign, and Nixon won re-election with 61percent of the popular vote, losing only Massachusetts and the District of Columbia.

When the burglary trial began on January 8, 1973, the prosecution charged that Liddy's legitimate political intelligence work for CRP had gone astray—an interpretation of the facts that was consistent with the White House's containment defense. The *New York Times* and the *Post* charged that hush money was passing from the administration through Hunt to the burglars, who variously pleaded—or were found—guilty on January 30. The containment strategy had been executed according to plan, but had it succeeded?

Judge John Sirica was distressed that "all the facts have not been developed by either side"; and Woodward and Bernstein bluntly reported that the "trial was marked by questions that were not asked of witnesses, answers that were not given, witnesses who were not called to testify, and some lapses of memory by those who were testifying under oath" (Bernstein & Woodward, 1974, p. 268). Unresolved questions and the professional interests of the opposition party and watch-dog journalists all combined to reduce the likelihood that these convictions would clear the administration.

January 1973 was a watershed month in American journalism. Along with the burglary trial and Nixon's inauguration, it was the month of the Supreme Court's *Roe v. Wade* decision, the death of Lyndon Johnson, and Nixon's announcement that the Vietnam War was over. The journalistic community had devoted tremendous resources to the coverage of the 1972 election, to the Vietnam War, and to the protests against it—and suddenly all those melodramas were ending. It was almost as though three long-running soap operas were being canceled in the same month. The war, the protests, and the campaign had been substantial line items in the budgeting of news space, time, and personnel; and those resources were now available for the coverage of other news. But what stories would interest the journalists and citizens in the wake of Vietnam and re-election? Watergate had all the elements of melodrama needed to fill the bill, especially when it moved from local Washington news into the U.S. Senate and national coverage.

The Senate had two arenas in which to investigate Watergate: the Judiciary Committee's confirmation hearings for Acting FBI Director L. Patrick Gray and the Select Committee on Campaign Practices chaired by Senator Sam Ervin (D-NC). Gray's confirmation hearings were pivotal because the president was publicly committed to the thoroughness of the FBI's secretly deflected Watergate investigation. Gray volunteered FBI reports confirming the link between the secret fund and the "dirty tricks" operations. Worse, he testified that Dean knew of the FBI's interview schedule and had seen their confidential reports. Still worse, Dean had given the contents of Howard Hunt's White House safe to Gray, who, on his own initiative, had destroyed this evidence.

As Gray's prospects for confirmation dimmed, interest in Dean's testimony increased. White House strategists knew that Dean's testimony would heighten the drama and undercut their containment strategy. The president therefore issued a statement on "executive privilege." Nixon would provide "all necessary and relevant information through informal contacts" but would not permit his staff to respond to congressional subpoenae (Nixon, 1973c) because they served at his pleasure and authorization, not by virtue of Senate confirmation (Price, 1977). He based his claim on President Washington's refusal to provide the House with documents related to the Jay Treaty, over which they had no statutory jurisdiction. But in this case the legislative committees and the special prosecutors *did* have statutory jurisdiction. Consequently, Nixon's claim was construed by many as an attempt to thwart the investigations—which, of course, it was.

The executive privilege statement was a rhetorical gamble involving three audiences. Nixon needed the public to believe that he had complied with his promise of cooperation. He needed the hostile Senate to believe either that he would fairly and honestly provide "all necessary and relevant" materials or that he had a solid constitutional basis for noncompliance. And he needed the federal judiciary to accept his legal arguments for executive privilege. Nixon's executive privilege statement underscores the seriousness of his break-in/cover-up transformation of August 29: by March, the break-in charges had become secondary to his promise to cooperate.

Whether executive privilege would have worked will never be known because the strategy was quickly overtaken by the flow of events. Dean warned the president on March 21, 1973, that "We have a cancer within, close to the presidency, that is growing" (*The White House Transcripts,* 1973, p. 134). He told the president what had been going on and said that Hunt wanted money to maintain his silence. Their discussion turned immediately to the logistics of getting and laundering the money (*The White House Transcripts,* 1973, pp. 146–149). Judge Sirica revealed defendant James McCord's charges that defendants had been pressured into silence and perjury. Then Gray's FBI nomination was withdrawn. The White House defense was no longer proceeding as planned.

The avoidance and containment strategies that had contributed to Nixon's landslide re-election had also allowed the accusers to establish their case. Where the Nixon people had once sought to prolong the scandal until after the election, they now wanted to end it and to get on with business as usual. But largely because they had failed to take the lead in the investigations, the offensive had been taken over by watchdog journalists, by the Senate, and, later, by the special prosecutors.

Victimization Mishandled

An April 17 press release signaled the end of the avoidance strategy in three ways. Nixon permitted his aides to testify in the Senate because they could claim executive privilege in executive session. He personally reported new developments that he attributed to his new personal investigation. And he acquiesced to televised Senate hearings. The April 17 statement radically changed the rhetorical climate. Dean announced that he would implicate others rather than become the scapegoat, and speechwriter Raymond Price recommended that Haldeman consider resigning to save Nixon. McCord, Hunt, and Dean were prepared to talk to the courts, the Senate, the press, and the public via television. The avoidance and containment strategies had collapsed, and Nixon decided that it was time for him to use television to end the scandal.

Richard Nixon was confident of his ability to persuade Americans with televised speeches. Had he not saved his 1952 vice presidential candidacy with the "Checkers" speech? Had he not been a pioneer of televised debates? Had he not undermined the antiwar moratoriums with his address on November 3, 1969? Had he not repeatedly gone to the public "over the heads of Congress" to enlist support for his legislative programs? Surely he must have felt that a prime-time address by one so recently and overwhelmingly re-elected, and by the one who had since ended "Johnson's War," could clear up the controversy over this third-rate burglary. Nevertheless, Nixon told speechwriter Raymond

Price to write a presidential resignation into the speech if he thought it necessary (Price, 1977), perhaps to test Price's loyalty.

Nixon's address of April 30, 1973, explained that he had become aware of new information on March 21. His account emphasized his personal effort to discover the truth: "I personally assumed the responsibility for coordinating intensive new inquiries into the matter, and I personally ordered those conducting the investigations to get all the facts and to report them directly to me, right here in this office" (Nixon [1973a], p. 329). Those efforts uncovered new facts that had led him to accept the resignations of Haldeman, John Ehrlichman, Kliendienst, and Dean, although he absolved Haldeman and Ehrlichman "of any implication of personal wrong-doing" (p. 329). Nixon pledged, once again, to "do everything in my power to bring the guilty to justice and to purify the political process." He also announced his nomination of Elliot Richardson, "a man of unimpeachable integrity and rigorously high principle" to whom "I have given absolute authority to make all decisions bearing upon the prosecution of the Watergate case," to be the new attorney general (p. 330).

By appearing on prime-time television Nixon publicly established his leadership, an impression underscored by his explicit statements of personal responsibility for the acts of his subordinates and for the conduct of future investigations:

For the fact that alleged improper actions took place . . . the easiest course would be for me to blame those to whom I delegated the responsibility to run the campaign. But that would be a cowardly thing to do. I will not place the blame on subordinates—on people whose zeal exceeded their judgment and who may have done wrong in a cause they deeply believed to be right. ([1973a], p. 330)

But the resignations undercut public confidence in Nixon's earlier categorical denials and made him seem either duplicitous or gullible, neither of which enhanced his personal legitimacy.

The final clause of the previous quotation captures the essence of Nixon's Watergate problem. His people, he said, *may* have done wrong in a cause they *deeply believed to be right*. For Nixon the seriousness of their transgression was still in doubt, and their motives were pure. This is not a good position from which to lead an investigation or to proclaim outrage, and his mixed signals undercut his acceptance of responsibility.

Nixon's condemnation of the break-in and his promise to prosecute the guilty allowed him to blame criminal actions on the convicted conspirators and to let Haldeman, Ehrlichman, and Dean take the blame for the cover-up, even as he took nominal responsibility for their actions. This might have worked if Nixon had transferred guilt for the Watergate offenses to the sacrificial victims. But he chose to use his waning credibility to absolve Haldeman and Ehrlichman. This absolution of his associates destroyed Nixon's effort to end the Watergate scandal through victimization. Indeed, the speech drove Dean toward the prosecutors because he saw himself becoming the scapegoat.

Even if guilt had been effectively transferred to the scapegoats, the victimization still would have been only partial because Price and Nixon misphrased the pledge to investigate. They said [italics added], "*I* pledge to you tonight from this office that *I will do* everything in *my* power to insure that the guilty *are brought* to justice and that such abuses *are purged* from our political processes in the years to come long after *I* have left this office" (Nixon [1973a], p. 331). Because he meant to pronounce the administration and the political order purified in the present by virtue of actions begun by Nixon in the past, Price needed to use the present perfect tense to make his point. Thus he should have written: "I *have done* everything in my power to insure that the guilty *have been* brought to justice and that such abuses *have been* purged." Had he done so, Price's Nixon might have been a political hero. Instead, Price's use of the future tense committed Nixon personally to a crusade against the very abuses of power that he had been engaged in for nearly a year—a crusade that he had no intent to conduct.

Moreover, Nixon's sweeping endorsement of Attorney General Richardson's integrity, principle, and authority narrowed the grounds on which later confrontations with him could be seen as legitimate. Given this endorsement, any attack on Richardson would undermine either Nixon's ability to judge character or his willingness to cooperate with him.

Thus the April 30 address brought Nixon personally into the Watergate scandal. It raised doubts about his early denials, it stripped him of his top aides, it pledged him to investigate, it increased public interest in the controversy, it drove an incriminating witness to the prosecution, and it limited the bases for future challenges to the new attorney general. It is difficult to imagine a less helpful speech. Perhaps Nixon forgot that the "Checkers" speech had earned him the "Tricky Dick" moniker, that his first debate with Kennedy was generally considered an important factor in his defeat, that Johnson's war had become Nixon's war long before he had ended it, and that his televised addresses had contributed to a deteriorating relationship with Congress. But in the rhetorical presidency presidents turn to public discourse, and Richard Nixon was an archetypal rhetorical president. During May a new presidential staff was assembled, the Ervin Committee hearings convened in the Senate, and Richardson appointed Special Prosecutor Archibald Cox.

The Campaign for Personal Absolution

The president began a campaign of personal absolution on May 22 (Nixon [1973e]). He denied knowledge of, or participation in, either the break-in or the cover-up. Early in the speech, Nixon answered his accusers in words that deserve to be quoted in full:

> With regard to the specific allegations that have been made, I can and do state categorically:
> 1. I had no prior knowledge of the Watergate operations.
> 2. I took no part in, nor was I aware of any subsequent efforts that may have been made to cover up Watergate.
> 3. At no time did I authorize any offer of executive clemency for the Watergate defendants, nor did I know of any such offer.
> 4. I did not know, until the time of my own investigation, of any effort to provide the Watergate defendants with funds.
> 5. At no time did I attempt, or did I authorize others to attempt to implicate the CIA in the Watergate matter.
> 6. It was not until the time of my own investigations that I learned of the break-in at the office of Mr. Ellsberg's psychiatrist, and I specifically authorized the furnishing of this information to Judge Byrne.
> 7. I neither authorized nor encouraged subordinates to engage in illegal or improper campaign tactics. ([1973e], p. 547)

Subsequent evidence seems to confirm that he did not know about the specific burglaries in advance, but that he knew of, and even initiated, some of the other plans.

Nixon's sudden need to clear *himself* was a direct consequence of his April 30 address, of his professed confidence in Gray's by then infamous FBI investigation, of the August 29 break-in/cover-up transformation, and of the discrepancy between executive privilege and the resignations. Moreover, Nixon again employed the risky form of categorical denials.

Nixon's statement reflected his conviction that the controversy was being spearheaded by Democrats and the liberal press. Although neither group had much incentive to clear Nixon prematurely, it was not they who had authorized the program of break-ins, buggings, dirty tricks, hush money, deflected investigations, and cover-ups. Nixon hoped to get the press off of the story without escalating his public involvement in the scandal. But his new categorical denials presented, for the first time, *verifiable* claims for reporters, prosecutors, senators, and citizens to explore: claims that allowed Nixon little margin for error.

The dismissed aides who testified before the grand jury and the Ervin Committee followed different rhetorical paths. Mitchell justified, Ehrlichman explained, and Haldeman sacrificed Dean, who cooperated by mortifying himself. This cafeteria of testimony did little to focus the hearings, but it did heighten the melodrama. As the president's chief accuser and the linchpin of the cover-up, Dean was both valuable and vulnerable. If he were discredited before the Senate, the public, the press, or the courts, he would be blamed for both Watergate and slander. But his testimony was detached, professional, and open. Through mortification Dean reserved the right to implicate those who professed innocence. By the end of Dean's testimony in late June, the Ervin hearings had become Dean's word against the president's. Then the dam broke.

The Battle over the Tapes

On July 16, 1973, presidential aide Alexander Butterfield told the Ervin Committee that President Nixon had secretly taped his meetings and telephone calls. Ervin and Cox requested the tapes as the evidence they needed to resolve the Nixon-Dean standoff, but Nixon invoked executive privilege. White House attorneys claimed that presidents are answerable to the nation, but not the courts. The Ervin Committee filed suit in federal court while Cox challenged the president's right to withhold evidence. Gallup reported that approval of the president had dropped to 31 percent—down 36 points since February 26 (King & Ragsdale, 1988).

When the Ervin Committee's hearings came to a close, Nixon tried to exploit his accusers' vulnerability with an August 15, 1973, address to the nation. He differentiated his nominal responsibility for the actions of his subordinates from his larger constitutional responsibility to defend the office against "false charges." He countercharged that the hearings had "become increasingly absorbed in an effort to implicate the President personally" ([1973b], p. 691). He reiterated his confidence in usually reliable investigative sources that had proved unreliable, and he justified withholding the tapes on the grounds that presidential confidentiality "is a much more important principle" than cover-up. Still unprepared to denounce his former aides, Nixon blamed the sociopolitical climate of 1972 for fostering understandable, if deplorable, misconduct. He further charged that urgent policy matters were being ignored by Congress, and he challenged the public to demand to know why (Nixon [1973b], p. 697).

This address was a short-term success. Nixon's popularity increased by 8 percent, temporarily turning the tide. The attempt to transfer guilt to Congress might have worked at the height of his popularity, but now it could only apply the brakes to his slide. Moreover, it exacerbated the country's problems by further undermining the public's confidence in government without creating any positive foundation for his own defense. Perhaps a strategy of mortification could have saved Nixon (Brummett, 1975), but Nixon's statements of October 5, April 30, and May 15 had created a climate in which he could hardly have reclaimed his innocence without admitting some degree of executive incompetence.

The pivotal element of the August 15 address was Nixon's assertion of confidentiality rather than executive privilege as his reason for refusing to release his tapes. Many of his supporters expected Nixon to produce the tapes and end the controversy. But because the tapes would have confirmed his early role in the cover-up, he could not permit their release. By choosing the dubious grounds of presidential confidentiality as his basis for withholding them, Nixon invited his adversaries to challenge him in court. Thus the debate moved into the courts during August, September, and October as the White House fought demands for its tapes. Even as Nixon gained leverage over Congress he shunted the debate into the courts, much as he earlier had opened the Pandora's Box of cover-up.

Nixon is reputed to have told his aides that he would not be impeached as long as Spiro Agnew was the vice president. This protection deteriorated significantly on October 10 when Agnew resigned and pleaded nolo contendere to charges of income tax evasion. By replacing the polarizing Agnew with Gerald Ford, Nixon increased the prospect of his own impeachment.

On the day of Ford's nomination the court ordered the release of the tapes. The White House complied by preparing transcripts and stipulating that Cox could subpoena no further tapes. Cox's insistence prompted his dismissal along with those of Richardson and Assistant Attorney General William Ruckelshaus in the "Saturday Night Massacre" of October 20, 1973. Characterized as an effort to "avoid Constitutional confrontation," the terminations raised a difficult question: if the constitutional arguments for confidentiality and executive privilege were legally sound, why did Nixon not give the Supreme Court an opportunity to uphold them?

Richardson's resignation juxtaposed Nixon's declining popularity with his earlier characterizations of Richardson's unimpeachable integrity and absolute authority. The "massacre" and Nixon's silence about it combined to undermine his personal pledge to get the facts, to cooperate with investigators, and to compromise on executive privilege wherever possible. By so strenuously arguing to retain the tapes, Nixon engendered suspicion that he might have tampered with, or withheld, important evidence (Nixon, 1973d).

The Impeachment Hearings

The first impeachment resolution had been introduced shortly after the president refused to release tapes to the Ervin Committee and Special Prosecutor Cox. Because Nixon's pledge to cooperate had become the issue, serious consideration of impeachment proceedings might have been delayed, or even avoided, by releasing the tapes to Cox. But the firing of Cox prompted the Democratic leadership of the House to authorize Judiciary Committee consideration of impeachment.

The Judiciary Committee tried to define the impeachment criteria of "high crimes and misdemeanors" with interpretations ranging from "clear treason" to "a clear pattern of misconduct." Majority Counsel John M. Doar's February 21, 1974, report argued that noncriminal actions could require impeachment from office for "undermining the integrity of the office, disregard of constitutional duties and oath of office, abrogation of power, [and] abuse of the governmental process." He further stipulated that impeachment required a "substantial" record of misconduct rather than separate or isolated incidents (Lukas, 1976, p. 645). The president predictably denounced Doar's grounds as too broad, and argued that criminality was necessary to justify impeachment (Nixon, 1974b).

But even the president's own standard for impeachment became tenuous on March 1, 1974, when he was named an unindicted co-

conspirator in charges of obstruction of justice, perjury, bribery, obstruction of a congressional committee, obstruction of a criminal investigation, and involvement in conspiracies to commit each of these crimes. Nixon was spared indictment only because a sitting president cannot be indicted (Jaworski, 1976). Even his own "criminality" standard for impeachment might have proven precarious.

Nixon made his last aggressive stand on April 29, 1974, with a televised address responding to a Judiciary Committee subpoena for sixty-four tapes. He recounted events since the break-in, asserted that "The basic question at issue today is whether the President personally acted improperly in the Watergate matter," and announced that his release of transcripts of forty-two tapes would "once and for all show that what I knew and what I did . . . were just as I have described them . . . from the beginning" ([1974a], p. 391). Reiterating his claims of executive privilege and confidentiality and deploring the leaks and rumors associated with the investigation, Nixon asserted that the transcripts contained all relevant portions of the tapes. He invited Senate Judiciary Committee Chairman Peter Rodino (D-NJ) and ranking Republican Edward Hutchinson (R-MI) to authenticate them. He specifically claimed that the transcripts would prove that he first learned of the cover-up on March 21, 1973, that he only considered paying money to Hunt for national security reasons, and that he was always trying "to discover what was right and to do what was right" (Nixon [1974a], p. 397).

Nixon's April 29 address crystallized the issues. As the president climbed further out on the limb he became critically vulnerable to a variety of likely developments, such as the discovery of omissions or inaccuracies in the transcripts, signs of any motives other than "what is right," or evidence of any presidential cover-up prior to March 21, 1973.

In twenty-two months of defensive rhetoric Nixon had set the stage for his own impeachment hearings. He himself had outlined the key issues, defined the evidentiary standards, and provided the evidence. When Rodino and Hutchinson found the transcripts incomplete and replaced them with Judiciary Committee transcripts, and when new Special Prosecutor Leon Jaworski subpoenaed sixty-four more tapes, Nixon's problems mounted.

Nixon's impeachment defense was devised by James St. Clair, a constitutional lawyer. Speechwriter Price felt that their defense of never having paid hush money to Hunt was legally sound, but "politically it proved woefully inadequate—and unfortunately what we were engaged in was a political rather than legal battle" (Price, 1977, p. 275).

The White House exploited the dual legal/political nature of the hearings, such that three conflicting versions of the hearings emerged from the White House. Nixon and Price treated the proceedings as a partisan confrontation with Democrats in Congress; but they did not allow the Committee to approach it in that way, demanding that the proceedings be nonpolitical, secret, stringent, and impartial. Meanwhile, Nixon's lawyer approached the hearings as a nonpolitical trial. These conflicting views made it difficult for the White House to cultivate a consistent and favorable media view of the hearings. The resulting confusion indirectly enhanced the impression that Nixon was "on the ropes."

The crushing blow came on July 24, when the Supreme Court ruled in *U.S. v. Nixon* that "The generalized assertion of privilege must yield to the demonstrated specific need for the evidence in a pending criminal trial" (White, 1975, p. 5). This required Nixon to provide Jaworski with sixty-four additional tapes.

Handed the issues, the evidentiary standards, the evidence, a narrow and technical White House defense, and the Court's unwillingness to accept Nixon's claim to confidentiality, the Judiciary Committee passed three Articles of Impeachment all derived from Nixon's own defense. Article I charged Nixon with obstruction of justice: a charge derived from his own condemnation of cover-ups, his vow of cooperation, his assumption of personal responsibility, his attempt to absolve his implicated aides, his dismissal of the special prosecutor, and his submission of incomplete and inaccurate evidence. Article II charged that he had abused his constitutional powers by using the IRS, the FBI, the CIA, and the "plumbers" to harass citizens, to frustrate investigators, and to interfere with executive operations. This article stemmed from his stonewall defense that had driven investigators to pursue every loose thread while offering no real defense for seemingly improper activities. Article III charged Nixon with willfully denying subpoenae related to Congress's constitutional powers of impeachment. That charge resulted from Nixon's tenacious commitment to executive privilege and confidentiality in cases where they did not apply.

The committee had been expected to pass at least one article because of its 21-17 Democratic majority, but Rodino and the White House both doubted that a partisan vote would lead to impeachment. Consequently, Rodino and the Democrats sought to persuade liberal and moderate Republicans such as Cohen, Fish, Railsback, Smith, McClory, and Butler, while the White House stressed partisanship. When a news story characterized Rodino's leadership as little more than crass partisan politics, the White House overreacted, offending several Republicans on the Committee (Lukas, 1976). Six of the Committee's seventeen Republicans—more than most observers had thought possible—ultimately voted for the first two impeachment articles. Nevertheless, Nixon would be safe until the House voted to impeach and the Senate voted to convict him. House debate was scheduled for August 19 with gavel-to-gavel television coverage. Speechwriter Raymond Price believed that the battle could be won in the Senate.

But before the impeachment resolutions could be debated in the full House, the public learned the contents of the tapes covered by the *U.S. v. Nixon* ruling. Most damaging was the tape of the June 23, 1972, meeting in which Nixon had told Haldeman to have the CIA deflect the FBI's investigation. Price, Haldeman, and Attorney J. Fred Buzhardt all acknowledged that this "smoking pistol" tape provided sufficient evidence to prove the obstruction of justice and abuse of power charges, and the Court's decision itself undermined Nixon's defense against the subpoena defiance charge. The transcripts were "at variance" with Nixon's statements and undermined his case considerably.

Nixon therefore moved to an even more restricted defense: "that when all the facts were brought to my attention, I insisted on a full investigation . . . and prosecution" (Nixon [1974c], p. 623). But the smoking gun revelations contradicted Nixon's defense, confirmed most of the charges against him, and embarrassed most of his supporters. As he saw any hope of winning in the House or Senate evaporate, Nixon resigned on August 8, 1974.

Summary

Why did the Watergate scandal unfold as it did? The Nixon White House and CRP were engaged in a program of activities that were at variance with Nixon's law and order rhetoric. They responded to the initial charges with strategies of avoidance, containment, and a concerted effort to deflect investigations. With those strategies working, Nixon for some reason made "cover-up" the more serious charge. Nevertheless, the containment strategy might have worked if the Vietnam War, protests against it, and the presidential campaign had not all ended at the very moment that Judge Sirica, Woodward and Bernstein, and Democratic senators called for more information about Watergate. When Nixon's aides were implicated in the cover-up he accepted their resignations halfheartedly and pledged personally to see that all the guilty would be brought to justice. Unwilling to fulfill that pledge, he fired those whom he had invested with public confidence. He then grounded his intransigeance in the dubious argument of presidential confidentiality, virtually assuring a legal challenge that he would lose. Because he said too much that was at variance with the facts, public disclosure of the facts foreclosed all options other than impeachment and resignation.

RONALD REAGAN AND THE IRAN-CONTRA CRISIS

The Iran-Contra scandal exploded in two stages during November 1986. First came reports that the United States had sold arms to Iran in exchange for hostages. President Reagan responded with a November 13, 1986, address trivializing the arms sale and characterizing it as an effort to reach moderate Iranian leaders rather than to release hostages. But the speech proved unsatisfying, and a rare press conference was called for November 19. The president's handling of the press conference suggested that he was ill-informed about our weapons, the deal, and the role of our allies (Reagan, 1986b, 1986c).

The second shoe dropped just as administration supporters were predicting that the controversy would abate during the Christmas season. Attorney General Edwin Meese revealed that the considerable profits from the Iranian arms deal had been secretly channeled to the Nicaraguan Contras. This was an apparent violation of the Boland Amendment prohibiting aid to the Contras without congressional approval.

President Reagan was on the ropes from the outset, and his public image suffered accordingly. His performance approval rating plummeted 16 points—from 63 percent in October to 47 percent by December (Gallup Organization, 1986, p. 11). President Reagan appointed the blue-ribbon Tower Commission and a special prosecutor to investigate the allegations.

The Tower Commission Report of March 4, 1987, identified a series of errors, misjudgments, and inappropriate practices. In his public remarks Reagan said that "it was a mistake" ([1987], p. 209), and in an interesting transformation of the problem, he said [italics added], "Now, what should happen when *you* make a mistake is this: *You* take your knocks, *you* learn *your* lessons, and then *you* move on. That's the healthiest way to deal with a problem" (1987, p. 210). In this speech

Reagan used the word "mistake," but he neither provided a clear referent for "it" nor said that "it" was in any way *his* mistake. Indeed, he obligingly instructed *us* about the healthiest way to deal with problems.

The Tower Report and continuing news coverage of the scandal did little to improve Reagan's public approval ratings, which remained below 50 percent through April 1987 (Gallup Organization, 1987b). Worse, his approval-to-disapproval margin shrank from +34 percent to +3 percent, and it recovered to only +13 percent by June. The Gallup poll found that 42 percent of those surveyed found in Iran-Contra some reason to question the president's stewardship, and the fact that their approval of his foreign policy performance dropped 17 percent suggests that Iran-Contra caused most of the damage.

Several congressional committees found cause to investigate the charges. A joint House-Senate committee was formed, and their televised hearings during the summer of 1987 received widespread attention. The centerpiece of the hearings was testimony by Lieutenant Colonel Oliver North and Admiral John Poindexter. The scandal wound down as it seemed that Poindexter had authorized the operations on the basis of his conception of the president's wishes, without specific approval.

Reagan's defenders found solace in three facts. First, approval of Ronald Reagan *himself* dropped only 5 percent during the scandal, and it remained at 75 percent with an astounding margin of 57 percent approval over disapproval. Second, at least 48 percent of those surveyed always approved of Reagan's performance, and he had been as low as 52 percent only twenty months before the scandal. Finally, 54 percent of those disapproving of Reagan's *performance* approved of him *personally* (Gallup Organization, 1986).

As Reagan prepared to leave office, the scandal remained unresolved. Vice President George Bush had a memorable on-air confrontation with CBS anchor Dan Rather when Rather pressed Bush about his role in the Iran-Contra affair. Questions later dogged the Bush administration, and the indictment of Reagan Defense Secretary Caspar Weinberger, the disclosure of Weinberger's memoranda indicating Bush's early support of the arms deal, and the trial of Deputy CIA Director Clair George undermined Bush's drive for re-election. Shortly thereafter, Reagan's Secretary of State George Schultz published his memoirs and toured the talk shows, saying unequivocally that Vice President Bush had been an active advocate of the Iran-Contra plan.

In short, Ronald Reagan survived Iran-Contra, but it undermined his ability to lead and it continued to hamper his successor. The Iran-

Contra scandal hurt the president's performance approval by 27 percent, his foreign policy approval by 17 percent, perceptions of his truthfulness and candor by 60 percent, and his perceived prospects for effectiveness by 32 percent; and trust in his stewardship dropped to 42 percent. How did the allegedly "Great Communicator" get into the rhetorical swamp of Iran-Contra? Why was he able to extricate himself without clearing either his presidency or his successor? The crisis was a short-circuit in Reagan's rhetoric, and the familiar and potent Reagan rhetoric was ill-suited to the defensive posture he chose.

Reagan's Pre-Scandal Rhetoric

Reagan's pre-scandal rhetoric was notable for its sheer pervasiveness. Even before Reagan, presidents had relied heavily on speechmaking. But no one could have foreseen the sheer amount of presidential talk that was to emanate from the Reagan White House. It requires three linear feet to shelve all fifteen volumes and 13,499 pages of *The Public Papers of the Presidents* for Ronald Reagan. Silence apparently was not in Reagan's repertoire. By saying so much Reagan said some things that need not have been said; and because he was Ronald Reagan, he said those things publicly and memorably.

Rhetorical presidents frequently create unnecessary problems for themselves because they speak so much. So it was for Reagan. Because the United States was negotiating with terrorists for the release of hostages, Reagan did not need to say that we would "never" deal with terrorists. Because adversaries can characterize any president's actions and rhetoric as contradictory, a certain measure of presidential silence is often prudent. But for Ronald Reagan the presidential role was a speaking part, and he made the most of it.

Reagan's early presidential discourse exhibited five characteristics. First, his logic simplified a perplexing world for his listeners. He made the complex comprehensible, and the implausible probable. In 1981, for example, he simplified fiscal policy with the notion that "tax and spend" policies had fueled inflation and that "tax cut and spend" policies would help America to outgrow inflation. His Strategic Defense Initiative proposed an invisible shield reminiscent of an old toothpaste commercial that would render the world's complicated defense technologies useless. Even more important, Reagan never complicated the apparently simple issues, as had President Carter. Reagan's simplification was a powerful tool for informing, persuading, and involving his public because it provided citizens with a variety of information short-cuts to understanding national politics.

Second, Reagan used extraordinarily vivid narratives to help his audience visualize his world (Fisher, 1987; Lewis, 1987; Ritter & Henry, 1992; Rogin, 1987; Smith, 1987). His early experience as a sportscaster had taught him how to recreate entire baseball games from a tickertape by imagining scenes and helping his listeners to see it all with him. Later, in Hollywood, he learned how to tailor his message to the cameras and microphones and how to enhance the dramatic power of a narrative. He also learned a host of movie plots and scripts, several of which found their way into his speeches as though they had actually happened (Rogin, 1987), as when he used his role as "The Gipper" in *The Knute Rockne Story* to frame his commencement address at Notre Dame. The confluence of these lessons produced a president who played well for the camera, who thought visually, and who helped his audience to envision his world. Vividness fails to capture fully the essence of Reagan's narrative language. It cinematically presented verbal film clips to a music-video, film-at-eleven culture. The result was a verbal style of such powerful visual images that his words often seemed to have been confirmed by visual inspection.

Third, Reagan created a community—"Mister Reagan's Neighborhood"—by weaving five threads into a seamless tapestry (Smith, 1987). His neighborhood was populated by "extraordinary ordinary Americans" defined by their interdependent jobs rather than by their demographic identities. There were no domestic adversaries in the neighborhood, and liberals, Democrats, and "doubting Thomases" were ignored into oblivion. These hard-working, productive, and cooperative neighbors had a proud heritage of freedom, faith, courage, determination, and generosity. Their heritage was replete with heroes who exemplified Reagan's belief in belief. His can-do Americanism taught that faith and belief are necessary and sufficient causes of success. Critics who pronounced his economic and defense programs unworkable were scolded for undermining faith in the neighborhood's can-do heritage.

Whenever Reagan's good neighbors who could do anything when they really believed also decided to act courageously, their actions were self-evidently moral. Responsible neighbors never question their neighbors' ethics or morals when they claim to be motivated by the neighborhood's heritage. Problems arose in his neighborhood only when the good people forgot to guard themselves against either the runaway train of impersonal government or foreign-based forces of evil.

The fourth characteristic of Reagan's rhetoric was its demonology. President Reagan brought back the moralistic Cold War rhetoric of the Eisenhower era (Ritter & Henry, 1992). This theme complemented his neighborly view that he had no domestic adversaries. The world's problems were due to evil forces loose in the world, and those evil forces controlled the Kremlin—a theme most prominently articulated in his response to the shooting down of Korean Airline flight 007 and in his 1983 address to the Evangelicals (Reagan [1983b], [1983c]). Later, as President Reagan began negotiating arms reduction treaties with Mikhail Gorbachev, he shifted the focus of evil toward smaller dictatorships like those in Iran, Libya, and Nicaragua. Americans were heroic, Reagan seemed to say, but heroic people test themselves against demons and villains. Not unlike a Hollywood horror film, the dramatic tension of the tale of Mister Reagan's Neighborhood came not from the heroes but from the frightening demons who endangered them.

The fifth characteristic of Reagan's rhetoric was his reliance on "refutative epideictic." Only rarely did Reagan respond to criticism with facts. Instead of the forensic discourse we expect in adversarial confrontations, he turned to ceremonial reflections on the essential meaning of America: our ability to endure and to prosper whenever we can believe in, and act worthy of, our heritage. This strategy transformed criticism of his leadership into implicit criticism of the neighborhood, its heritage, and its citizens (Smith, 1987).

In short, Reagan used frequent cinematic narratives to simplify complex subjects, to foster a sense of community, and to deflect criticism of his leadership. At his characteristic best, President Reagan approached Americans as a charming storyteller ready to frame the troublesome events of the day in simple, cinematic stories based on familiar values, premises, and images that reinforced his audience's sense of community.

Reagan and the Rhetorical Dilemmas of Iran-Contra

Why did President Reagan's usually persuasive rhetoric apparently fail during Iran-Contra? His problem was unlike that of Nixon, who had opened a new can of rhetorical worms every time his defense seemed to be working. Reagan's predicament was that the rhetoric that had been the key to his success did not fit the lock of Iran-Contra exculpation. Moreover, his efforts to use his rhetorical prowess where it was inappropriate undermined his presidential leadership. Reagan faced a series of dilemmas.

To speak or not to speak? The sheer quantity of Reagan's previous rhetoric caused problems for him in Iran-Contra. His propensity to talk had created a public expectation of more talk, making it difficult for Reagan to keep silent. Nixon had used the strategy of avoidance with some early success, but Reagan could not avoid the allegations without becoming a very different kind of leader.

On the other hand, for Reagan to talk about the charges would be to put at risk his image of trustworthy leadership. Of course, Reagan spoke—defending his administration in addresses to the nation. This was an odd approach for a president who would later claim to have been out of the decision-making loop, but it was the only choice that Reagan's personal style allowed him to make. An archetypal rhetorical president like Reagan cannot help engaging in public rhetoric. This proved problematic.

To admit or to refute? Reagan was described as being mad as a hornet when he heard about Iran-Contra, but the object of his anger remains unclear: was it the arms sale? the diversion of profits? the lack of congressional consultation? the lack of personal consultation? the lack of success? or something else? The president may not have been directly involved in the scheme, but his protestations of outrage seemed to clash with his earlier rhetoric.

Reagan's outrage sounded hollow because the allegations were fully consistent with the major themes of his pre-scandal rhetoric. The operation was alleged to have been conducted by ordinary people acting heroically, rather than by high level diplomats or generals. The alleged operation was self-evidently moral and well intentioned because good Americans had thought of it. They had expected it to succeed because they had truly believed in their mission. Most important, it was a bold initiative in a good cause that had been executed decisively to avoid the dilatory red tape of Congress and the bureaucracy.

Reagan therefore had two basic options. He could defend his rhetoric by bolstering the actions of his aides and arguing for the transcendent importance of their mission. Or he could retreat from his prior rhetoric by conceding, explicitly or implicitly, that the alleged actions went beyond his conception of bold action. He chose the latter path, thereby undermining the themes of his bold rhetoric of the early 1980s. His defense broke with his prior rhetoric in three ways.

First, Reagan could not use his cinematic narrative style to advantage in Iran-Contra. He could hardly describe vividly a series of meetings that he claimed not to remember. Nor could he describe meetings among national security personnel and arms dealers without helping his accusers. His subsequent descriptions of his meetings kept the hot potato in the White House.

Second, Reagan's military anecdotes and calls for decisiveness had to be tempered. His rhetoric's devaluation of careful deliberation had taken on ominous implications, among them the possibility that a presidential advocate of bold and decisive action might encourage, or even approve, rash acts by his subordinates that could jeopardize both long- and short-term interests. His critics in the House and Senate charged that the Reagan administration had rejected responsible deliberation and had authorized the project without congressional consultations—a course of action that was defended by Colonel North in his congressional testimony. Once again, Reagan's rhetoric could not refute the charges because the charges fit the logic of his prior rhetoric.

Third, Reagan could not use his characteristic strategy of simplification because there was no simple explanation for Iran-Contra that was publicly acceptable. Every simple question like "Why did we do this?" or "Who approved it?" drew complex and confusing answers. He began his first explanation in the familiar style. The Iranian initiative, he explained, "was undertaken for the simplest and best of reasons." But he proceeded to explain four reasons that were not connected in any obvious way: (1) "to renew a relationship with the nation of Iran," (2) "to bring an honorable end to the bloody 6-year war between Iran and Iraq," (3) "to eliminate state-sponsored terrorism and subversion," and (4) "to effect the safe return of all hostages" (Reagan, 1986c, p. 1559). Few of his listeners could reasonably be expected to repeat this purportedly simple reason the next morning, and an America accustomed to digestible news developed a severe case of information heartburn.

Reagan's inability to simplify the allegations nurtured such confusion that he held a press conference to try again. But the president's confusion and uneasiness at the November 19 press conference seemed only to sharpen the impression that Reagan himself was unable to take charge of this problem. The president's defense was that he did not remember approving the plan. But Americans accustomed to Reagan's mythic stature found it difficult to reconcile that image with his professed ignorance, despite his ample efforts to demonstrate it. Belief-to-disbelief comparisons ran heavily against Reagan across all demographic groups: -33 percent among Republicans, -60 percent overall, and -70 percent among independents (Gallup Organization, 1987a).

But recall that Reagan's overall personal approval dropped only 5 percent, presumably because the public's general trust in him transcended this incident and the delicacy of the subject required presidential discretion.

To use epideictic or forensic themes? President Reagan's usual tendency to construe policy criticism as an attack on our heritage was unworkable in this case. In the Beirut truck-bombing speech, for example, the president had deflected questions about his policy with references to the courage and spirit of the martyred marines (Reagan, 1983a). But Iran-Contra offered little for him to work with: memories of the Ayatollah, slick deals, shrewd planning, and his long-standing pledge *not* to deal for hostages. Although he embellished the heroic persona of Colonel Oliver North to some advantage, North himself was responsible for most of that embellishment. For Reagan to make the Iran-Contra confrontation the epitome of his story of the American experience would have been to put that narrative and its persuasive power at risk. Moreover, Reagan's rhetoric had long emphasized the confidence borne of perceived morality, wisdom, and invulnerability. The Iran-Contra decision makers' confidence in their planning resonated with Reagan's can-do rhetoric, their ethical overconfidence resonated with his theme of self-evident morality, and their confidence in their own wisdom resonated with Reagan's faith in America's proud heritage and ordinary people.

For President Reagan to use this theme for exculpation, he would have had to distinguish between confidence and overconfidence—a term not to be found in the Reagan lexicon. It was the planners' overconfidence that had led them into difficulty, but much of Reagan's rhetorical appeal had been grounded in the limitless potential of faith. Iran-Contra was inappropriate for refutative epideictic because Reagan could neither narrate nor write a story of the American experience with the danger of overconfidence as its theme.

Reagan's alternative to refutative epideictic was traditional forensic argument. But propositions and facts had never been his strong suits, and he was renowned for falling asleep at Cabinet meetings and for making factual errors. To address the charges against him in a linear propositional form, armed with a mass of detailed evidence, would have made Reagan look foolish and uninformed. And that turned out to be his best approach.

Reagan's address to the nation, his press conference, and his response to the Tower Commission Report all made him look inept. He quickly proved to be misinformed about the kinds of weapons sold to

Iran, about the size of the shipment, about the role of third countries, and about the rechannelling of funds to the Contras. By responding to the charges in a rhetorical form in which he was basically inept, Reagan dramatized his unfamiliarity with the entire operation and staked out his claim to innocence.

To fight the demons or to tame them? Initially President Reagan's foreign policy rhetoric had been demon-oriented. Early in his second term Reagan began the rhetorical rehabilitation of the Soviet Union and its new leader, Mikhail Gorbachev. For Reagan, Gorbachev was sufficiently different from his predecessors to permit negotiations between them. Before long "Gorby" was hailed by Americans and their magazines as a reasonable and moral world leader.

But Iranian leaders received no such rhetorical rehabilitation prior to the news that the administration had sold arms to them. Since Reagan had said, "I don't know whether reconciliation [with Iran] would be possible" (Reagan, 1981) nine days after his inauguration, there was only one public statement by the president about American-Iranian relations.

Reagan did discuss Iran with the covert initiatives under way, and he could have begun the process of revising Americans' perceptions of Iran in ways that would have better fit his administration's policy. But he chose a very different path, telling members of the 1985 convention of the American Bar Association that:

The American people are not—I repeat, not—going to tolerate intimidation, terror, and outright acts of war against this nation and its people. And we're especially not going to tolerate these attacks from outlaw states run by the strangest collection of misfits, looney tunes, and squalid criminals since the advent of the Third Reich. ([1985], p. 898)

Were we now to accept the covert sale of arms to such people without doubting the president? This speech neither enhanced our relations with Iran nor prepared Americans for rapprochement with moderate Iranian leaders.

Moreover, the president had annually renewed his emergency powers toward Iran. The last of these renewals had been sent to Congress just three days before the president's revelation of the diplomatic efforts and arms sales. "The crisis has eased, but it has not been fully resolved," President Reagan told Congress, and "it is necessary to maintain in force the broad authorities that may be needed to respond to the process of implementation" (1986a, p. 1551) of the original Carter agreement. If his requests for authorization were sincere, why was he selling arms to them? On the other hand, if the situation had improved sufficiently to justify the arms sale, why was the president using this justification to extend his emergency powers?

Surely Ronald Reagan and his 75 percent approval rating could have improved the Iranians' image, much as he had improved Gorbachev's image, had he chosen to do so. But he did not. Consequently, most Americans could interpret this deal only through the nightmarish memories they retained from the 1979–1980 hostage crisis.

Instead, Reagan again shifted the focus of evil in the modern world. As Evil had fled the Kremlin for Libya and Iran, it now fled the Middle East for Nicaragua. With Daniel Ortega and his Sandinistas as the embodiment of Evil, Reagan could emphasize his efforts to defeat them and to minimize his dealings with the Iranians (Stuckey, 1990). Over the long haul Reagan's commitment to the Nicaraguan Contras failed to persuade the public, which, by a 69-29 percent margin, eventually favored cancelling the authorized aid to the Contras. But in the short term it kept attention on Contra aid, the hemispheric component of the Iran-Contra operation, the component that could best be defended.

Executive versus Legislative Branches

Reagan described his philosophy of executive management for a *Fortune* magazine cover story that appeared just before the scandal broke. The following statement appeared three separate times in the interview: "Surround yourself with the best people you can find," said the president, "delegate authority, and don't interfere as long as the policy you've decided upon is being carried out" (Dowd, 1986, pp. 33, 36). This approach to management was a logical extension of Reagan's respect for extraordinary ordinary people and for can-do Americanism. When his system of delegated responsibilities worked, his administration worked well and the president got the credit. The unusual Reagan style of delegation entailed more delegation than supervision, and that was hardly lost on those who worked in his administration. Admiral Poindexter, Colonel North, and CIA Director William Casey apparently inferred that the president's delegation of authority to them was sufficient to permit implementation of their plans without either full consultation or specific presidential authorization.

Reagan's problem was that Iran-Contra revealed the difficulties inherent in his management style. The public had seen his statement of management philosophy on the cover of *Fortune* magazine just the month before, and they could apply it: Had Reagan really surrounded himself with the best people he could find? Had he really delegated so much authority? Could he really not have supervised this operation at all? Was this a policy that he personally had decided upon? Was it possible not to interfere "as long as the policy you've decided upon is being carried out" without considerably more knowledge than Reagan was willing to admit? On the other hand, the insulation of Reagan from knowledge about the Iran-Contra operation implied that he also had little knowledge about previous successful operations.

The Iran-Contra scandal compelled President Reagan to salvage either his trustworthiness by sacrificing his perceived competence, or his perceived competence at the expense of his trustworthiness. Those who had perceived Reagan as a strong and informed leader were driven to question his trustworthiness, and those who had perceived him as a paragon of integrity were compelled to reassess his managerial competence. It was not a pretty choice for Reagan's supporters, and their anguish was savored by his opponents.

The president's management problem was compounded by his relations with Congress. Because the immediate charge was that his administration had proceeded without congressional authorization, Congress was directly involved in the affair from the outset. The administration's legislative strategy had for years been to use Reagan's frequent discourse to induce public pressure on Congress. As it had for Presidents Wilson, Roosevelt, Johnson, and Nixon before him, this strategy brought Reagan short-term legislative victories and a sour executive-legislative relationship. The strategy of going public had helped Reagan to achieve policy victories like the tax cut, but it fostered an adversarial relationship between Reagan and the Congress.

This institutional conflict was exacerbated by the president's intensive campaign efforts on behalf of 1986 Republican senatorial candidates Paula Hawkins, Jeremiah Denton, Jim Broyhill, and others—all of whom lost. The incoming Senate was newly Democratic, and it included senators like Bob Graham and Terry Sanford who arrived knowing that this president had failed in his bid to undercut them with their constituents. Perhaps they also realized that any president's leverage depends on his popularity in the legislator's home district (Edwards, 1980), a test that Reagan had just failed. Consequently, the reports that the president had not fulfilled his legal obligation to work with the Congress surfaced in a relational context most unfavorable to his exculpation.

The Iran-Contra revelations were shocking to many people, but they should not have been surprising. Why would anyone who had been listening to Reagan's rhetoric have been surprised to hear that his administration might have attempted to achieve its agenda with a bold initiative that circumvented governmental procedures? The characteristics of Reagan's successful pre-scandal rhetoric were ill-suited to his new task.

Summary

Iran-Contra was a rhetorical crisis for the Reagan presidency because the otherwise successful Reagan rhetoric was ill-suited to the crisis. Toward the end of his first press conference on Iran-Contra the president was asked, "What would be wrong in saying that a mistake was made on a very high-risk gamble so that you can get on with the next [two] years?" Like Nixon before him, President Reagan insisted on vindication: "Because I don't think a mistake was made. It was a high-risk gamble, and it was a gamble that, as I've said, I believe the circumstances warranted. And I don't see that it has been a fiasco or a great failure of any kind" (1986d, p. 1590). Had Reagan admitted then that "mistakes were made," the court of public opinion might not have returned its indictment. Had he embarked on a rhetoric of prudence, of cautious deliberation, and of a neighborhood of kinder and gentler people who sometimes erred in the process of trying to do what they thought to be right, he might have turned the corner. But that would not have been Ronald Reagan. It was, however, the early rhetoric of George Bush.

CONCLUSIONS

Presidents who rely on public persuasion to lead will periodically create problems for themselves. This chapter has analyzed the rhetorical crises faced by Richard Nixon and Ronald Reagan—two archetypal rhetorical presidents. Each achieved early success because of his rhetoric, each talked himself into trouble, and each spent most of his administration's final years trying to resolve his rhetorical crisis. Our analyses lead us to four conclusions.

First, a rhetorical crisis is most likely when a president's rhetoric is out of step with his administration's actions. Richard Nixon stressed law and order but knew in general terms of efforts by his supporters to engage in illegal acts, and he himself obstructed justice. He denied any White House involvement whatsoever in the break-in but led the cover-up from the Oval Office. He pledged to cooperate with investigators so that the guilty would be punished after ordering his aides to deflect those investigations. Ronald Reagan said repeatedly that the United States would never negotiate for hostages even while his administration was negotiating for the release of hostages. He warned about dangerous Iranians and then sold arms to them. He spoke about the importance of bold and decisive efforts by people who truly believe in a good cause, but he hedged when confronted with allegations of just such an operation.

Perhaps the Nixon and Reagan administrations should have paid more attention to their prior rhetoric when formulating their policies. Perhaps they should have tempered their rhetoric so that it could better match their actions. In any case, both administrations were rhetorically driven by themes and arguments that they could not enact. But this is not to equate the Nixon and Reagan crises.

Richard Nixon's defensive rhetoric accounted for most of his trouble. By publicly misrepresenting and overstating his position time after time, Nixon defined the culpable acts, legitimized investigative efforts, defined the charges against himself, steered the conflict into the courts, and, finally, ended his own presidency. Perhaps Nixon's critics finally got him, or perhaps his obsession with outfoxing his critics led him to do their work for them.

Ronald Reagan's case was quite different. He did not make his predicament worse by talking about it; he simply could not use the rhetoric that had served him so well. To talk of bold actions, for example, simply made the charges seem more plausible. The contrast between the Nixon and Reagan predicaments points toward a second conclusion.

A successful rhetorical president has become so by developing three resources: public trust, an image of managerial competence, and a coherent rhetoric that unites trustworthiness and competence into a vision that coordinates public choices. When one of the horses in this troika pulls up lame, the other two compensate in ways that change the behavior of all three.

Richard Nixon focused on his image of competence at the expense of trust. He denounced the stupidity of the Watergate break-in. He claimed that he and his White House aides had been unaware of the project, and he later attributed his misstatements to inept investigations.

Some presidents would have denounced the break-in as illegal, immoral, unethical—perhaps especially, if they had been unaware of it—but not Nixon. He invested his waning credibility in the half-hearted effort to excuse the fine public servants who had made mistakes, and he pledged publicly to pursue an investigation that he had privately ordered to be deflected. Such choices by Nixon guaranteed that the facts, when revealed, would prove him guilty of a breach of trust. Moreover, by using his rhetorical skills to defend his indefensible position, he put those skills at risk—sharply curtailing his opportunities for speeches and press conferences. Ironically, Nixon's political miscalculations regarding his accusers eventually undermined his image of competence as well.

Unlike Nixon, who never felt well liked, Ronald Reagan liked to be liked, and he was. Reagan focused on his personal image of trustworthiness. By design or by accident, Reagan salvaged his image of trustworthiness by sacrificing his image of executive competence. In his first Iran-Contra speech and press conference he sounded like a person who thought himself well informed, but a spate of White House corrections and retractions made it clear that he was not. Many of his accusers relished this proof of his managerial "detachment," even as they failed to see that it preserved his essential image of trustworthiness. Reagan's supporters could sustain their faith in him, believing that he would not knowingly have approved of the operation.

But in pursuing this line of defense Reagan tempered the rhetoric that had made him successful. Indeed, most of his core supporters liked Oliver North and the operation, and they continued to support President Reagan. But they might well have supported him even more strongly if he had boldly defended the operation in his pre-scandal rhetoric. This would not have resulted in a breach of trust because his actions would then have been consistent with his rhetoric. By tempering his rhetoric, Reagan diluted his ability to lead public opinion during his final two years, and he bequeathed to George Bush a less forceful rhetorical posture.

What could Presidents Nixon and Reagan have said or done to better handle their crises? Ideally, they could have insured that their words and actions were congruent. But like so many ideal standards, this one is deceptively simple. Both crises concerned inconsistencies between public words and private actions, and between the words of the presidents and the actions of their subordinates. Still, better efforts could have been made. Nixon need not have pledged to help investigations that he had already worked to deflect; Reagan need not have backed off from an operation that was consistent with his rhetoric.

Let us give Richard Nixon the benefit of the doubt regarding his role in the Watergate break-in. What could he have done from the moment he heard about it? First, he could have denounced any unauthorized entry into any political headquarters as an illegal and improper disruption of the democratic process. Second, he could have refrained from encouraging a cover-up; short of that, he could have refrained from making "cover-up" the culpable act. Third, he could have demanded, rather than accepted, the resignations of those implicated in either the break-in or the cover-up, and he could have attributed to them full responsibility and guilt for their transgressions. Finally, he and Price could have used the present perfect tense to describe their commitment to investigate the break-in, thus semantically closing the book on Watergate and shifting the burden of justifying further investigations to his accusers. Had he made these four rhetorical choices, perhaps even only two or three of them, Nixon might have saved his presidency.

Ronald Reagan's crisis proved less damaging to his presidency, and his alternatives were, accordingly, less difficult. Reagan could have salvaged his perceived competence and his rhetoric by defending and justifying the Iran-Contra operation. North, Poindexter, and the others had incorporated a strategy of "plausible deniability" into their plan in the hope that the president would be shielded from scandal. But Reagan's problem was that such denials were incongruent with his prior rhetoric. Reagan could conceivably have used that rhetoric to justify the entire operation. Specifically, the president could have expressed his grave doubts about the constitutionality of the Boland Amendment and underscored his obligation to direct foreign policy. If he were to lose a court battle over the point, then Reagan, unlike Nixon, could have apologized for making a judgment error in a national security context that demanded secrecy and urgency. The irony is that Reagan used these very arguments to disavow the operation rather than to justify it. And because he disavowed the logical extension of his own rhetoric he unnecessarily undermined that rhetoric as well as public regard for his managerial competence.

The Watergate and Iran-Contra episodes reveal a significant danger inherent in the rhetorical presidency: the danger of talking too much. Roderick P. Hart, the most penetrating and acerbic critic of this trend toward presidential speechifying, observed that:

The natural inclination of one who speaks for a living is to become audience driven, to become less and less inclined to examine one's own thoughts analytically and more and more attentive to the often uncritical reactions of popular assemblages. . . . [E]xtensive public speaking begets repetition since there are only a limited number of topics confronting any given president . . . [and] Repetition, in turn, begets (1) a dulling of the intellect, (2) a growing sense that one's views are correct, and (3) the feeling that rhetorical action is equivalent to empirical action. . . . All of this leaves few moments for the other sorts of things we expect a president to do—namely, to think. . . . It is axiomatic that the more one speaks, the less time one has to reflect. (Hart, 1987, pp. 195–198)

It is also axiomatic that a president who leads through public persuasion can talk too much. Too much talk can betray a president's vulnerabilities. Too much talk can exhaust a president's rhetorical resources. Too much talk can create contradictions to be exploited by presidential adversaries. Too much talk can lead to stylistic carelessness—saying the right things badly.

Watergate and Iran-Contra are not the only instances of presidents in rhetorical crisis. Woodrow Wilson's campaign to pressure the Senate toward ratification of the Treaty of Versailles and Lyndon Johnson's Vietnam rhetoric have many of the earmarks of rhetorical crises. Richard Nixon and Ronald Reagan reached the presidency largely because of their success with political rhetoric, and each seemed especially well suited to the job description of the rhetorical presidency. Perhaps their crises, their choices, and their tragic falls show that even the best equipped presidents are susceptible to rhetorical crises. But a more plausible hypothesis is that rhetorical crises are an occupational affliction of rhetorical presidents: those who live by the word die by the word.

REFERENCES

Associated Press. (1993, May 18). Public gets three more hours of Nixon tapes. *Winston-Salem Journal*, p. 5.

Bernstein, C., & Woodward, B. (1974). *All the president's men*. New York: Simon & Schuster.

Brummett, B. (1975). Presidential substance: The address of August 15, 1973. *Western Speech Communication, 39*, 249–259.

Dean, J. (1976). *Blind ambition*. New York: Simon & Schuster.

Dowd, A. R. (1986, September 15). What managers can learn from manager Reagan. *Fortune*, pp. 33–41.

Edwards, G. C., III. (1980). *Presidential influence in Congress.* San Francisco: W. H. Freeman.

Fisher, W. R. (1987). *Human communication as narration: Toward a philosophy of reason, value, and action.* Columbia: University of South Carolina Press.

Gallup Organization. (1986, December). *Gallup Report* (Report No. 255). Wilmington, DE: Scholarly Resources.

Gallup Organization. (1987a, January–February). *Gallup Report* (Report No. 256–257). Wilmington, DE: Scholarly Resources.

Gallup Organization. (1987b, June 23). *Gallup Report* (Report No. 261). Wilmington, DE: Scholarly Resources.

Haldeman, H. R. (1978). *The ends of power.* New York: Dell.

Harrell, J., Ware, B. L., & Linkugel, W. A. (1975). Failure of apology in American politics: Nixon on Watergate. *Speech Monographs, 42,* 245–262.

Hart, R. P. (1987). *The sound of leadership: Presidential communication in the modern age.* Chicago: University of Chicago Press.

Jaworski, L. (1976). *The right and the power.* Houston: Gulf.

King, G., & Ragsdale, L. (1988). *The elusive executive: Discovering statistical patterns in the presidency.* Washington, DC: Congressional Quarterly.

Lewis, W. F. (1987). Telling America's story: Narrative form and the Reagan presidency. *Quarterly Journal of Speech, 73,* 280–302.

Lukas, J. A. (1976). *Nightmare: The underside of the Nixon years.* New York: Viking.

Nixon, R. M. (1972a). The president's news conference of June 22. *Weekly Compilation of Presidential Documents, 8,* 1078–1079.

Nixon, R. M. [1972b]. The president's news conference of August 29. *Public papers of the president* (pp. 827–838). Washington, DC: U.S. Government Printing Office.

Nixon, R. M. (1972c). The president's news conference of October 5. *Weekly Compilation of Presidential Documents, 8,* 1489.

Nixon, R. M. [1973a]. Address to the nation about Watergate, April 30. *Public papers of the president* (pp. 328–333). Washington, DC: U.S. Government Printing Office.

Nixon, R. M. [1973b]. Address to the nation about the Watergate investigation, August 15. *Public papers of the president* (pp. 691–698). Washington, DC: U.S. Government Printing Office.

Nixon, R. M. (1973c). Executive privilege. *Weekly Compilation of Presidential Documents, 9,* 253–255.

Nixon, R. M. (1973d). Presidential tapes and documents. *Weekly Compilation of Presidential Documents, 9,* 1329–1331.

Nixon, R. M. [1973e]. Statements about the Watergate investigations, May 22. *Public papers of the president* (pp. 547–555). Washington, DC: U.S. Government Printing Office.

Nixon, R. M. [1974a]. Address to the nation announcing answer to the House judiciary committee subpoena for additional presidential tape recordings, April 29. *Public papers of the president* (pp. 389–397). Washington, DC: U.S. Government Printing Office.

Nixon, R. M. (1974b). President's news conference of February 25. *Weekly Compilation of Presidential Documents, 10,* 250–256.

Nixon, R. M. [1974c]. Statement announcing availability of additional transcripts of presidential tape recordings, August 5. *Public papers of the president* (pp. 621–623). Washington, DC: U.S. Government Printing Office.

Nixon, R. M. (1978). *RN: The memoirs of Richard Nixon*. New York: Grosset & Dunlop.

Price, R. (1977). *With Nixon*. New York: Viking.

Reagan, R. (1981). The president's press conference of January 29. *Weekly Compilation of Presidential Documents, 17*, 65.

Reagan, R. (1983a). Events in Lebanon and Grenada. *Weekly Compilation of Presidential Documents, 19*, 1502.

Reagan, R. [1983b]. The Korean Airline massacre, September 5. In C. A. Smith & K. B. Smith (Eds.), *The president and the public: Rhetoric and national leadership* (pp. 283–289). Lanham, MD: University Press of America, 1985.

Reagan, R. [1983c]. Remarks at the annual convention of the National Association of Evangelicals, March 8. *Public papers of the president* (pp. 359–364). Washington, DC: U.S. Government Printing Office.

Reagan, R. [1985]. Remarks at the annual convention of the American Bar Association, July 8. *Public papers of the president* (pp. 894–900). Washington, DC: U.S. Government Printing Office.

Reagan, R. (1986a). Extension of emergency powers toward Iran, November 10. *Weekly Compilation of Presidential Documents, 22*, 1551.

Reagan, R. (1986b). Independent counsel to investigate the arms sale to Iran. *Weekly Compilation of Presidential Documents, 22*, 1613–1614.

Reagan, R. (1986c). Iran–United States relations. *Weekly Compilation of Presidential Documents, 22*, 1559–1561.

Reagan, R. (1986d). The president's news conference of November 19. *Weekly Compilation of Presidential Documents, 22*, 1583–1591.

Reagan, R. [1987]. Address to the nation on the Iran arms and Contra aid controversy, March 4. *Public papers of the president* (pp. 208–211). Washington, DC: U.S. Government Printing Office.

Ritter, K., & Henry, D. (1992). *Ronald Reagan: The great communicator*. Westport, CT: Greenwood.

Rogin, M. (1987). *Ronald Reagan, the movie: And other episodes in political demonology*. Berkeley: University of California Press.

Smith, C. A. (1987). Mister Reagan's neighborhood: Rhetoric and national unity. *Southern Speech Communication Journal, 52*, 219–239.

Stuckey, M. (1990). *Playing the game: The presidential rhetoric of Ronald Reagan*. New York: Praeger.

White, T. H. (1975). *Breach of faith*. New York: Atheneum.

The White House Transcripts. (1973). New York: Bantam Books.

9

Conclusions:
Presidential Leadership in the 1990s

The previous chapters have explored various aspects of presidential leadership as persuasion. This chapter summarizes the major findings and uses them to illuminate presidential leadership during the remarkable period of George Bush's fall and Bill Clinton's first hundred days.

MAJOR FINDINGS

This book has covered a variety of topics in a variety of ways, and a number of presidents and scholars have had speaking parts. This chapter can best begin with a curtain call for the major ideas—a moment for us to see them all together on the stage.

1. Presidential leadership in the modern era entails persuasion. In Chapter 1 we summarized nine of the major works on presidential leadership written by political scientists to establish the central role played by persuasive communication. It is only through communication that issues and people can be discussed and understood; thus it is only through persuasive communication that presidential candidates can develop and sustain their electoral and governing coalitions.

But communication between presidents and their citizens has rarely been easy. After all, not until Warren Harding's administration in the 1920s did presidents have microphones, amplifiers, and speakers to help them reach their audiences. Today, of course, presidents have radio, television, satellite links, fax machines, and electronic mail as well. But not all this change has helped rhetorical presidents. When Roosevelt spoke of the Depression and war he had access to three radio networks owned by two corporations through which to reach his listeners. Presidents Kennedy, Johnson, Nixon, and Ford had access to three commercial television networks as well as radio. But Presidents Bush and Clinton talk to a society that is familiar with satellite dishes, fifty-channel cable systems, video rentals, and remote channel changers with add and delete features. Most of these channels engage in narrowcasting—continuous programming of similar programs to a target audience—as opposed to the broad-based broadcasting of old. Because of this proliferation of channels, no president can command the public's attention as presidents once could.

Moreover, when presidents are discussed in the news the coverage rarely includes much of the president's own message. Hart (1987) found that presidents were seen during other people's discourse: the voice track amounted to reporters, 46.8 percent; the president's contemporaries, 45.3 percent; and presidents, 7.9 percent. As a result, most national stories are visually associated with the president while others are providing the narrative. The dilemma facing contemporary presidents is that they can no longer command the attention of all their citizens, and they have only one chance in thirteen of having their words narrate their own actions. Even when a president appears on television to frame the nation's choices, that appearance is framed by the network anchors. C-SPAN and C-SPAN 2 provide unframed messages, but only to those people with cable television who do not delete it from their viewing menu. In short, contemporary presidential leadership entails persuasion in an era when public persuasion is increasingly difficult.

2. The presidential job description constrains presidents' personal rhetorical flexibility. Constitutional responsibilities, presidential precedents, and public expectations have combined to create a twentieth-century rhetorical presidency that is a striking contrast to the Framers' presidency. In the mold of Woodrow Wilson and the Roosevelts, contemporary presidents employ eight distinct genres of presidential discourse; they use language that differs from that used by candidates, corporate executives, social activists, and religious leaders even though it evidences elements of each. Presidents speak, and they speak in ways that are characteristically presidential.

3. Presidents create electoral and governing coalitions by helping others to interpret social and political realities. The interpretive systems approach to political communication described in Chapter 2 holds that all individuals have four innate, involuntary interpretive processes—needing, symbolizing, reasoning, and preferencing—which they coordinate by creating and adopting four kinds of social interpretive structures: laws, language, logic, and ideology. As people use these interpretive processes and structures in their communication with others they find moments of convergence and divergence that help them to feel themselves members of some interpretive communities rather than others. These overlapping, incongruent interpretive communities struggle for the right to interpret social and political realities for everyone else. Presidents use discourse to create and sustain interpretive coalitions, such that presidential rhetoric is a melting pot of needs, words, arguments, and priorities.

4. The breadth and heterogeneity of presidents' interpretive coalitions impinge directly on their latitude to lead, and vice versa. In Chapter 3, our examination of Gerald Ford's attempt to create presidential coalitions revealed his dilemma: Ford could say neither that the pardon established Nixon's guilt nor that it denied him the protection of self-incrimination because he needed the Nixon loyalists to keep his administration afloat. Moreover, Ford had to reach out with bold initiatives such as the earned pardons for Vietnam-era draft evaders because he had neither the loyalty of the Nixon holdovers nor solid support from those who might challenge him for the 1976 nomination.

Theoretically, the broader the president's coalition the more latitude the president has to lead. However, sociological and technological changes have made American society more pluralistic and its messages more available. The net effect of these changes has been that broad coalitions can no longer be as homogeneous as they were in the days of a white male electorate. Consequently, broad electoral coalitions are heterogeneous, with diverse communities perceiving selectively the candidates' messages. Once a president has been elected, his latitude to lead is constrained by the heterogeneity of his electoral coalition because each community in that coalition has been primed for disappointment. The elusive key to presidential governance in the late twentieth century is visionary rhetoric that unifies diverse Americans around specifics rather than abstractions.

5. Presidential coalitions are built around both convergence and divergence. Unity and division, identification and polarization are interdependent. They can best be understood as unifying *around* and dividing *from*, as identifying *with* and polarizing *against*. Ford preferred to heal, rather than to exploit, the wounds of the Vietnam and Watergate turmoil, whereas George Bush created his electoral coalition by polarizing conservatives and moderates against liberals. The fact that both administrations ended in electoral defeats should underscore the point that neither approach is strategically superior. Presidents Roosevelt, Truman, Eisenhower, Kennedy, Johnson, Nixon, Ford, Carter, Reagan, and Bush had the rhetorical option of polarizing Americans against the common enemies of Depression, Fascism, and Communism. But the end of the Cold War impoverished American political rhetoric by denying rhetors an object of fear and hatred beyond our borders. The demise of the Soviet Union defused both the rhetoric of the Evil Empire and much of the fear of World War III, and the quick and easy defeat of Iraq (billed as the world's fourth largest army) has made it more difficult to arouse public passions with foreign policy rhetoric. Indeed, the public seemed almost in a daze when President Bush declared a no-fly zone in Iraq and sent relief troops into Somalia and when President Clinton considered military action in Bosnia-Herzegovina. In short, presidents since Franklin Roosevelt have often unified Americans by polarizing them against external demons that, for better and worse, are not salient features of the 1990s. Without external demons President Clinton has only Americans converging and diverging with other Americans.

6. *Presidents can seek convergence and divergence on individual or community levels.* President Truman's antifamine program succeeded because it offered a wide variety of personal reasons for people to conserve food, and because it mobilized around existing interpretive communities such as business, labor, and schools. Carter's attempts to persuade people to conserve energy failed because he ignored his citizens' personal needs and because he largely ignored existing interpretive communities in favor of new federal agencies.

7. *Presidential persuasion can succeed or fail because of its timing.* Kennedy's address on civil rights worked well, in part, because he spoke just hours after Governor Wallace had defied the federal mandate to desegregate the University of Alabama. The Roosevelt and Reagan inaugurals worked, in part, because they used their first speeches to frame the issues and principles that would guide their administrations. On the other hand, Gerald Ford's address justifying the Nixon pardon was delivered without warning on a Sunday morning, thus inviting both the judgment that he wanted to slip it past the public and extensive news coverage on Monday, normally the slowest news day. Jimmy Carter's unexplained postponement of his energy address from July 5 to July 15 contributed to the suspicion that he was indecisive and raised expectations for the address. And the decision to delay Carter's Panama Canal address from September until February gave the New Right time to strengthen and disseminate their arguments against the treaties. Each

of these addresses either met or failed to meet a political problem at a rhetorically appropriate moment.

8. Presidential persuasion is adversarial, and competing rhetors play important roles. American presidents lead in relation to aspiring leaders with whom they must jockey for support. Each presidential argument implies one or more opposing arguments with which it must cope. Kennedy tried to allay the fears of foreign policy conservatives in his American University commencement address, and he transcended the segregationists' response to his legal arguments by reframing civil rights as a moral issue. Although Presidents Ford and Carter both supported the renegotiated Panama Canal treaties, Ronald Reagan and Phillip Crane advanced a more compelling narrative that persuaded the Republican Party to move toward an antitreaty position, partly to mobilize their resources to challenge Carter and the Democrats in 1980. By winning the narrative conflict the New Right won the right to interpret foreign policy for the 1980s. Nixon stonewalled the Watergate investigation effectively for several months, but he was unprepared to simultaneously protect himself in the courts, the Congress, and in the court of public opinion.

9. The rhetorical form of a presidential address has political consequences. President Reagan was a master storyteller who generally avoided using propositional logic. His addresses unified most Americans by telling their story in a way that invited them to see his policy proposals as reasonable and preferable to their alternatives. When he did use propositional arguments in response to the first Iran-Contra charges his ineptitude with the form invited his audience to perceive him as utterly uninformed about the operation, a perception that worked to his advantage. A particular kind of narrative, the jeremiad, merges presidential authority with the first American sermonic form to elevate presidents and to undercut their adversaries, to encourage social cohesion and optimism while undermining the Framers' checks and balances on the presidency, and to advocate social change in terms of historical continuity.

10. Presidential language, especially self-references, can be crucial to effective leadership. Because people think with symbols, a figure of speech is a figure of thought. Hart's (1984) work on presidential language, discussed in Chapter 1, found that contemporary presidents employ an unusually high frequency of self-references. This is a two-edged sword. Self-references accentuate presidents' personal leadership, but they also link those presidents to positions and actions for which they receive blame as well as credit. Ford justified the Nixon

pardon with a string of references to "my" responsibility, "my" decision, and "my" conscience when impersonal references to the presidential authority to pardon would have insulated him from unnecessary
criticism. Nixon pledged personally to cooperate with those investigating the Watergate affair when he had no intention of doing so; a grammatical choice for which, it can be argued, he was driven from office.
Carter's energy jeremiad spoke of a crisis of public confidence, then
dwelled on what he personally would do to solve it. All three presidencies were injured, perhaps even critically, by these language choices.
On the other hand, Ronald Reagan avoided using any self-references
when he admitted that "mistakes were made" in the Iran-Contra scandal. Indeed, he even spoke about what "you" do when "you" have a
problem.

*11. Successful presidential leadership requires presidential rhetoric
that evolves to meet changing political circumstances.* Political situations invite rhetorical choices that have political consequences. Unless
the presidents' rhetoric adapts to evolving political situations, the presidents will be left behind. George Bush's discourse failed to adapt to the
changes in America and the world, and the problems and divisions
around which Americans had diverged in 1988 were largely irrelevant
by 1992. Nixon was able to sustain his electoral coalition throughout
1972 by avoiding and containing the Watergate scandal, but he devoted
too little attention to the effects of his choices on his governing coalition and it collapsed. Indeed, his Watergate rhetoric amounted to one
bad choice after another. Reagan chose not to use his familiar rhetoric
to justify Iran-Contra, so he changed his language and logic abruptly.
These presidents might have recognized more clearly the ratcheting
effect of their words on their political circumstances. This leads to our
final point.

*12. The contemporary rhetorical presidency requires presidents to
use public persuasion that often backfires.* Ford's speech justifying his
potentially explosive decision to pardon some Vietnam-era draft
evaders facilitated public acceptance, but his remarks justifying the
Nixon pardon plague him still. George Bush's attempts to polarize
Americans with conservative rhetoric against congressional intransigence, liberal permissiveness, and Saddam Hussein helped him in
the short term, but they invited the candidacy of Pat Buchanan who
promised actions to match the rhetoric. Jimmy Carter went to the public
in support of the Panama Canal treaties, but in doing so he provided
more words for the New Right to use in their critique of his interpretive
vision. And as Richard Nixon talked more and more about his role in

the Watergate case, he gave his adversaries more and more ways to trip him up. To these cases we should add the experiences of Woodrow Wilson and Lyndon Johnson, who found that rousing public rhetoric alienated some of the swing votes in Congress whom they might better have persuaded personally and in private.

In short, modern presidential leadership entails persuasion. It matters greatly who says what to whom, when, why, how, and with what evolutionary political results. Let us end the book by using our perspective to illuminate the surprising fall of George Bush and the first one hundred days of the Clinton presidency.

THE END OF THE BUSH ADMINISTRATION

In just four years George Bush went from being perceived as a vice presidential "wimp" to being the most popular president in the annals of American polling to being a defeated president. The reasons for Bush's dramatic rise and fall center around his persuasive efforts.

In Chapter 4 we examined Bush's successful use of polarization to induce conservatives and moderates to prefer him to Michael Dukakis. Conservatives were induced to support him because of his conservative rhetoric and his choice of young conservative Senator Dan Quayle as his running mate. Those conservatives and moderates were induced to prefer Bush to Dukakis on the basis of their shared dislikes. But Bush's 1988 campaign rhetoric sowed the seeds of his demise.

The first problem for Bush was that he was elected on the basis of a clear, coherent electoral rhetoric that provided him with no basis for forming a governing coalition. The Democrats still controlled both houses of Congress, and Bush's divisive rhetoric had not paved the way for conciliation. Thus, his efforts at identification were always suspect, and the polarizing rhetoric was never far away. Although he had run as part of "Reagan-Bush," George Bush was no Ronald Reagan.

The second problem for Bush was that he was never able to use his impressive coalition-building skills to build a domestic coalition. Bush was able to build an international coalition of unprecedented breadth to defeat Saddam Hussein. But the coalition that included Americans and Soviets, Arabs and Israelis was based on their shared distaste for Iraq's invasion of Kuwait, its effect on the stability of the Middle East, and the atrocities reportedly being carried out by Iraqis in Kuwait. President Bush unified Americans by attributing to Saddam Hussein a wide variety of dislikes that included allusions to Hitler, aggression, human atrocities, eco-catastrophes, anti-Semitism, terrorism, greed, and Islamic fundamentalism. There was, in Bush's rendition of Saddam Hussein's Iraq, a little something for everyone to despise. In the process, Bush was able to unite Americans against Iraq and to end the war with 89 percent public approval—the highest level of presidential popularity ever recorded. But he was not equally successful in uniting a majority against a domestic enemy.

Bush's third problem was that he abdicated the rhetorical presidency well before the 1992 election. The Bush years were marked by momentous events and by presidential speeches that were not given. Political situations rich with rhetorical potential were repeatedly ignored by Bush. Where was the historic address when the Berlin Wall was demolished? Where was his speech about the death of the Soviet Union? Where was his speech in praise of the courageous Soviet republics striving for freedom and democracy? And where was the speech on the 1990 budget deal with Congress?

In the entire corpus of presidential addresses not given by Bush, the most important, surely, is the speech he did not give to the American people about his shift on taxes. Tired of saying that he would not raise taxes, Bush had underscored his campaign's point with the famous "Read my lips: No new taxes" pledge. But by autumn of 1990 it was clear that his budget would not pass without some sort of tax increase, and the president reluctantly agreed to one. The situation demanded discourse to re-orient people toward the tax increase as preferable to the alternatives; and when the president failed to explain his preferencing behavior, others did. Democrats such as Paul Tsongas, conservative Republicans such as Pat Buchanan, and even the maverick businessman H. Ross Perot readily provided unflattering narratives that explained Bush's actions.

The rhetorical situation facing Bush was not difficult, and the speech that should have been given seems fairly obvious. First, Bush could have reminded us of his pledge not to institute new taxes. Second, he could have shown us a simple graph of the economic trends at the time of his pledge. Third, he could have contrasted for us the economic trend that he had expected to see with the up-to-the-minute forecast based on existing tax rates. Fourth, he could have laid out the alternatives facing him: (1) to keep his pledge not to raise taxes despite the growing deficit, or (2) to take the courageous and responsible step of agreeing to Congress's tax increase to help the country. Fifth, he could have pointed out that he was not agreeing to any "new taxes," but only to increases in existing taxes. Sixth, he could have outlined publicly the terms of his bargain with Congress, and he could have stressed the shared responsibility of citizens and reporters to monitor congressional compliance with the agreement. With such a speech President Bush could better have (1) defined political and economic realities, (2) provided dramatic tension for journalists, and (3) made himself the hero of the story.

Ironically, perhaps even tragically, President Bush said most of these things in one way or another, at one time or another, to disparate audiences. But he failed to seize the moment by pulling these points together into a coherent discourse that demanded public attention and congressional compliance. The president had reasons for suddenly preferring to raise taxes, but he failed to satisfactorily explain those reasons to the American people. Consequently, Buchanan began to woo the conservative community away from Bush, thereby fragmenting Bush's electoral and governing coalitions alike.

Bush's fourth problem was that he became too popular for his own good. Because Operations Desert Shield and Desert Storm crowded coverage of most domestic issues off the front pages of America's newspapers, it seems unlikely that Bush owed his 89 percent approval to his domestic leadership. But domestic problems festered while he and the public concentrated on the Gulf War.

It is almost inconceivable that any president could achieve 89 percent public approval, much less sustain or increase it. The spiral of public opinion was bound to unwind, and as it did, Democrats and the media seized on it. Americans began paying more and more attention to the recession and other domestic problems that had been ignored during the war. The more Bush slipped back to mortal stature, the more vulnerable he became to criticism; and the more he was criticized, the more vulnerable he became.

Bush's fifth problem was his inability to capitalize on his incredible popularity. Some presidents would have used the cessation of war address to mobilize support for domestic programs, but George Bush did not. He could have used the cessation address to reflect on the ability of Americans to overcome their differences in emergencies and to defeat their enemies. He could have identified any of the pressing domestic problems as the new target of that brave army of ordinary Americans, and he could have pledged to lead us in a dramatic assault on that problem. In doing so President Bush would have capitalized on his popularity as a decisive leader, on the newly fashionable language of war, and on the news media's relative inattention to domestic issues that invited *someone* to define the domestic agenda. By not doing these things in his cessation address Bush encouraged the perception that he was purely a foreign policy president, and he encouraged others— Democrats, pundits, and conservatives—to define the domestic agenda. They were glad to oblige.

When President Bush did try to use his Gulf War success it was late and misdirected. His 1992 State of the Union address reflected on the weak economy and reprised the line first used in relation to Iraq's invasion of Kuwait: "This will not stand." Again Bush drew his line in the sand, this time setting an arbitrary deadline for congressional action on his economic plan. Again Bush pledged that after the deadline the battle would be joined. But the speech made many mistakes. First, it made Congress, rather than economic problems, his foe; this was an imprudent way to win votes in an election year. Second, he could not really follow through on his pledge to join the battle after the deadline, unless he planned to launch air strikes on Capitol Hill to soften them up for the ground offensive. Third, the general programs that he announced in the address did not match the legislative package introduced by House Republicans. Majority Leader Richard Gephardt, therefore, introduced a bill that was billed as "The President's Package"; and Ways and Means Committee Chairman Dan Rostenkowski had the Committee consider the bills as entire packages, ostensibly to facilitate action within the president's timetable. Finally, the speech and its initiatives were several months too late either to define the domestic agenda or to capitalize on Bush's high popularity, which had dropped from 89 percent to below 50 percent.

By abdicating the rhetorical presidency Bush sowed the seeds of presidential failure. Citizens accustomed to visionary orienting messages from President Reagan began to seek their orienting narratives from other authority figures. By not talking to his people Bush allowed his relationship with them to weaken. By avoiding public discourse Bush enabled others to charge, credibly, that he was not in charge, that his policies were not coherent, that he did not care about domestic policy, and that he was out of touch with America. In the post-Reagan era conservatives and moderates disappointed in Bush's lack of leadership turned increasingly to a variety of conservative and homespun pundits for guidance, people such as Rush Limbaugh, Ross Perot, and Pat Buchanan. When these mavericks found responsive chords, the president was unable to use their language and logic to flavor his speeches.

The rhetorical difficulties of the Bush presidency came to fruition during the campaign. Alex Castellanos (1993) of the November Group, the 1992 Bush campaign advertising firm, reflected on the campaign at a special conference of the International Communication Association. The central problem, said Castellanos, was that "to have a campaign you have to have a message . . . something you want to do." Because Bush had no such message of his own he had run in 1988 as Ronald Reagan, and the contradiction between Bush's conservative promises and his performance invited conservatives to defect. Because Bush had no central message his struggle with Congress seemed to be bickering. It was "not wrong to bicker," said Castellanos, "it was wrong to have nothing to bicker about."

One sign of the rhetorical failure of the Bush presidency was his challengers' successful use of popular communication media in 1992. Bill Clinton's public forums, Ross Perot's town meetings, and the widespread use of talk shows such as the Larry King and Arsenio Hall shows all suggested that citizens wanted interaction with their leaders. Roughly 63 percent of the voters in 1992 preferred (1) candidates who talked with them, who listened to them, and who symbolically demonstrated their attachment to them, as opposed to (2) President Bush, who had rarely addressed them about their shared difficulties, who refused to debate Pat Buchanan in the Republican primaries, and who nearly refused to debate the issues with Clinton and Perot.

THE EARLY CLINTON PRESIDENCY

Perhaps Bill Clinton won the presidency in 1992 because he was not President Bush, but he was one of many people who was not George Bush. Indeed, Clinton was the one person who used the campaign to dramatize four of the ways in which he differed from George Bush.

First, Clinton used the politics of inclusion rather than division. His announcement speech of October 3, 1991, introduced his themes of change and inclusion. He reflected on his state's experience with race-baiting and promised not to let "them get away with it." In this and subsequent speeches Clinton provided an umbrella for any citizens tired of the divisiveness of the Bush era. But other challengers did this, too, and it alone did not account for the success of Clinton's candidacy.

The second difference concerned what President Bush had often referred to as "the vision thing." In contrast, Clinton's announcement speech advanced a vision in jeremiadic logic. He explained how he had learned the ancient truth at Georgetown University (a Catholic university in the nation's capitol). That truth, he said, was that "America was the greatest country in human history because at critical times we have always believed in two simple ideas. One, that the future can be better than the present, and two, that each and every one of us has a personal moral responsibility to make it so" (1991). But America had recently been led astray from that ancient truth by leadership that was "afraid to change in a world that is changing so fast." As a result of that leadership, "Our country is headed in the wrong direction fast—it's falling behind, it's losing its way. And all we've gotten out of Washington is status quo paralysis—neglect and selfishness and division—not leadership and vision."

To end America's tribulations a new prophet was needed to help America rediscover the ancient truth. "Make no mistake: This election is about change," said Clinton. "We need a new covenant to rebuild America. A solemn agreement between the people and their government. Government's responsibility is to create more opportunity for everybody. Our responsibility is to make the most of it" (Clinton, 1991). Clinton has yet to articulate his message so clearly since his announcement, but the jeremiadic logic of that speech framed his campaign, his acceptance speech, and his inaugural address.

Clinton's jeremiad articulated an ancient truth, spoke to people's need for optimism, justified his life-long pursuit of the presidency, and challenged each citizen to assume more personal responsibility for the condition of life in America. It also reserved a potential escape route for him: the campaign/presidency would not succeed unless citizens lived up to their responsibilities to make tomorrow better than today.

A third contrast with President Bush was Clinton's proclivity for answering questions with multi-point programs. At a time when citizens suspected that all politicians had only glittering generalities to offer, Clinton was a candidate with policy specifics to boggle most minds. Moreover, most of his specific policies were linked logically in fairly specific ways. This was a conscious decision. The campaign believed that the public was more concerned with action than personality, so it took the unusual step of introducing "The Plan" before introducing the candidate (Greer, 1993). Indeed, the language and logic of Clinton's policy discussions created for him an image of expertise that contrasted sharply with Bush's willingness to wait out the recession and with Perot's readiness to implement what he referred to as some of the many good proposals floating around Washington.

A fourth contrast between candidates Bush and Clinton was Clinton's ability to lend coherence to problems and solutions. Much of this ability stemmed from his jeremiadic logic, but there were other sources as well. When Bush and Quayle were campaigning hard on the theme of "family values," for example, Clinton turned the tables on them. In his address at Notre Dame Clinton said that "We need more than a president who talks about family values. We need an administration that values families" (1992). He then used that premise to frame his discussion of the Family Leave Bill, health care, education, and the need for an economic stimulus.

Clinton won election by turning 43 percent of the popular vote into two-thirds of the electoral votes. As a result, Clinton's early presidential footing was dramatically different from that of Ronald Reagan. Both Reagan and Clinton amassed 43 million votes, but Bush and Perot amassed 18 million votes more than had Carter and Anderson, combined. Clinton consequently lacked any appearance of widespread public support. Moreover, he had won by running against the Washington establishment, and he had difficulty staffing his administration with experienced Washingtonians. As a result, Clinton took office with weak electoral and governing coalitions and a commitment to a dramatic first hundred days.

It was no surprise to anyone that Bill Clinton relished the role of rhetorical president. He had always liked to engage people in conversation and to explain his ideas to them. That trait, by itself, set him apart from George Bush, who had neglected a variety of promising rhetorical opportunities. President Clinton went on national television on February 15, 1993, to prepare the nation for his economic address to Congress on February 17. The president and members of his administration then crossed the country immediately to build support for his deficit reduction plan. By taking his message outside Washington, the administration courted the local and regional media. Clinton himself gave seventeen public speeches around the country in support of his plan, and it passed in record time.

But when it came time for the president to build support for his economic stimulus plan—the centerpiece of his campaign to jumpstart the economy—Bill Clinton gave only five public speeches, two of which were national radio addresses that attracted little attention. Meanwhile his Republican adversaries, led by Senate Minority Leader Bob Dole, dominated the news and talk shows with their opposition to his plan. When conservative Democrats began to defect, it became impossible for the leadership to stop a Republican filibuster and the stimulus package fell to defeat.

Clinton's inability to win passage of the economic stimulus package revealed several weaknesses in his governing coalition. It suggested that the president could not count on the Democratic majorities in the House and Senate to enact his programs because of Senate Republicans' ability to filibuster and an insufficient number of supportive Democrats to end it. This left him with a series of rhetorical dilemmas.

First, the president could negotiate with Senate Republicans, such as Dole and Phil Gramm of Texas, who could help him avoid future filibusters. But they were widely regarded as his most likely challengers in 1996, and he would have to negotiate with the greatest of care.

Second, Clinton could go public to build public support. But rhetorical presidents since Woodrow Wilson had repeatedly found that the broad arguments needed to win public support were rarely compatible with the technical compromises needed to win swing votes in Congress. Moreover, the time and energy he would devote to traveling and speaking would be time taken from his other responsibilities and initiatives.

Third, the president had achieved rhetorical coherence during the campaign by linking his policy proposals together into a package. He continued to do this in his major addresses of the first hundred days. But each of these bills required separate legislative action. Thus, precisely because his proposals on taxing, spending, health care, national service, education, and the environment were interconnected he could not press one without undermining the attention available for the others. Although he tried diligently in his public remarks to stress the interconnectedness of these proposals, each required a separate vote and, therefore, a separate coalition and, consequently, a separate blend of needs and reasons.

The president emphasized on several occasions the importance of understanding and supporting his policies as a whole. He told Congress, for example, that "The economic plan can't please everybody. If the package is picked apart, there will be something that will anger each of us, won't please anybody. But if it is taken as a whole, it will help all of us" (1993b, p. 223). He told the middle class that he would be able neither to cut nor to retain their income tax rates, but he assured them that by raising modestly their taxes "Our comprehensive plan for economic growth will create millions of long-term, good-paying jobs. . . . Our national service plan will throw open the doors of college opportunity to the daughters and sons of the middle class" (1993a, p. 208). And he explained to Atlanta business people that:

There are millions and millions of Americans who, in the first 6 months of this year, will save more money in interest payments than they'll pay in the energy tax I propose for the full 4 years of this administration. That is what happens if you gain control of your economic destiny. (1993c, p. 461).

But as Clinton pressed each proposal in its time, his adversaries predictably sought to defeat it by breaking the package into parts and mobilizing the potential opponents of each part. They were aided by the legislative realities that have frustrated all rhetorical presidents, as well as by the bitter nature of many of Clinton's prescriptions and by the growing perception that Clinton was an old-style tax-and-spend liberal marketing snake oil cures.

Our reading of the speeches from President Clinton's first hundred days leads us to observe that the speech texts were not his problem. Many of them, such as his February 26 address on the "Global Economy" at American University and his March 1 "Remarks on National Service" at Rutgers University, were quite well conceived and argued. Nor can we fault his efforts to communicate directly with voters in his town meetings, a format that enabled Clinton to hear from "real people" and to dramatize his interest in them. What, then, were his problems?

President Clinton's first rhetorical problem was that his discourse did not always reach the politically important interpretive communities. Two of his most important addresses were delivered at universities, and he has spoken to several civic groups in addition to town meetings. But he addressed the nation via television only twice during his first four months, and one of those was his address to Congress. Word of his other addresses reached the public only through the news media and talk shows, and that is his second problem.

The news media and talk shows thrive on controversy, with the effect that Clinton and his policies have become the subjects of other people's conversations. The more Clinton makes his persuasive case, the more he is pummelled by Rush Limbaugh, *Crossfire*, and *The Capitol Gang*. Whereas President Reagan narrated political life for Americans, Clinton, like Bush, has been mainly a character in other people's narratives. This is especially problematic for Clinton, who is sufficiently charismatic to handle the role of narrator.

Being a character in other people's stories is problematic for President Clinton because his presidency is dedicated to reorienting the American people—a task he cannot perform if his adversaries tell the story. As the drama built toward the May 27, 1993, House vote on Clinton's budget that would "make or break" his presidency, it was his adversaries who made the news. When it passed by a scant margin of 219-213, CNN's reporters told the story over Clinton's mute gestures.

Clinton's problem is the same as Bush's: How can the president communicate with the public if they cannot hear him?

The contemporary presidency, with its emphasis on public persuasion, has devoured several presidents to date. Wilson failed to win Senate support for his League of Nations, Johnson could not find the right combination of arguments to resolve the Vietnam question, Nixon almost talked his way into impeachment, Ford failed to satisfactorily justify his pardon of Nixon, Carter encountered a host of rhetorical problems, and Bush basically abdicated the role. Only Roosevelt, Kennedy, and Reagan can be considered successful rhetorical presidents.

Bill Clinton has many of the qualities required by the rhetorical presidency: he enjoys public speaking and the give and take of argumentation, he has the ability to articulate other people's thoughts and feelings and to incorporate their experiences in his remarks. Moreover, he is able to do so in a positive way that builds convergence around shared beliefs rather than in a negative way that emphasizes shared disbeliefs. Nevertheless, his first four months have been only moderately successful.

From the vantage point of May 31, 1993, it appears to us that President Clinton will need to make seven rhetorical adjustments if he is to exercise persuasive presidential leadership. *First, President Clinton will need to speak to the nation on television more frequently.* The only way for him to get more control over his message transmission is to address the public directly. Addresses from the Oval Office, televised press conferences, town meetings, and live telecasts of addresses to selected audiences all allow the president to convey his full message to a large audience in his own way, and they permit the public to hear the president for themselves. Televised addresses to Congress enable him to reach legislators and citizens alike, without disenfranchising Congress.

Second, President Clinton needs to establish himself as the public narrator of his slice of American history. He can do this by shifting from his overwhelmingly propositional logic of multi-point plans toward somewhat more use of narrative logic. Ever since the announcement of his candidacy Bill Clinton has been the subject of other people's stories—from Gennifer Flowers to the draft to not inhaling marijuana to his slickness to his $200 haircut. That drew attention to his candidacy by making him interesting, and therefore professionally useful, to the journalistic community. But it hurt him badly during his first hundred days as president. Ronald Reagan had been successful because he himself drove the news by telling America's story, the story of John

Winthrop's "shining city on a hill." The Clinton group's potential for doing the same thing was evident in their convention film and commercials about "a place called Hope," but they dropped the story before his inauguration and blurred the vision in which sacrifice and investment made sense.

Third, President Clinton needs to do a better job of tailoring his speeches to the professional needs of journalists. News is story-driven, and if he does not provide journalists with interesting stories they cannot do their jobs in a way that fulfills *his* needs as president. Instead, they do their jobs by reshaping, rather than conveying, his message. Presidents will continue to be news pegs for national and international stories. It is up to presidents like Clinton to provide interesting and dramatic storylines in which they are the protagonists that satisfy the journalists' timetable and appetite for drama.

Fourth, President Clinton needs to reinvigorate his jeremiadic logic to demonstrate that there is nothing as traditional as change. This was the message to which his voters responded, and it is the logical framework in which his plans make sense. Without it, his plans can be more easily picked apart and defeated. The prevailing diagnosis during April and May 1993 was that the president needed to "focus" his message, but had he done so he would have played into the hands of his opponents. Instead, President Clinton needed to remind his people, repeatedly, of the larger, unifying vision that guides him. If he wants us to "make change our friend" he must frame it for us, and his jeremiad provides him with a good frame.

Fifth, President Clinton needs to make it less easy for others to oppose him. He can do this by discontinuing his Carteresque tendencies to admit flaws and to invite disagreement. The conflict-driven journalistic community provides politicians with incentives for attacking presidents in the form of publicity and an image of independence. The president needs to provide his peers with some disincentives to challenge him publicly. This is especially important since the decline of party discipline in the House and Senate. The danger to presidents is that they can easily become the object of other people's polarization efforts. Short of engaging in nasty politics, presidents can provide these disincentives by heaping less praise on disagreement with their points of view. The president also needs to allow himself some distance from the most unpopular issues, recognizing (1) that his advocacy of a proposal will draw opposition as well as support, and (2) that his four-year responsibility for presidential leadership is more important than any single issue.

Sixth, President Clinton needs to mobilize people by working with existing organizations and interpretive communities. The kinds of change that Clinton seeks are comparable to those sought by Presidents Truman and Carter. In Chapter 7 we suggested that Truman was more effective than Carter because he addressed people's personal needs as well as their humanitarian needs and because he worked through existing groups and governmental structures. Because this was the strategy used by the 1992 Democratic campaign to reach Latino voters (Echaveste, 1993), it seems likely to be the model for the Clinton administration.

Seventh, President Clinton needs to realize that he can say so much that people stop listening, and that he can talk himself into a state of rhetorical crisis. This is the danger facing people who are well suited, by nature, to the demands of the rhetorical presidency. And it is a potential problem for the talkative Bill Clinton, whose 1988 speech nominating Michael Dukakis ran on and on to the consternation of the convention and network scheduling people. It is also a potential problem if Clinton continues to speak to a wide variety of audiences in a way that invites people to rely on news reports of the speeches. If he addresses the nation on television with some regularity to emphasize his vision and its relationship to his policies, and if he monitors more carefully the fit between his words and actions, he can make presidential persuasion his friend.

CONCLUSION

In the final analysis, the key to contemporary presidential persuasion is that the White House speaks. It speaks with many voices, on many topics, with varying degrees of success. But this variability seems tightly organized in comparison with the increasing disunity of the American public. Interpretive communities—both linked with and divided from one another by satellites, fax machines, cellular telephones, desktop publications, and cable television—continue to proliferate. Arthur Schlesinger, Jr. (1992), has written that "The American population has unquestionably grown more heterogeneous than ever in recent times. But this very heterogeneity makes the quest for unifying ideals and a common culture all the more urgent" (p. 19).

The twentieth-century rhetorical presidency developed hand in glove with the media of mass communication that made it possible for humans to communicate across time and space. Some people stayed up into the wee hours listening for faraway voices on their crystal radios. But as we approach the twenty-first century we find that we have developed our communication technologies to the point at which we can *avoid* communicating across time and space. We listen to personal stereos in crowded places and at home, we delete unwanted television stations from our lives, we rent videos so that we need not be bothered by unwanted messages, and we stay up into the wee hours watching the television channel targeted at people just like us. In the process of making communication technologies more sophisticated, we have lost many of the opportunities to communicate with people who are unlike us.

The compartmentalization of interpretive communities has complicated the task of presidential leadership. Some recent presidents have turned to deception and dirty tricks, some have turned to the politics of division, some have withdrawn into silence, and some have sought unity in glittering generalities and simplistic solutions—but the underlying problem continues to worsen.

If the contemporary federal system is to work, the White House must speak. But it must speak responsibly, and to all corners of the community. It must speak clearly and persuasively of the problems facing us individually and collectively, and of the technical complexities and moral implications of the possible solutions. It must address the needs, symbols, reasons, and preferences that provide personal coherence and the laws, languages, logics, and ideologies that provide social coordination. It must balance our tendency to diverge with our need to converge. And, for now, it must find a way to unite these disunited communities without the help of foreign bogeymen. The task is difficult but not impossible for presidents who understand that presidential leadership requires them to build interpretive coalitions out of the needs, words, reasons, and preferences that make sense to their citizens.

REFERENCES

Castellanos, A. (1993). Remarks on developing the political advertisements, Pre-conference on "Communication in the 1992 presidential campaign." International Communication Association.

Clinton, W. J. (1991). Announcement of candidacy for president, October 3. Purdue University Public Affairs Video Archives.

Clinton, W. J. (1992). Campaign appearance at the University of Notre Dame, September 11. Purdue University Public Affairs Video Archives.

Clinton, W. J. (1993a). Address to the nation on the economic program, February 15. *Weekly Compilation of Presidential Documents, 29*, pp. 207–209.

Clinton, W. J. (1993b). Address before a joint session of Congress on administration goals, February 17. *Weekly Compilation of Presidential Documents*, *29*, pp. 215–224.

Clinton, W. J. (1993c). Remarks to the business community in Atlanta, March 19. *Weekly Compilation of Presidential Documents*, *29*, pp. 458–463.

Echaveste, M. (1993). Remarks on connecting with the audience, Pre-conference on "Communication in the 1992 presidential campaign." International Communication Association.

Greer, F. (1993). Remarks on developing the political advertisements, Pre-conference on "Communication in the 1992 presidential campaign." International Communication Association.

Hart, R. P. (1984). *Verbal style and the presidency: A computer-based analysis*. New York: Academic Press.

Hart, R. P. (1987). *The sound of leadership: Presidential communication in the modern age*. Chicago: University of Chicago Press.

Schlesinger, A., Jr. (1992). *The disuniting of America*. New York: W. W. Norton & Company.

Bibliography

BOOKS

Adorno, T. W., Frenkel-Brunswick, E., Levinson, D. J., & Sanford, R. N. (1950). *The authoritarian personality*. New York: Harper.

Bales, R. F. (1970). *Personality and interpersonal behavior*. New York: Holt Rinehart.

Barber, J. D. (1985). *The presidential character: Predicting performance in the White House* (3rd ed.). Englewood Cliffs, NJ: Prentice-Hall.

Bercovitch, S. (1978). *The American jeremiad*. Madison: University of Wisconsin Press.

Bernstein, C., & Woodward, B. (1974). *All the president's men*. New York: Simon & Schuster.

Billig, M. (1991). *Ideology and opinions*. Newbury Park, CA: Sage.

Bochin, H. (1990). *Richard Nixon: Rhetorical strategist*. Westport, CT: Greenwood.

Bormann, E. G. (1985). *The force of fantasy: Restoring the American dream*. Carbondale: Southern Illinois University Press.

Bosmajian, H. A. (1983). *The language of oppression*. Lanham, MD: University Press of America.

Bowers, J. W., & Ochs, D. (1971). *The rhetoric of agitation and control*. Prospect Heights, IL: Waveland Press.

Broesamle, J. J. (1990). *Reform and reaction in twentieth century American politics*. Westport, CT: Greenwood.

Buchanan, B. (1978). *The presidential experience*. Englewood Cliffs, NJ: Prentice-Hall.

Buchanan, B. (1987). *The citizen's presidency*. Washington, DC: Congressional Quarterly.

Burke, K. (1969). *A rhetoric of motives*. Berkeley: University of California Press.

Burns, J. M. (1978). *Leadership*. New York: Harper Colophon.

Campbell, C. (1991). The White House and Cabinet under the "let's deal" presidency. In C. Campbell & B. Rockman (Eds.), *The Bush presidency: First appraisals* (pp. 185–222). Chatham, NJ: Chatham House.

Campbell, K. K., & Jamieson, K. H. (1990). *Deeds done in words: Presidential rhetoric and the genres of governance*. Chicago: University of Chicago Press.

Carr, D. (1986). *Time, narrative, and history*. Bloomington: Indiana University Press.

Carter, J. (1982). *Keeping the faith: Memoirs of a president*. New York: Bantam.

Corwin, E. S. (1957). *The president: Office and powers* (4th rev. ed.). New York: New York University Press.

Crane, P. M. (1978). *Surrender in Panama: The case against the treaty*. New York: Dale Books.

Dean, J. (1976). *Blind ambition*. New York: Simon & Schuster.

Deutsch, K. (1966). *The nerves of government*. New York: The Free Press.

Dworkin, R. (1977). *Taking rights seriously*. Cambridge, MA: Harvard University Press.

Easton, D. (1965). *A systems analysis of political life*. New York: John Wiley.

Edwards, G. C., III. (1980). *Presidential influence in Congress*. San Francisco: W. H. Freeman.

Edwards, G. C., III. (1983). *The public presidency: The pursuit of popular support*. New York: St. Martin's.

Erickson, P. D. (1985). *Reagan speaks: The making of an American myth*. New York: New York University Press.

Fisher, W. R. (1987). *Human communication as narration: Toward a philosophy of reason, value, and action*. Columbia: University of South Carolina Press.

Ford, G. R. (1979). *A time to heal: The autobiography of Gerald R. Ford*. New York: Harper & Row.

Germond, J. W., & Witcover, J. (1981). *Blue smoke and mirrors*. New York: Viking Press.

Graber, D. A. (1992). *Public sector communication: How organizations manage information*. Washington, DC: Congressional Quarterly.

Greenstein, F. I. (1969). *Personality and politics: Problems of evidence, inference, and conceptualization*. Chicago: Markham.

Greenstein, F. I. (Ed.). (1983). *The Reagan presidency: An early assessment*. Baltimore: The Johns Hopkins University Press.

Haldeman, H. R. (1978). *The ends of power*. New York: Dell.

Hart, R. P. (1984). *Verbal style and the presidency: A computer-based analysis*. New York: Academic Press.

Hart, R. P. (1987). *The sound of leadership: Presidential communication in the modern age*. Chicago: University of Chicago Press.

Hartmann, R. T. (1980). *Palace politics: An inside account of the Ford years*. New York: McGraw-Hill.

Hinckley, B. (1990). *The symbolic presidency: How presidents portray themselves*. New York: Routledge.

Jamieson, K. H. (1988). *Eloquence in an electronic age: The transformation of political speechmaking*. New York: Oxford.

Jaworski, L. (1976). *The right and the power*. Houston: Gulf.

Kamler, H. (1983). *Communication: Sharing our stories of experience*. Seattle: Psychological Press.

Kernell, S. (1993). *Going public: New strategies of presidential leadership*. Washington, DC: Congressional Quarterly.

Kessel, J. H. (1992). *Presidential campaign politics* (4th ed.). Pacific Grove, CA: Brooks Cole.

King, G., & Ragsdale, L. (1988). *The elusive executive: Discovering statistical patterns in the presidency*. Washington, DC: Congressional Quarterly Press.

Koenig, L. W. (1986). *The chief executive* (5th ed.). New York: Harcourt Brace Jovanovich.

Lasswell, H. H. (1962). *Power and personality*. New York: Viking.

Lipset, S. M. (1960). *Political man: The social bases of politics*. Garden City, NY: Doubleday.

Lowi, T. J. (1985). *The personal president: Power invested, promise unfulfilled*. Ithaca: Cornell University Press.

Lukas, J. A. (1976). *Nightmare: The underside of the Nixon years*. New York: Viking.

Miller, P. (1953). *The New England mind: From colony to Providence*. Cambridge, MA: Harvard University Press.

Miroff, B. (1976). *Pragmatic illusions: The presidential politics of John F. Kennedy*. New York: Longman.

Mollenhoff, C. R. (1980). *The president who failed: Carter out of control*. New York: Macmillan.

Neustadt, R. E. (1980). *Presidential power: The politics of leadership from FDR to Carter*. New York: John Wiley. Originally published in 1960.

Nixon, R. M. (1978). *RN: The memoirs of Richard Nixon*. New York: Grosset & Dunlop.

Noelle-Neumann, E. (1984). *The spiral of silence: Public opinion—our social skin*. Chicago: University of Chicago Press.

Polsby, N. W., & Wildavsky, A. (1991). *Presidential elections* (8th ed.). New York: The Free Press.

Popkin, S. L. (1991). *The reasoning voter: Communication and persuasion in presidential campaigns*. Chicago: University of Chicago Press.

Price, R. (1977). *With Nixon*. New York: Viking.

Rawls, J. (1971). *A theory of justice*. Oxford: Oxford University Press.

Ritter, K., & Henry, D. (1992). *Ronald Reagan: The great communicator*. Westport, CT: Greenwood.

Rogin, M. (1987). *Ronald Reagan, the movie: And other episodes in political demonology*. Berkeley: University of California Press.

Rokeach, M. R. (1960). *The open- and closed-mind*. New York: Basic Books.

Rossiter, C. (1956). *The American presidency*. New York: Harcourt, Brace & World.

Ryan, H. (1993). *The inaugural addresses of twentieth-century American presidents*. Westport, CT: Praeger.

Sandel, M. (1982). *Liberalism and the limits of justice*. Cambridge: Cambridge University Press.

Sanders, A. (1990). *Making sense of politics*. Ames: Iowa State University Press.

Schlesinger, A., Jr. (1992). *The disuniting of America*. New York: W. W. Norton & Company.

Seligman, L. R., & Covington, C. (1989). *The coalitional presidency*. Chicago: Dorsey Press.

Shogan, R. (1992). *The riddle of power: Presidential leadership from Truman to Bush*. New York: Plume Book.

Simons, H. W., & Aghazarian, A. A. (Eds.). (1986). *Form, genre, and the study of political discourse*. Columbia: University of South Carolina.

Smith, C. A. (1990). *Political communication*. San Diego: Harcourt Brace Jovanovich.

Stewart, C. J., Smith, C. A., & Denton, R. E., Jr. (1994). *Persuasion and social movements* (3rd ed.). Prospect Heights, IL: Waveland.

Stuckey, M. (1990). *Playing the game: The presidential rhetoric of Ronald Reagan*. New York: Praeger.

Tulis, J. K. (1987). *The rhetorical presidency*. Princeton, NJ: Princeton University Press.

Turner, K. J. (1985). *Lyndon Johnson's dual war: Vietnam and the press*. Chicago: University of Chicago.

Turner, V. (1982). *From ritual to theatre: The human seriousness of play*. New York: Performing Arts Journal Publications.

Viguerie, R. A. (1981). *The New Right: We're ready to lead*. Falls Church, VA: The Viguerie Company.

Weiler, M., & Pearce, W. B. (Eds.). (1992). *Reagan and public discourse in America*. Tuscaloosa: University of Alabama Press.

White, T. H. (1975). *Breach of faith*. New York: Atheneum.

The White House Transcripts. (1973). New York: Bantam Books.

Wills, G. (1987). *Reagan's America: Innocents abroad*. Garden City, NY: Doubleday.

Windt, T. O. (1990). *Presidents and protesters: Political rhetoric in the 1960s*. Tuscaloosa: University of Alabama Press.

Windt, T. O., & Ingold, B. (Eds.). (1987). *Essays in presidential rhetoric* (2d ed.). Dubuque, IA: Kendall-Hunt.

Zarefsky, D. (1986). *President Johnson's War on Poverty*. Tuscaloosa: University of Alabama Press.

JOURNAL ARTICLES AND BOOK CHAPTERS

Basile, P. S. (1982). U.S. energy policy. In W. Kohl (Ed.), *After the second oil crisis* (pp. 195–224). Lexington, MA: Heath.

Bellah, R. N. (1967). Civil religion in America. *Daedalus, 96* (Winter), 1–21.

Berry, N. D. (1981). The foundation of presidential leadership: Teaching. *Presidential Studies Quarterly, 11*, 99–105.

Bormann, E. (1977). Fetching good out of evil: A rhetorical use of calamity. *Quarterly Journal of Speech, 63*, 130–139.

Bormann, E. G. (1972). Fantasy and rhetorical vision: The rhetorical criticism of social reality. *Quarterly Journal of Speech, 58*, 396–407.

Brock, B. L. (1988). Gerald R. Ford encounters Richard Nixon's legacy: On amnesty and the pardon. In H. R. Ryan (Ed.), *Oratorical encounters: Selected studies and sources of twentieth-century political accusations and apologia* (pp. 227–240). Westport, CT: Greenwood.

Brummett, B. (1975). Presidential substance: The address of August 15, 1973. *Western Speech Communication, 39,* 249–259.

Buchen, P. W. (1989). The making of an unscheduled presidential transition. In J. P. Pfiffner & R. G. Hoxie (Eds.), *The presidency in transition* (pp. 65–73). New York: Center for the Study of the Presidency.

Davis, D. H. (1979). Pluralism and energy: Carter's national energy plan. In R. Lawrence (Ed.), *New dimensions in energy policy* (pp. 191–200). Lexington, MA: Heath.

Delia, J. G., O'Keefe, B., & O'Keefe, D. J. (1982). The constructivist approach to communication. In F. E. X. Dance (Ed.), *Human communication theory: Comparative essays* (pp. 147–191). New York: Harper & Row.

Edsall, T. B. (1992). Why Bush accentuates the negative. In S. J. Wayne & C. Wilcox (Eds.), *The quest for national office* (pp. 200–204). New York: St. Martin's Press.

Edwards, G. C., III. (1991). George Bush and the public presidency: The politics of inclusion. In C. Campbell & B. Rockman (Eds.), *The Bush presidency: First appraisals* (pp. 129–154). Chatham, NJ: Chatham House.

Fairbanks, J. D. (1981). The priestly function of the presidency: A discussion of the literature on civil religion and its implications for the study of presidential leadership. *Presidential Studies Quarterly, 11* (Spring), pp. 214–232.

Fisher, W. R. (1973). Reaffirmation and subversion of the American Dream. *Quarterly Journal of Speech, 59,* 160–167.

Gallup Organization (1986, December). *Gallup Report* (Report No. 255). Wilmington, DE: Scholarly Resources.

Gallup Organization. (1987a, January–February). *Gallup Report* (Report No. 256–257). Wilmington, DE: Scholarly Resources.

Gallup Organization. (1987b, June 23). *Gallup Report* (Report No. 261). Wilmington, DE: Scholarly Resources.

Gottlieb, D. (1978). Texans' response to President Carter's energy proposals. In S. Warkov (Ed.), *Energy policy in the United States* (pp. 33–44). New York: Praeger.

Hahn, D. F. (1980). Flailing the profligate: Carter's energy sermon of 1979. *Presidential Studies Quarterly, 10,* 583–587.

Hahn, D. F., & Gustainis, J. J. (1987). Defensive tactics in presidential rhetoric: Contemporary topic. In T. Windt & B. Ingold (Eds.), *Essays in presidential rhetoric* (2d ed.), (pp. 43–75). Dubuque, IA: Kendall-Hunt.

Harrell, J., Ware, B. L., & Linkugel, W. A. (1975). Failure of apology in American politics: Nixon on Watergate. *Speech Monographs, 42,* 245–262.

Hershey, M. R. (1989). The campaign and the media. In Gerald M. Pomper (Ed.), *The election of 1988: Reports and interpretations* (pp. 73–102). Chatham, NJ: Chatham House.

Holland, J. W. (1990). The great gamble: Jimmy Carter and the 1979 energy crisis. *Prologue* (Spring), 63–79.

Johannesen, R. L. (1986). Ronald Reagan's economic jeremiad. *Central States Speech Journal, 37,* 79–89.

Kassabaum, N. L. (1979). The essence of leadership. *Presidential Studies Quarterly*, *9*, 239–242.

King, A. A., & Anderson, F. D. (1971). Nixon, Agnew, and the "silent majority": A case study in the rhetoric of polarization. *Western Speech*, *34*, 243–255.

Klumpp, J. F., & Lukehart, J. K. (1978). The pardoning of Richard Nixon: A failure in motivational strategy. *Western Journal of Speech Communication*, *41*, 116–123.

Leathers, D. G. (1973). Belief-disbelief systems: The communicative vacuum of the radical right. In G. P. Mohrmann, C. J. Stewart, & D. F. Ochs (Eds.), *Explorations in rhetorical criticism* (pp. 124–137). University Park: Pennsylvania State University Press.

Lewis, W. F. (1987). Telling America's story: Narrative form and the Reagan presidency. *Quarterly Journal of Speech*, *73*, 280–302.

Maslow, A. (1943a). A theory of human motivation. *Psychological Review*, *50*, 370–396.

Maslow, A. (1943b). The authoritarian character structure. *Journal of Social Psychology*, *18*, 401–411.

McWilliams, W. C. (1989). The meaning of the election. In G. M. Pomper (Ed.), *The election of 1988: Reports and interpretations* (pp. 177–206). Chatham, NJ: Chatham House.

Miller, D. (1992). Community and citizenship. In S. Avineri & A. De-Shalit (Eds.), *Communitarianism and individualism* (pp. 85–100). Oxford: Oxford University Press.

Milstein, J. (1978). How consumers feel about energy. In S. Warkov (Ed.), *Energy policy in the United States* (pp. 79–90). New York: Praeger.

Murphy, J. J. (1990). "A time of shame and sorrow": Robert F. Kennedy and the American jeremiad. *Quarterly Journal of Speech*, *76*, 401–414.

Olsen, M. (1978). Public acceptance of energy conservation. In S. Warkov (Ed.), *Energy policy in the United States* (pp. 91–109). New York: Praeger.

Pastor, R. (1976, June). In the Canal Zone: Who should be sovereign? *Harvard Magazine*, pp. 38–43.

Pomper, G. M. (1989). The presidential election. In G. M. Pomper (Ed.), *The election of 1988: Reports and interpretations* (pp. 129–152). Chatham, NJ: Chatham House.

Quirk, P. J. (1991). Domestic policy: Divided government and cooperative presidential leadership. In C. Campbell & B. Rockman (Eds.), *The Bush presidency: First appraisals* (pp. 69–92). Chatham, NJ: Chatham House.

Ritter, K. (1980). American political rhetoric and the jeremiad tradition: Presidential nomination acceptance addresses, 1960–76. *Central States Speech Journal*, *31*, 153–171.

Ritter, K. (1993). Lyndon Johnson's inaugural address: The jeremiad and national policy. In H. R. Ryan (Ed.), *Rhetorical studies of presidential inaugural addresses* (pp. 195–209). Westport, CT: Greenwood.

Rockman, B. A. (1991). The leadership style of George Bush. In C. Campbell & B. Rockman (Eds.), *The Bush presidency: First appraisals* (pp. 1–36). Chatham, NJ: Chatham House.

Smith, C. A. (1987). Mister Reagan's neighborhood: Rhetoric and national unity. *Southern Speech Communication Journal*, *52*, 219–239.

Smith, C. A. (1988). Richard M. Nixon and the Watergate scandal. In H. R. Ryan (Ed.), *Oratorical encounters: Selected studies and sources of twentieth-century political accusations and apologia* (pp. 201–226). Westport, CT: Greenwood.

Smith, C. A. (1992). Interpretive communities in conflict: A master syllabus for political communication. *Communication Education, 41*, 415–428.

Smith, C. R., & Hyde, M. J. (1991). Rethinking "the public": The role of emotion in being-with-others. *Quarterly Journal of Speech, 77*, 446–466.

Smith, K. B. (1981). The representative role of the president. *Presidential Studies Quarterly, 11* (Spring), pp. 203–213.

Taylor, C. (1973). *Hegel and modern society*. Cambridge: Cambridge University Press.

Zulick, M. (1992). The agony of Jeremiah: On the dialogic invention of prophetic ethos. *Quarterly Journal of Speech, 78*, 125–148.

Index

ABOUT THE AUTHORS

CRAIG ALLEN SMITH is Professor of Communication at the University of North Carolina at Greensboro, where he teaches courses in political communication, rhetorical criticism, and speechwriting. His previous works include *Political Communication* (1990), *Persuasion and Social Movements* (3rd ed., 1994) written with Charles J. Stewart and Robert E. Denton, Jr., and *The President and the Public: Rhetoric and National Leadership* (1985) edited with Kathy B. Smith, as well as book chapters and journal articles. He was the first chairperson of the Speech Communication Association's Political Communication Division.

KATHY B. SMITH is Associate Professor of Politics at Wake Forest University, where she teaches courses in the American presidency, politics and the mass media, and seminars in political communication. In addition to *The President and the Public: Rhetoric and National Leadership* (1985), her work has been published in a variety of academic books and journals.